Surviving in Ministry

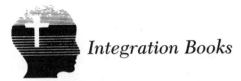 *Integration Books*

STUDIES IN PASTORAL PSYCHOLOGY,
THEOLOGY, AND SPIRITUALITY
Robert J. Wicks, General Editor

also in the series

Surviving in Ministry

*Navigating the Pitfalls,
Experiencing the Renewals*

Robert R. Lutz, M.Div., D.P.C.
Bruce T. Taylor, M.D.
editors

Integration Books

paulist press/new york/mahwah

Acknowledgement

BV
660.2
.S86
1990

The editors would like to thank
Virginia Levin and Melissa Hayden
for their assistance
in preparation of the manuscripts.

Excerpt from "The Brown Bottle" by Penny Jones, copyright © 1983, by Hazelden Foundation, Center City, MN. Reprinted by permission.

Excerpt from "The Road Not Taken" by Robert Frost from *Mountain Interval*, copyright © 1916 by Holt, Rinehart and Winston, Inc. Used by permission of Henry Holt and Company.

Library of Congress Cataloging-in-Publication Data

Surviving in ministry: navigating the pitfalls, experiencing the
  renewals/editors, Robert R. Lutz, Bruce T. Taylor.
    p.   cm.—(Integration books)
  Includes bibliographical references.
  ISBN: 0-8091-3156-0
  1. Clergy—Office. 2. Rabbis—Office. 3. Pastoral theology.
  4. Pastoral theology (Judaism) I. Lutz, Robert R., 1946–   .
  II. Taylor, Bruce T., M.D. III. Series.
  BV660.2.S86   1990
  253'.2—dc20   90-39430
                                                              CIP

Published by Paulist Press
997 Macarthur Boulevard
Mahwah, New Jersey 07430

Printed and bound in the
United States of America

Contents

Dedication

In memory of Roger, a colleague in ministry, whose untimely death was perhaps a response to some of the issues discussed in this book.

Foreword

Surviving in Ministry is a book written by committed religious leaders for committed religious leaders. It is an ecumenical work that brings forth the candid views of Jewish and Christian women and men called to minister to others. Broad in scope, practical in content, it helps us realize that even though there are no easy methods of dealing with ministerial tension, we must not cease to ask pertinent questions on the topic of the relationship between stress and spiritual leadership. Likewise, we must recognize that with deep faith comes deep doubt; the chaff and the wheat grow together. Therefore, there is no final or permanent way to remove the anxieties and tensions that are a natural outgrowth of true involvement in a covenant with God.

Just before his death in 1981, Urban Holmes, the Dean of the School of Theology of the University of the South in Sewanee, Tennessee, wrote what appears to be, on first blush, a very puzzling and paradoxical phrase: "The opposite of detachment is not compassion, it is seduction."[1] By this I believe he meant that we are seduced by our own crazy expectations and the impossible expectations of others, rather than merely walking in faith with our eyes on what God wants of us. Too often we are more concerned with our image than with what is best. Too often we preoccupy ourselves with avoiding misunderstandings and looking like failures in the eyes of others rather than taking care to discern which tasks we are being called to undertake and which ones we are not.

The question of *presence* or *availability* to others as a part of living out a commitment to ministry is certainly not easy. "Availability is a great gift; it is a gift to behold, a gift to cherish, gift to share. Yet, as in any living gift, availability must be nurtured if it is to thrive and be a continual source of joy. The challenge [though] is [in] knowing how and when to do this; and the satisfaction is in knowing that if we continually try to be open to God we will never lose it."[2]

Surviving in Ministry helps us to maintain our availability to others in spiritual and emotional need by offering a wide variety of perspectives on "navigating the pitfalls and experiencing the renewals" in ministry. To accomplish this a number of key topics are covered including ones such as:

- major spiritual and theological issues and dilemmas in the life of the minister;
- appreciating the dangers of unrecognized anger and guilt and how they can be dealt with constructively;
- the tensions caused by personality disorders when they occur among religious professionals;
- the problems inherent in inadvertently basing one's self-esteem too much on the approval of others and on one's achievements in ministry;
- women's perspectives on ministerial pressures;
- the need for a support group for religious leaders;
- psychological/spiritual aspects of burnout;
- knowledge and use of the concept of "transference" in dealing with ministerial tension;
- the clergy family;
- children and spouses of religious professionals;
- clergy couples;
- the congregation as a family system.

In dealing with the above topics, as in any work—and in an edited volume in particular—there is naturally some variability in approaching the subject. In *Surviving in Ministry*, given the different backgrounds of the authors, the treatment is naturally from different points of view. In addition, although many chapters are general in nature, a significant portion, on the surface, may appear to have less *direct* application for Catholic (celibate, male) clerics. However, having noted these two points, I feel that given the richness of the volume as a whole and the value of each of the contributions, I would not hesitate to recommend *Surviving in Ministry* to all persons in ministry. There is much contained in the lessons shared—and even more in the Spirit with which they were obviously prepared.

Rabbi Tarphon, a contemporary of Jesus, once said: "The day is short, the work is great, the laborers are sluggish, the wages are high, and the Master of the house is insistent. It is not your duty to *finish* the work, but you are not free to neglect it." *Surviving in Ministry* certainly helps us to remain committed to this call to be faithful, and for this I am indeed grateful to both editors of this volume and the fine contributors who joined them in preparing such informative material.

Robert J. Wicks
Series Editor

Notes

1. Urban T. Holmes, *Spirituality for Ministry*, San Francisco: Harper & Row, 1982, p. 150.
2. Robert J. Wicks, *Availability: The Problem and the Gift*, Mahwah, New Jersey: Paulist, 1986, p. 103.

Preface

This book is a valuable resource for ministers of all faiths as well as those who work closely with any religion professionals; it is a direct outgrowth of the Isaac Taylor Institute of Psychiatry and Religion at Taylor Manor Hospital. The Institute offers inpatient, outpatient and consultative services for those religion professionals who are experiencing difficulties with work, addiction, emotional or personal issues. The Institute itself is a development of the professional work of its Director, Dr. Robert McAllister. The Isaac Taylor Institute of Psychiatry and Religion is also an embodiment of the lifelong motto of my grandfather, Isaac Taylor, for whom the Institute is named. "Live, let live, and help others to live" is the philosophy which has helped Isaac Taylor, his son, Dr. Irving Taylor, and his grandson shape and develop Taylor Manor Hospital and its programs for adolescents and adults since 1939.

The utility of this book should not, however, be limited to the religious or a strict religious definition of the word minister. All those in the "ministering professions" including health-care professionals, public leaders or others whose work is to serve the needs of our community should be able to identify with and learn from the ideas and lessons presented here. While the chapters are written with the religion professional in mind, one can easily transpose most of the ideas and concepts to others who face many similar dilemmas in their day-to-day work. As such, this book can be used as a valuable guide to a truly mature life in any ministering profession.

Bruce T. Taylor, M.D.

Robert R. Lutz, M.Div., D.P.C.

Surviving in Ministry: A Theological Dilemma

At age seventy, a chaplain became severely depressed and was hospitalized. Prior to this, he had the chaplaincy position in a large city hospital for sixteen years, working alone, six days per week, twelve hours per day. He lived at the hospital and wore a pager in order to be accessible at all times.

A minister, ordained about ten years, found that he absorbed the pain of other people and had great difficulty setting reasonable limits on the demands of others. Serving as formation director of a large seminary, he was responsible for the spiritual direction of about thirty students. When this became overwhelming he sought help. "Now don't forget to reach out to those needy people!" admonished his mother, who had visited him at the treatment facility, as she was taking her leave.

I was involved in surveying two hundred Lutheran ministers about their use of leisure time. When we were receiving the questionnaires by return mail, the pastor of a large congregation telephoned to tell me he would not fill out his questionnaire because he had no leisure time. How sad! I could not help wondering how he was surviving in ministry and what kind of example he was to his people.

Hulme, Brekke, and Behrens (1985), in a study to determine the state of health of parish ministry, concluded that this question is closely related to the health of the parish pastor. From their sample, they discovered the greatest need for pastors is for improved self-care.[1]

The Dilemma

I am convinced that many if not most ministers do not take adequate physical and emotional care of themselves. My first inkling that

1

this might be true came when I looked closely at my own life in parish ministry and discovered that I could have been taking much better care of myself. I also found that I am not much different from colleagues I know, from ministers who are psychiatric patients whom I counsel, and from research findings in this area.

The topic of self-care has been approached in a variety of ways. Time management, maintaining integrity, understanding power dynamics, and other useful topics have been explored. But from a theological perspective, self-care of one in ministry has been addressed only indirectly, as far as I can ascertain. In pondering this with a colleague, he remarked, "If ministers start taking good care of themselves, much less ministry is likely to be accomplished." I am not convinced this is true. If those in some of the examples cited above had taken better care of themselves over the years, some fewer ministry tasks may have been accomplished. This, however, seems minimal compared with the "down time" in the months of hospitalization those vignettes represent.

But my friend perhaps unknowingly put his finger on the theological dilemma which seems inherent in the issue of clergy taking care of their own needs in healthy ways. Biblical imagery depicting those in the Lord's service does not seem to allow much room for self-care. We are characterized as shepherds willing to lay down our lives for the sheep, servants seeking first the kingdom of God, followers denying ourselves to take up our cross of suffering, expected to be all things to all people. However, a closer look at some key words in the Bible may reveal more room for self-care than might be supposed.

MINISTRY—The terms "minister" and "ministry" come from a translation of the Greek word *diakoneia* which means "to serve." The nature of Christian ministry follows from the person and the work of Jesus Christ who emphasized that greatness is measured in willingness to serve (Lk 22:25–27) and who declared that he came not to be ministered to, but to minister even unto death (Mk 10:45). Thus the term "ministry" came to mean a service to God and the community which might culminate in a total sacrifice like that of Christ. The concept of responsible authority is also associated with "ministry" (cf. Acts 20:28; 1 Pet 5:2–4; 2:25). This pastoral overseeing or shepherding has a rich heritage in both the Old Testament and in the Lord's own ministry. The shepherd was responsible in the widest sense for the flock. This involved gathering, searching for the lost, tending the sick, guarding from attack, and leading to good pasture.[2] Nothing in the meaning of this term seems to indicate that being in ministry requires neglecting adequate self-care. Even when ministry calls us to dangerous or extreme circumstances, I do not believe that lack of routine, healthy self-care and ministerial sacrifice can be equated.

SERVANT—Ministers are often called servants of Christ, or, less frequently, servants of God. The Hebrew word for servant, *'ebed*, occurs almost eight hundred times and means "worker." Sometimes *'ebed* meant slave, but the term does not carry the negative sense that to be a servant or slave was to be in a despised or deprived situation. Many slaves held positions of trust, responsibility, and even authority as Joseph did in Egypt.[3]

SUFFERING SERVANT—Four passages in Isaiah are concerned with "the Servant of the Lord" in a special sense (Is 42:1–4; 49:1–6; 50:4–9; 52:13–53:12). In these passages, the servant fulfills his divine mission to the world through suffering and death for the sins of others, is raised from death, and is exalted by God. Regardless of Isaiah's original meaning for these texts, the Christian church has seen them as prophesying the coming of Jesus Christ. Most scholars agree that Jesus was deeply influenced by the servant passages in Isaiah.[4] Indeed, Jesus fulfilled the mission of the suffering servant of Isaiah. And as distinct from those who suffer as a consequence of their ministry, suffering and death were the means by which Jesus fulfilled his mission.[5]

Those who are called to ministry are called to participate in the Lord's sufferings. "If they persecuted me, they will also persecute you" (Jn 15:20). Being in ministry involves suffering and sacrifice, but I do not believe this equates with neglect of self. One of the ways I participate in suffering is to be with clients as a pastoral counselor. Sometimes the pain of my client is very real to me and I am emotionally exhausted at the end of the session. If I repeatedly ignore this exhaustion, I will become less able to be with others in their pain because of my own emotional depletion. By ignoring my needs I not only lessen the effectiveness of my ministry, but I possibly set the stage for it to come to a grinding halt when my body or emotions override my intentions and say "Stop!" in the form of a physical or emotional disorder. Ministry brings people into contact with a variety of suffering, and even danger. We need to work at being physically and emotionally fit for this type of service.

CARE—An attitude held by almost all clergy and professed religious psychiatric patients with whom I have worked is that to be in ministry means to deny self-feelings, wants, and needs in order to reach out to others. They cite passages such as Matthew 6:24–34 in which Jesus exhorts us not to worry about food or clothing but to seek first the kingdom of God, and similar passages. The common word in such passages is the Greek *merimna* (noun) or *merimnao* (verb) which means anxious concern for self, life and others. These warnings are not an admonition against all human concern. The New Testament presupposes that it is natural to be concerned for self. Rather the warnings are directed against the false orientation of these concerns and against anxiety about them. Their intention is not to forbid us to share in ordinary concerns of self-care, but that we ought not to become preoccupied with these things, thereby losing sight of God and others. Our concern for ourselves is freed from anxiety when we give up the idea that we can, by ourselves, control the future and make ourselves secure, and when we learn to commit our concern to God with thanksgiving (Phil 4:6; 1 Pet 5:7).[6]

To engage in ministry to people is to take on the role of a loving servant. This will lead to active participation in the suffering of others. It will often require placing the needs of others before our own. For some, actual persecution and even physical harm may be a consequence of ministry. Stress over long periods of time not only comes from being in the position of ministering to others but also is inherent in the organizational and emotional structure of the church. None of this, however, negates one's taking adequate emotional or physical care of self. To participate in such care can in fact be one of the ways ministers equip and prepare themselves for the demands of their calling. To avoid such care will diminish effectiveness and ultimately the duration of one's work.

In my experience, what often passes for a self-giving style of ministry are such things as the inability to set limits, a need to please others, and difficulty in maintaining ego boundaries. These resemble suffering servanthood outwardly. Inwardly, however, they can represent angry, frustrated, unhappy, resentful, and worn-out clergy people. Some of this seems to be fostered by an unhealthy perception of the expectations of the church, and some seems to be the inherent traits of those who enter ministry. I would submit, however, that it is not related to the biblical concepts of ministry, servanthood, suffering, or care.

Surviving in Ministry

So perhaps the dilemma is one of practical theology. As William Hordern points out in his book, *Living by Grace*, practical theology is the discipline of looking at the practice of the church in the light of its theology.[7] This must necessarily include the practice of the clergy of the church. And with Hordern, I believe, ". . . our practice all too often refutes our theological theory."[8]

In the rite of ordination of the Evangelical Lutheran Church in America, not unlike those of other church bodies, a candidate is set apart for the office of ministry with a series of charges and admonitions. Among these are some things the ordinand is expected to do for himself or herself which may tend to be lost or overlooked. The minister is not only to give, but also to receive comfort, to discipline himself or herself in life and to ". . . tend the flock by being an example . . . (1 Pet 5:2–4)."[9] Being an example is of crucial importance, not only for effective ministry but, I suggest, for surviving in ministry. It encompasses both self-discipline and the receiving of comfort and is probably the single most powerful tool the minister has with which to witness. The gospel needs to be read, preached and taught. The sacraments need to be administered. But none of these is as powerful in itself as it is when combined with doing the gospel. One need only look to Jesus to see the power released by the example of his life in combination with his teachings and preaching.

How then should we be examples that will not only facilitate a theologically sound ministry, but will also enable survival in ministry over the years of our service? This is a tricky question. The answer, of course, is unique to each person in ministry. God forbid we should all be carbon copies, losing the uniqueness that is God's gift to each of us.

The trickiness lies in the sources of our answers. Not all the factors impacting on our life in ministry are healthy, nor are they necessarily consistent with the theologies we proclaim verbally. Those who tend toward "workaholism" might jeopardize their health in addition to modeling a belief in salvation by works. Strong needs for approval can not only sidetrack effective ministry and create unnecessary stress, but can also witness to a belief that God is looking over our shoulder waiting to catch us doing something wrong—an angry, judgmental God.

For Christians, Jesus is the supreme model of the godly life, from whom much can be learned for our own lives. But Jesus had a calling in ministry unique to himself and unlike that of anyone else. Jesus was set apart to be the savior of the world, to die for the sin of humankind. His whole life was directed toward that end. This, however, is not my calling, nor the focus of my life. While it sounds "right" to say Jesus is my model for a life of ministry, it is just not that simple. Our God-given purposes in life are very different. Similar caution exists in raising Paul or one of the other saints to the position of role model. In this situation the humanity rather than the divinity of the model is the problem. Paul, for example, exhibited some characteristics which do not seem exemplary. His addiction to his work, his difficulty relating to females, and his impossibly high standards may not be helpful modeling for you and me. Yet much that is positive can be learned from the life of St. Paul and other significant figures in the life of the church.

Perhaps another approach to ministry by modeling could be suggested based on the belief that we are created in God's image and that God was pleased with what was created. I have in mind a model which will provide the latitude to grow toward being the unique people God made us to be, the space to take adequate care of ourselves in order to stay healthy in ministry, and the example for those we are called to serve that will be life enhancing. We can lead by being examples of:

Whole persons,
Empowered by God's grace,
To live and serve authentically, and
Be freed by that grace to accept our limits.

I shall comment briefly on the aspects of this model as an attempt to provide an orientation rather than a blueprint. The other chapters in this volume address many of the issues inherent in such an orientation as food for thought about surviving in ministry.

We can be healthy examples for the people we lead by modeling wholeness. The Bible understands persons only as whole persons. The Greek idea that body and soul are separate was certainly prevalent during the time of the writing of much of the Bible. However, it was never part of the biblical understanding of persons. Both the Greek and Hebrew words for soul and body, taken in context, refer to whole persons. As Harbaugh says in his book, *Pastor as Person*, "While a person may be addressed in terms of his or her body, mind, emotions, or in a variety of other ways, when God or the believing community speaks, the appropriate response is that of the whole person with all our heart, soul, mind, and strength (Mark 12:29ff.)."[10]

Wholeness of self cannot occur in isolation. The biblical concept of whole person is always a person in relationship to others and to God. The Israelite person was complete only in relationship with the Israelite people. We likewise only grow toward wholeness in relation to others. But beyond this, we creatures can not be understood except in relation to our creator. Harbaugh sums it up well saying, "The biblical view is of a person called to a life of love and peace with one's self, others and God."[11]

For virtually all Protestants salvation by God's grace alone is a central belief. Indeed, it was the keystone of the reformation. So the model with which we lead would do well to reflect this central concept. If it is part of our tradition, then we need to live as whole persons saved by God's grace alone. The doctrine teaches that a Christian's relationship with God is not based on merit. Therefore the ministry we do is out of love and not for the sake of any reward. This may seem very basic and obvious. However, as I reflect on my own parish ministry, I am painfully aware that at times I modeled salvation by works. I do not think that I am alone in this tendency. Ministers are always busy, busy, busy. It is inherent in the job. The way we handle that business provides a powerful role model for parishioners to follow. The drivenness of my own personality style could hardly have testified to a belief in this central doctrine though I would like to think I believe it at some level. Drivenness in ministry not only models a foreign doctrine of salvation, it is proven to be unhealthy physically and emotionally.[12]

AUTHENTICITY—I think there are at least two ways we can model salvation by grace which will be consistent with our beliefs and provide a healthy footing for our lives. The first is living as authentically as possible. An example: after about eight years of parish ministry Reverend Joe discovered that he was being not himself but rather his image of a good pastor. Basically, this meant doing everything well, when it needed to be done. Anyone who has done ministry knows there is always more to do than can possibly ever be accomplished. One must be a jack-of-all-trades. It also stands to reason that one will do some things better than others and that some aspects of ministry will be more fulfilling and enjoyable than others. No matter! On Reverend Joe charged into the work, first with enthusiasm and later with steadily growing anger and emotional weariness.

When Reverend Joe became aware of his emotional state, the words of Henri Nouwen spoke profoundly to him. "When the imitation of Christ does not mean to live a life like Christ, but to live your life as authentically as Christ lived his, then there are many ways and forms in which one can be a Christian."[13] He decided to seek counseling, realizing he was as far from being who he really was as he could get. For example, the church he served was located in a fast-growing suburban community. Reverend Joe followed moving vans making house calls, inviting people to church. He perceived that this was expected by the board, by the bishop, and by his image of the good pastor. But, in truth, he said, "I hate to make cold calls, whether it be for Christ, for Electrolux, or for the Encyclopaedia Britannica. It is impossible to be authentic while praying that no one be home." In addition, the parish was recovering from serious wounds encountered in a power struggle which had occurred before he came there as pastor. The corporate self-esteem and level of commitment seemed all but non-existent. As he explained, "What I really wanted to say when someone did answer the door was, if you're looking for a place to worship, don't come to my parish. I wouldn't go there either if I weren't the pastor."

The words of Nouwen were like a theophany for Reverend Joe. It was as if God were telling him it was all right to be who he really was. A change in his ministry began taking place. He stopped making new member calls and began to trust his feelings about what he could give from himself in that place and time. He provided a lot more pastoral care, teaching, and affirming of the members. He shifted from a stance of doing for congregation to one of being with the people. In the two years Reverend Joe remained with that congregation, the people, including Joe, grew in their sense of identity as Christians and began seeing themselves in a more positive light. When Reverend Joe began to value who he was and what he had to offer, the members began to value themselves and their life together as a congregation. Consequently, the congregation became more attractive to some of the newcomers to the community.

LIMITATIONS—Closely related to authenticity, the second way to model a belief in salvation by grace is by discovering limitations. If giving himself permission to be authentic marked the first stage in Reverend Joe's journey toward a healthier life and ministry, finding and accepting his limits characterized the next stage. In fact, encountering our limitations is a natural consequence of being who we really are. Since no one does everything well and with equal fulfillment, once we are willing to admit this to ourselves and those we serve, we quickly find our limits. Sometimes we do know, accept and share our limits intellectually. Both Reverend Joe and his congregation knew he struggled with neighborhood visiting. He participated in numerous training events and knew how to do mission development work. But not until Reverend Joe was willing to say to himself and the congregation, "This is not me," was he able to be freed from the tyranny of the notion that any pastor in a growing suburb should make new member calls.

At least two discoveries were made by Reverend Joe in this process. First, the limits turned out to be gifts. Through them he learned more about who he was as a person and as an ordained minister. He discovered a peace and a sense of competency which he had never felt before—a feeling of belonging or of having a niche in life. Second, he found the more authentic he was the more effective his ministry was. Narrowing the scope of what he did in God's service enabled him to know himself more completely, and to bring that self to his work, using his personality rather than denying it or striving to change it. The accepting of limits tends to be a freeing rather than a constricting experience through which many opportunities for growth and development emerge. It also models God's unconditional acceptance of his people, salvation by grace rather than by deed.

The other side of Reverend Joe's story also needs to be shared. What happens to pastor and people in a small, struggling congregation in a rapidly growing community when the pastor decides he is not cut out to be an evangelist or mission developer? I would not suggest that the invitation to accept limits is an invitation to selectively ignore that which is not comfortable. That would be to model irresponsibility. Rather it is a challenge to do something constructive with the discomfort. Both Reverend Joe and the congregation realized they could not ignore the steady influx of new residents to their community. But they came to this realization from the fresh perspective of becoming excited about sharing the gospel and themselves with others. Reverend Joe chose to move, enabling the congregation to call a successor with gifts and talents compatible with the now genuine need and desire to reach out to the community. He became free to choose a ministry setting more suited to his abilities and less dependent upon those skills he either lacked or had no heart for using.

Conclusion

Perhaps it is true that those of us in ministry have a difficult time taking care of ourselves. It seems however, that self-care is not so much a dilemma of theology as it is of practice. In fact, the theology of much of the Judeo-Christian tradition frees us to take adequate care of ourselves in the work of ministry. To the extent that we exercise this freedom we not only approach our work in a physically and emotionally prepared way. We also show others by example that we accept and value ourselves as God's creatures and take seriously the enormous, at times even dangerous task of ministering, by using the resources that God gave us to be ready for it.

Notes

1. William E. Hulme, Milo L. Brekke, and William C. Behrens, *Pastors in Ministry: Guidelines for Seven Critical Issues* (Minneapolis: Augsburg, 1985), p. 152.

2. Alan Richardson, *A Theological Word Book of the Bible* (New York: Macmillan, 1976), pp. 146–147.

3. Ibid., p. 223.

4. Ibid., p. 224.

5. Ibid., p. 251.

6. Ibid., p. 41.

7. William Hordern, *Living by Grace* (Philadelphia: Westminster, 1975), p. 7.

8. Ibid.

9. *Occasional Services: A Companion to the Lutheran Book of Worship* (Minneapolis: Augsburg, and Philadelphia: Board of Publication, L.C.A., 1982), p. 197.

10. Gary L. Harbaugh, *Pastor as Person* (Minneapolis: Augsburg, 1984), p. 19.

11. Ibid., pp. 19–20.

12. Hulme, p. 152.

13. Henri J.M. Nouwen, *The Wounded Healer* (New York: Doubleday, 1972), p. 103.

Rea McDonnell, S.S.N.D., Ph.D.

The Spiritual Life of the Minister

Through many dangers, toils and snares
We have already come. . .
Grace will lead us home.

Each of us could name a variety of dangers, snares and pitfalls which we have navigated in our spiritual life, for each of us experiences the life of the Spirit, its grace and its stumbling blocks, in unique ways. Yet we do hold in common our belief and our experience that our ministry is initiated, empowered, renewed by the Spirit of God. This life in the Spirit is the spiritual life, that is, the foundation, the core, the energy which propels our service with and to the people of God. The most obvious pitfalls stand at both ends of the spectrum: either neglect of the spiritual life or spiritualizing of human life so as to reinforce dualism and, subtly or blatantly, negate the human.

In this chapter I will first focus on the Spirit of God and the rhythms of that Spirit's energy which can be uncovered in very human situations. I will show how a spiritual life, far from denying the human, enriches and empowers all that is human. Secondly, I will center our reflection on God, for if we do tend to neglect our spiritual life it may be more a crimp in our relationship with God than a lack of time or leisure or discipline. Finally, I will offer some suggestions for spiritual discipline, that is, disciple-making activity.

My assumptions are simple: survival in ministry is not enough. We are called and the energy is already within us to witness, even to embody God's love for the world. We are indeed called to reexamine the pitfalls, but the work of renewal, the refreshment of our inner energy, belongs to the Spirit who is often called the *dynamis* (the energy, the power, in Greek) of God.

The Spirit

The source, center, renewer of our spiritual life is the Spirit of God. "You send forth your spirit and we are recreated," sings the psalmist (Ps 104:30). More, the psalm continues: "You renew the face of the earth." We come to ministry originally because there burns in our heart a desire to see the earth and all its people renewed, loved into new possibilities, recreated.

At times, throughout a lifetime of service, our desire ebbs, our work turns chaotic, the abyss within and without threatens to swallow us. Then we remember: "In the beginning . . . the earth was a formless chaos and darkness covered the abyss. A mighty wind (*ruah*) swept over the waters" (Gen 1:1–2). God's creativity begins with chaos, darkness, the abyss and the breath (*ruah*) of God hovering over the waters. That *ruah* of God is named the Spirit.

Once we too were immersed in "the waters." In our mother's womb we were enclosed in water, gently rocked by two major rhythms of life: our mother's breath and our mother's heartbeat. These two rhythms are imprinted deep in our own psyches, memories of peace and nurture and safety. To discover the breath of God within us is to touch back into our deepest needs for love and peace.

To breathe in tune with God, however, to move into God, is to move into permanent insecurity. Where the Spirit of God is, there is freedom. For example, exodus and resurrection are the major paradigms of freedom in our Judeo-Christian traditions. The Spirit of God cannot be controlled. To breathe, however, in union with this Breath is to share the creativity, freedom, energy, and power of the Spirit.

Breath is one biblical image of God's life within us (Ez 37:5ff) and among us, "wrapping us 'round" with power (Jgs 3:10), and gifting us to speak on God's behalf (Jl 3:1–2). Heart, in biblical imagery, is where the Spirit breathes. Heart is the human center of the Spirit's creative, freeing action. The breathing and heartbeat which we have felt from the womb unites our human/spiritual energies.

Heart in the Jewish scriptures is the organ of human thought, the wellspring of human action, the seat of human passion. In a biblical spirituality, the heart stands for the whole person. For example, the heart of Jewish faith is the *Shema*, an appeal to love the Lord with our whole heart. We hear of stony, hard, fleshy, uncircumcised hearts; we hear of hearts leaping, clenching, grieving, joyful, tender, vengeful, loving. Jeremiah describes his heart as on fire with the word of God (Jer 20:9).

In our younger years in ministry, our hearts too undoubtedly burned within us. What is it which can drain the energy of God from our hearts? It may be the sin pointed out so frequently in the scripture: forgetting—forgetting that the spirit is the source and center of our ministerial life, our spiritual life, even and especially our human life.

Idols have no breath of life (Hab 2:19), no heart. We may have cluttered our life with idols, good works, projects which have little or no spirit-breath to motivate them, no heart-energy to sustain them. We may discover in mid-life, mid-ministry, that there is only fragmented, hurried, harried heart in what we do, in how we minister. We may have forgotten how very good our God finds everything created, everything human. We may have tried to deny, repress, the fundamental rhythms of being human. We may have dichotomized heart and head, flesh and spirit, and tried to subdue our hearts, all in the name of fostering a spiritual life. Stoic philosophy, for example, gave western religion some categories for spiritual development which were quite removed from, even antithetical to, a biblical spirituality. Stoics taught that God's chief attribute was *a-pathos*, to be without passion (note the English "apathy"). The God of Jews and Christians is portrayed as very passionate, but through the centuries recurring philosophies reinforced beliefs that to be like God is to be without passion, without desire. To be spiritual, even "angelic," meant to repress all that God created good, the human, especially the heart.

Our saints were not so repressed in their spiritual lives, offering a corrective to the "escape from the body" ways of "holiness." Psalmists, Ambrose, the Wesleys sang of God's passionate love. Rabbis and Teresa of Avila danced in response to God's love. Augustine, Francis of Assisi, Martin Luther were men of great heart, deep passion, loving all of life as God's way of coming very close to us.

An exercise, using our imagination, may help us remember how much God wants to heal and free and make whole our hearts, our humanity.

First, sit comfortably and quietly, two feet on the floor.

Breathe deeply.

Feel the energy of the earth penetrate your feet, grounded in the earth. Feel the energy move up your legs, into your torso, your heart, neck, head.

Continue breathing deeply for a while as you relax into an energy which is also *shalom*, peace, wholeness.

Hear God speak directly to you through the words of Isaiah: "I have carved you on the palms of my hands" (Is 49:16).

Now image your heart, torn with worries, hurts, rejections, fears. It may be bleeding, swollen, gouged out, puffed up.

Image God standing before you. God holds out a hand for your heart.

You notice God's hand. It is wounded, carved with your name. This wound pours out gold and glory and fire.

Now, God calls your name and directly asks for your heart— just the way it is.

You give it to the Lord.

The fire of God's hand cauterizes your wounds, burns away old bitterness and resentments. Healing begins.

Watch as God caresses your heart. The fire is not painful, but healing, energizing. The fire of God's hand is powering your heart.

Breathe out . . .

Breathe in . . .

Feel the rhythm . . .

Now God gives you back your heart.

Respond as you are so moved.

To be spiritual is to be human. To be human is to participate in the Spirit of God. The glory of God, Irenaeus, theologian of the second century, proclaimed, is the human being fully alive.

God

Who is this God who enjoys and is glorified by our becoming ever more fully human? God is mystery—one whom we will continue to discover for all eternity. Mystery is that which is infinitely knowable. Our words and images of God are mere attempts to know. Yet our God wants to be known. Our God is characterized by desire to reveal to us God's own self.

When we make any response to God's self-revelation we are expressing a "spiritual life." Spirituality simply means our unique response to God's initiative in our lives. Our spirituality is simply our relationship with God.

An exercise, using our memory, may make this more clear.

Again, sit quietly, feet grounded, feeling the earth's energy flood you, as you breathe deeply, slowly . . .

Remember your dearest, deepest human relationship.

How did you become close? What were you afraid of as you moved closer to each other?

What melts you, what angers you in your relationship?

How do you continually grow closer? What blocks intimacy with this person?

What do you admire in her/him? What are you grateful for? What do you regret in the relationship? What more do you want?

Be concrete, as specific as you can be in your remembering.

Jot your insights, memories and feelings down on paper.

What you have experienced in this relationship and in pondering it in your heart should reveal much of what you experience in relating to God. The best image and experience we can have of God is often that which we call "bigger than both of us," our love.

God is love. God is characterized particularly in the psalms, prophets and gospels as faithful to us (*'emet*) with a kindness, mercy, abundant and extravagant love which defies translation from the Hebrew word, *hesed*. If we are neglecting our spiritual life in ministry, it may be that we are neglecting our love life. If intimacy with a human person can wither because of our busy-ness, our scattered heart, how much more our intimacy with God.

In our human loves, intimacy may never even begin or may be cut short because we are afraid: afraid to be vulnerable or generous or

mutual, or even afraid to let ourselves be loved. In our relationship
with God the same fears may keep us distanced, withering our life in
the Spirit. No wonder that in the Jewish scriptures and New Testament the usual exhortation is "Be not afraid."

If we are often afraid of our own depths of passion, sometimes it is
the passion of God, especially anger as we read of it in scripture,
which frightens us away from God. Notice your own anger as you
remembered it in your dearest relationship. Doesn't anger often express intimacy? Isn't the aftermath of an angry exchange often a
deeper understanding and love? We might rethink, refeel God's
anger, now that we are adults. Of course, children are afraid of the
power of an adult's anger, no matter how just the authority, the parent. But in mutual relationship, the kind to which God invites adult
ministers, anger is an expression of trust, trust in the other and in the
strength of the relationship. God's anger may be an expression of
God's trust in us and a passionate desire for our growth. Because
intimacy is mutual, we can perhaps begin to acknowledge our angers
with God.

In our human loves, anger which is unexpressed can cool a relationship. Misunderstanding, expectations, hurts can build into buried
rage. Our unexpressed anger with God, too, can block our mutual
exchange of love and life. For example, some people expect God to
rescue them from suffering and misfortune. "Our God is a God who
saves," the psalmist assures us (Ps 68:20). We, however, might
equate saving with rescue, whereas from the Hebrew it means God's
giving us space, room, freedom. Instead of plucking us from our pain,
our God stays with us in our pain. "God bears our burdens day after
day; our God is a God who saves" (Ps 68:19–20).

In our human loves, a willful ego can damage a relationship. We
call actions flowing from such egocentricity sin. Sin surely can destroy our taste for God. The willful ego can be passive; then sin can
pose as a spirituality so dependent on God that the human person is
effaced—hardly the glory of God! The willful ego can be active, involved in projects which can pose as the "work of God" but are
motivated primarily by needs for human and/or divine acceptance,
approval, applause.

Another block in our relationship with God (and there are as
many as there are those consciously relating with God!) may be our
image of God, or our understanding of God's will. Muslims have one
hundred names for God. The Hindus recite one thousand names of
God. The Jewish scriptures teem with images of God as rock, dew,
fortress, nurse, etc. God offers us two special names in the book of

Exodus. In Exodus 3 we are told that God is like a burning bush. God is unending energy, something which the eastern churches have not forgotten. God's name emphasized God as Being: I am who am.

In Exodus 34:5-6, God reveals another name to Moses: "The Lord, the Lord, a God merciful and gracious, slow to anger and abounding in steadfast love." This is a passionately loving God. "Merciful" is a word reminiscent of the womb, that peaceful, nourishing, safe space. "Gracious" includes all that we mean by grace: free gift, abundant life, God's own self. "Steadfast love" links *hesed* (extravagant, unconditional mercy, kindness, tenderness, love and compassion of God) and *'emet* (usually translated "truth" but meaning a firm, steady, true, consistent and everlasting fidelity).

What is the will of such a God? If we change "will of God" to "what God passionately desires" we may cut through centuries of obfuscation, often in the name of spirituality, of the good news of the scriptures. God passionately desires life, life in abundance! God hates death, injustice, pain, sickness, and devotes divine energy and exhortation to destroy them. "This is what I want: releasing those bound unjustly, untying the thongs of the yoke, setting free the oppressed, breaking every yoke, sharing your bread with the hungry, sheltering the oppressed and the homeless, clothing the naked when you see them, and not turning your back on your own" (Is 58:6-7). "Choose life!" is a deeply heartfelt cry of our God to us (Dt 30:19).

Instead, we and our ancestors in the ways of holiness may have chosen death, suffering, as "God's holy will." If the circumstances of life did not offer us enough pain, we may have taken "sacrifice" into our own hands, mortifying ourselves and feeling quite spiritual and holy indeed. The meaning of discipline changed, so that difficulties were not only embraced but longed for as a sign of God's special favor. The practice of virtue replaced the free response to God's guiding Spirit. Works of justice were replaced by works of law by which we thought to secure our spiritual status.

"Choose life!" We who are carried ever deeper into relationship by our unconditionally loving, faithful God are invited to choose life, to let the Lord bear us up on eagles' wings (Ex 19:4), to let God set us free. Our unique response to this devoted initiative of God is also our spiritual life.

Discipline

Some have equated the spiritual life with the various disciplines associated with it, marking their progress in prayer, fasting, almsgiv-

ing, works of justice and charity, contemplation, communal worship,
reflective reading of scripture, "quiet time," and many more. Discipline almost always, despite the age-old debate about works and
grace, means work, and sometimes has even meant any self-chosen,
self-inflicted difficulty, borne with stoic courage. As much as this may
seem a caricature, religion professionals do seem uneasy, even guilty,
if they are not working at their spiritual life, if they have not provided
discipline for their spiritual journey.

Discipline has at its root, however, the Latin *discipulus/a,* a
learner. Discipline is all activity and attitude which alerts our ears,
eyes, hearts, selves, to the attitudes and actions of God. Discipline is
disciple-making activity, that which fosters our learning of God and
from God. We will center in the chapter on two foundational disciplines which open us to God: a contemplative attitude and compassionate action. Then we will examine the fruit of these disciplines,
since, according to the gospel, the richness of our life in the Spirit is
known by its fruits.

To study scripture is to worship, Jews believe. To learn God not
only from the revealed word but also from every human situation,
every human encounter, is to grow in a more intimate knowledge of
God. Even sin, our personal sin and evil in the world, can show us God
both in vivid contrast and also at work within the sin, transforming
even that into grace. Life is knowing God, a wholehearted knowing
which includes our whole person, not just our intellect. Knowing in
this way, according to scripture, is union with God. Thus, a fundamental discipline which can allow the Spirit to renew us and deepen
our union with God is to develop a contemplative attitude.

A contemplative attitude need not be religious. A baby coos for
hours, watching the leaves dance in the wind outside its bedroom
window. A sudden sunrise between dingy city buildings catches our
eye, and our throat, with awe. A comtemplative attitude means simply paying attention, but it does require an eye, ear, mind, heart
which is open, alert, receptive. The wonder/awe/openness which is
religious knows that "the world is charged with the grandeur of
God!" (Gerard Manley Hopkins). The contemplative heart receives
and treasures not only God, scripture, holy things, but everything.
Nothing is too base, too earthy, if the Spirit lights up creation from
within.

It is consciousness of the Spirit's movement, light, rhythm, work,
which adds the religious element to the contemplative attention we
give persons, events and environments. The Spirit finds us in the

midst of our daily activities and teaches us of God's heart, God's desire, in the midst of what we are doing, thinking, feeling.

To foster a contemplative attitude is to become quick of heart. Throughout Jewish scripture the great gift of God is wisdom, the listening and understanding heart, a heart alert to hear God's word, a receptive heart. To be receptive to God, God's word and Spirit, in even the most ordinary experiences of human living and loving is to develop a contemplative attitude.

A contemplative attitude undergirds our prayer. Asking God for the needs of our people is an important way to pray. So is waiting for the Spirit to bubble up from deep within us, putting our inarticulate groans, praises, hopes, needs, thanks, into words which God can understand and receive into God's own contemplative heart of womb-compassion.

A second fundamental discipline in the spiritual life, one which makes us learners from the heart of God, is compassion. There are so many good works, some of which can pose as compassion but which eventually leave the minister dis-spirited, compulsive, burned out, dissatisfied, greedy for recognition and/or gratitude. Compassionate action which twins with contemplative attitude, however, flows from a passion shared with God.

Com-passion, from the Latin, means literally to have passion with, as does *em-pathos* from the Greek. No seminary class, no lay ministry training program, can teach this way of being with. Granted, we can learn and renew and retool our skills for listening, responding, and choosing to love those whom we serve. Choosing to love can eventually lead to a more spontaneous kindness and tenderness, pruned of patronizing pity, as we enter their anger, fear, despair or joy. What steadies our love, what fuels us with an enduring flame, however, is to share God's own passion for people: for their life and health and wholeness (*shalom*).

Because we are living life in the Spirit we are invited to put flesh on God's heart, to embody God's own tender (*hesed*) faithfulness (*'emet*) toward the world and the human family. When God notices people who are lost, we search for them; when God discovers the strays, we bring them back; when God sees the injured, we bind them up; when God finds the sick, we tend them; when God rejoices in the strong and healthy, we set them out to play (paraphrase of Ez 34:16).

The gospel according to Luke, which offers a portrait of God as compassionate, hands on Jesus' exhortation: "Be you compassionate as your heavenly Father is compassionate" (Lk 6:36). Share the passion of our God, Jesus encourages us—God's passion for justice, peace, love, life, God's passion with people. The energy for that passion and com-passion is the Spirit who breathes within us, re-creates and continually renews our spiritual life.

Finally, we experience the fruits of a contemplative attitude and compassionate action. Fruits are not virtues to be admired, chosen and practiced, worked at. Fruits grow simply and steadily, almost imperceptibly, as the Spirit transforms us gradually. Love, joy, peace, kindness, faithfulness, patience with ourselves and others blossom, solidify, become a source of nourishment for others. We are less driven, more free, taking responsibility for our lives, ministries, interpersonal boundaries. We become humble, we become wise.

Our minds and hearts throb with the attitudes, energies, loves of God's own self, and, without effort on our part, throb with love for God's own self. We are fascinated with the mystery which powers the core of our own being. We enjoy God, the goal of the spiritual life.

Bibliography

Laurence Dunlop, *Patterns of Prayer in the Psalms* (New York: Seabury, 1982).

Joseph Grassi, *Healing the Heart* (New York: Paulist, 1987).

Merle R. Jordan, *Taking On the Gods* (Nashville: Abingdon Press, 1986).

Rea McDonnell, S.S.N.D., and Rachel Callahan, *Hope for Healing* (New York: Paulist, 1987).

Rea McDonnell, S.S.N.D., *Prayer Pilgrimage Through Scripture* (New York: Paulist, 1984).

Ann Ulanov and Barry Ulanov, *Primary Speech* (Atlanta: John Knox Press, 1982).

Glenn E. Ludwig, M.Div.

And at the Center: Integrity

"Ban Saturday Night Specials—They Kill"

It could be a newspaper headline about a proposed gun control law—in which case, there would be much debate over the nature of the ban, what is to be banned, and the protracted indicative postulated as to its authenticity (i.e. do they, indeed, kill?).

But it is not about guns. It is about Saturday night specials, and those of us who wear special collars or certain titles and have a very specific calling to live out. Is it becoming clearer? How about an illustration that will touch the nerve?

It is 11:00 p.m. on Saturday night. A particularly tough week has slipped by and tomorrow is Sunday. People from around the community will gather to hear something that will give meaning to their lives, something that will inspire or move or motivate them. And you sit at the keyboard staring at a screen or a blank sheet of paper. The week has been lost to details and meetings and administrations and letters and mail and a whole host of demons that have kept the profound from finding a place to rest in the mind. It is now time (actually, past time) to conjure forth those profundities and to form them gracefully (full of grace) into a creation known as a sermon. But you and I both know that from Saturday Night Specials profound religious truths rarely flow. The life, the energy, and indeed, the faith have been drained away from the one from whom much is now required.

Is it true that Saturday Night Specials kill? You bet—they kill the Spirit and the witness to the Spirit. The messenger, as in days of old, is killed because he or she does not come with good news.

Perhaps you will excuse the excesses in imagery in the illustration. But the reality of which I speak is true nonetheless. How does one handle the complexity of busy schedules and still find time for studying, pondering, and stewing over the word?

Some would perhaps suggest that the answer lies in time management. Speed Leas, author of a book entitled *Time Management*, would disagree. Writes Leas: "Time is not manageable. However, it is possible to manage oneself in time and to be responsive to circumstances as they arise."[1]

The real answer, I would contend, lies deeper than uses of time. In fact, how we use our time, the choices we make in ministry, the priorities we set for ourselves, all have their roots at the center of where we do our living. And at the center lies the issue of personal integrity. That is what this particular chapter is all about—integrity.

Integrity

It comes from the Latin, *integer*, meaning "anything complete in itself; entity; whole." It carries the connotation of being complete, of wholeness, of soundness. It is a quality or state of being whole, not fractured.

Actually, it is a hard word to clearly define. Maybe it is like rhythm—if you have to ask, you don't have it! Or maybe it is one of those phenomena in a person's life that is more easily known in its absence than in its presence. We have all known people who have lacked it and in its lacking it is all too obvious.

Although the Bible makes few references to integrity, it is clearly bound up in the concept of wholeness, a concept the Bible does make much of. Actually, the scriptural references to integrity all confirm our present day understanding of it. Used in scripture, integrity is a state or quality of being complete or well adjusted. It implies sincerity of heart and motive, singleness of purpose, genuineness, truthfulness and uprightness. The psalmist makes much of "walking in my integrity" (Ps 26:11) and "walk with integrity of the heart" (Ps 101:2). It is clear that one does "walk" in this state of wholeness and that the seat for such a quality lies in the heart, the center of one's life.

While the term scarcely appears in the New Testament, the concept is clear enough. We read about "purity of heart," "singleness of eye," "purity of motive," and the numerous injunctions to truthfulness, sincerity and genuineness as fundamental to Christian character and conduct.

If it is the concept of wholeness that forms the center out of which we function as leaders in a religious community, then a large part of our function *to* the community is to assist others in their quest for that same wholeness. "If we, as pastors, are seriously concerned to make possible for modern people that quality of liberated life promised in the Gospel, then we must acquire a new competency that cuts across any traditional role of the pastor—the vision and skill to search and assist others in their struggle to find wholeness and to work for wholeness in society."[2]

The importance of living in or walking in integrity can not be overstated. For those who serve as ministers and proclaimers of truth, the injunction to live in the truth of which we proclaim is always upon us. And we know the demands upon us and what they can do to us. Although writing about spirituality, Jay C. Rochelle in a recent journal article is making something of the same claim. He writes: "People in the ordained ranks continue to be chewed up into little bits and pieces, a process which cannot help but wear away at the quality and the depth of their ministry. We need constantly and fervently to return to the center of our faith if we are not to be chewed up into little bits. Such maceration always starts at the edge, but it proceeds to the center if you are not careful to maintain and deepen and freshen that center. If the center holds, you can afford ragged edges."[3]

Integrity and Priorities

The edges do get frayed, don't they? Well, how can we keep that from chewing into the center of our lives where faith, hope, love, and integrity abide? The answer? Being clear about priorities.

It is a strange and wonderful calling we enjoy. On the one hand, there is the freedom of movement, freedom in daily activities, freedom to make choices, freedom to decide our own schedules, and freedom to set priorities. On the other hand, we live under the mandate of our creeds, our faith, our belief system, and our communities who have called us to serve. We all know of the pressures there are, both internal and external. The vagueness of our calling contributes to those pressures. Hulme et al., writing in their marvelous little book, *Pastors in Ministry*, make the same point using the term "boundaries." As they claim, there is much "vagueness in many parish settings regarding these boundaries which, in turn, leads to unnecessary pressures of guilt."[4]

Developing priorities for one's ministry is based on a four step process. First, we need to assess our own skills. What is it we do well? What gifts and talents have been given to us to use and develop? Knowledge of self and honest appraisal of one's gifts are essential if we are to serve others in creative and faithful ways. Second, we need to assess the needs and assumptions of those whom we are called to serve. We cannot serve effectively if we do not know whom we are

serving. What are the needs around us? What expectations do people
have of us in meeting those needs? As Hulme comments: "Clergy and
congregations need to be clear about what each expects of the other.
The boundaries need to be drawn, assumptions need to be verbalized,
and a consensus reached on all of these expectations."[5] Third (and
this may sound a little strange to the ears), where is your heart? Do
you have the heart to do the specific ministries, to meet the needs of
those who have called you? Are the skills you possess matched with a
will to use them creatively? For instance, I know that I have neither
the heart nor the skills to do effective social ministry. I thank God that
there are those who do and I certainly support their efforts when and
where I can. But do not put me in the front line of such activities. This
is not to say that these ministries are not important or crucial. It is to
say, honestly, that my heart rests in other equally pressing areas of
ministry. Where is your heart? That is an honest, confessional question that needs to be answered as priorities are established for yourself in ministry. Fourth, and finally, all of the above need to be
matched together. How do the gifts God has given match the needs of
the community we are called to serve? And, further, how do those
needs reside in our hearts? Do we possess the will, even if we have the
skills, to meet those needs?

Writing in his fine book, *Pursuing Excellence in Ministry*, Daniel
V. Biles underscores the importance of self-awareness for both pastors and congregations. "Mission is knowing who you are and what
God expects you to do. Good pastors and congregations have this
self-awareness. It is a clear and commonly-held understanding of
what ministry is and how it is to be carried out in a given parish."[6]
Further on in the same book, in writing about the foundations of
excellence in parishes, he makes a similar point as it relates to leadership. He says that leadership is "rooted in a pastor's self-awareness of
being called by God to exercise that office of ministry and refined by
training in the various disciplines and tasks of pastoral ministry. It is
exercised through an ordained minister's constant interaction with
people in pursuit of bringing the Gospel to bear on their lives."[7]

The clear setting of priorities in a pastor's life enables him or her
to make sense out of conflicting and competing demands for time and
attention. It is clear priorities that will help keep a focus on what
needs to be done and how it is to be accomplished. This requires a
great deal of discipline and self-governance as well as self-awareness.
But the result, if we do not keep clear priorities, is a fragmentation of
our energies and a fragmenting of our lives. And fragments are not
wholeness!

Writing about autonomy and its importance, Harris is stressing the same point. "What our situation requires is pastors with the capacity for autonomy. Autonomy is an extremely over-used word today, with many definitions. . . . Autonomy has to do with people's inner ability to govern themselves. The concept of autonomy, as I see it, does not mean noisy self-assertion, adolescent rebellion against authority, or rugged lonerism. The autonomy of pastors, for me, is a capacity to balance and resolve opposing demands within themselves and between them and their congregations. It is the ability to do so in keeping with their personal values and intelligent self-interest and with the interests of the congregations in which they work. . . . In order to sustain a creative degree of tension, to take risks, to be out front about their hopes and intentions, to tolerate ambiguity, to stand criticism, to challenge prevailing norms, pastors must have within themselves the ability to be autonomous persons."[8]

Integrity and Professionalism

Now we come to an area that has raised controversy in religious circles—namely, the use of the term "profession" as it applies to ministry. Biles writes: "Fundamentally, the ordained ministry is not a profession; it is a calling. Different values are at work. The values and priorities of a career are simply incompatible with those of a *vocatio,* calling."[9]

While I would agree on theological principle with that argument, I want to clarify my use of "professionalism" before more theological flak is thrown. By professionalism, I mean really three things.

First, we are professionals if by that we mean that we are a body of persons engaged in a particular calling. That is one of the valid definitions of the word. And, what it means is that we have a level of conduct and performance (another bad word) that are expected of us by virtue of that calling. In some religious circles, there are codes of ethics that are required if one is to remain in the calling. To say we are professionals is to say that as a body, we are part of those codes of ethics where certain behaviors or activities are expected of us. This is not meant to deny the reality of the call and all the implications of service and ministry that go with it. It is meant to emphasize that we share as clergy in a profession that places expectations.

Second, those expectations are both from without and from within. The community of faith that calls us expects us to be effective ministers and faithful persons. They have a right to expect some degree of competency in ministerial tasks that we are called to do. A professional is one who knows what those expectations are and who faithfully seeks to be responsive to them. This means that we spend as much time preparing for a sermon to be preached to fifty persons as we would to a crowd of five hundred. It means that we give our attention to worship leadership whether it is the first service of the day or the fifth.

Chris Argyris maintains that there are three ingredients which make possible the expression of competence and personal effectiveness in individuals, regardless of the nature of their work. Self-acceptance: the degree to which the individual has confidence in himself or herself. Confirmation: when others experience me as I experience myself, that is, when I am able to gauge accurately the effect of my behavior on others. And essentiality: the more I am able to use my central abilities and express my central needs, the greater will be my feeling of essentiality to myself and to the setting involved.[10]

Third, professionalism involves motivation of the self. This is what Harris meant by "autonomy." It is the ability to do when one feels like not doing. It is the discipline needed to serve when one is hurt or hurting. It is the faithfulness to the calling that pushes one to go where angels may fear to tread. It is being true to the calling that we share in a way that continues to motivate us to serve in creative and effective ways.

Professionalism may be a dirty word in some theological circles, but I think it becomes an expression of integrity when understood in the right way. There are certainly expectations of duties, of conduct, of ethics we share in this calling. To live in them is to live in integrity.

Integrity and Decision Making

"Pastors are not likely to lead the way in risk taking."[11] So writes Gary Harbaugh in his fine book, *Pastor as Person*. He goes on to write: "However, the pastor is chosen by God to lead God's people. . . . So the pastor is called to provide pastoral care, but also to call God's people to choose a faithful future. . . . If faith is a choice forever and today, then pastors as persons need to become more attuned to risk taking. The reason is simple: there is no choice without risk. . . . When you say yes to one thing, you must inevitably say no to another."[12]

With our priorities all sorted out, and an understanding that we live with expectations and needs, the proverbial rubber hits the road when decisions are made. Making decisions means taking risks. We will please some with the decisions we make; we will earn the disdain and disapproval of others. How do we live with the fact that we can't please everyone whom we are called to serve? The answer by now should be self-evident—we live out of our own integrity. This integrity has been forged and molded by our calling, by the gifts God has given us, by the careful assessment of the needs around us, and by our desire to respond to those needs with what God has given us. No one can expect more. To stay true to ourselves, to live in the wholeness we own, means that we must make decisions at times that will not please others. But we can live with those decisions and the flak they bring if we have made those decisions out of our own sense of integrity.

Hulme et al. have some instructive words for those who wrestle with decisions. "In the midst of your challenges in your ministry, you really have nothing to prove. . . . Our goals should be inspirations for our action, not measurements for our self-judgment."[13]

It is, indeed, true that to say yes to some things is to say no to others. Even the choices of our priorities show that we have made decisions. Given the plethora of demands and expectations, the only way to maintain sanity is to be clear about who we are, what God is calling us to do where we are, and how we are to go about doing it. Otherwise, we get chewed up and out in the process of daily ministry. Truly autonomous persons must act out of their own sense of integrity so that important and necessary tasks get done and the peripheral tasks are left to another time.

For a fuller examination of this area, I highly recommend Gary L. Harbaugh's *Pastor as Person*. His subtitle, "Maintaining Personal Integrity in the Choices and Challenges of Ministry," describes what he lays out in the book. He provides an excellent schematic way to understand the holism required of today's pastors.

Integrity and Limits

It was Alfred North Whitehead who said: "A man has to ignore much to get on with something." Anyone who has lived under the constraints of a twenty-four-hour day and a twenty-five-hour work load knows the truth of that statement. We often have to ignore much to get any work done at all. This is called setting limits, and it is admittedly hard to do in a calling such as the ministry.

Writing in *Pulpit Digest*, C. Neil Strait offers some suggestions for what to ignore in the ministry. He says that in order for us to get on with our task of ministry, we must ignore the following temptations: to compare, to compromise, to become critical, to center everything on self, to carelessness, to commit to more than can be done, to conformity, and to cynicism.[14]

In his list is one that is crucial for all of us—to avoid the temptation to commit to more than can be done. Have any of us ever done that? Maybe the question should be: Have any of us ever *not* done that?

It is hard, is it not, to set limits? Harris thinks the problem rests in our fears. "Keeping busy makes you less vulnerable to criticism in a job few laity understand, and by keeping busy you show you have something to do; fear of not being needed; fear of the retribution we dream comes like the Furies to all pastors who say 'No' fear of owning up to your limits and thus revealing to everyone that you cannot be counted on (unlike your predecessor) to reassure them in their wish to be invulnerable to life."[15]

A sense of integrity can speak calming words to those fears. Operating our lives out of the wholeness we know and living with the self-knowledge of our own capabilities and limitations, we can learn to say "no" when appropriate. And it is appropriate to say "no" on occasion.

The whole notion of planned neglect postulated by Hulme is intriguing. "All of us need to learn to accept our limits. . . . Since accepting our limits is really accepting who we are as children of God, we can see in this challenge God's call to us. Learning, in this context, means growing. . . . Therefore, it is not more time that we need but a different attitude toward time, one that would enable us to deal with it realistically. . . . So we have to work, reducing the demands to which we need to respond. One commentator called this reducing process 'planned neglect'."[16]

Limit setting is really part of the process of knowing oneself and taking responsibility for oneself. We can begin to do that when we live in our integrity, knowing that in our priorities there is the need to take care of ourselves. Leas reminds us: "Overworked pastors are trying to do the best they know how, and the best they know is never to let up. They forget that there is no relation between the amount of time and effort that goes into the minister's work and its effectiveness —none whatsoever. In God's work, rewards are not related to the amount of labor."[17]

Part of the answer to setting limits is in learning to apply the old maxim: to work smarter, not harder. It is a lesson that those of us who confess to compulsiveness need to relearn.

And at the Center: Integrity

We are back to the center from which this essay started. Integrity is not only a rich word, it is a freighted word; a word that carries implications throughout our lives and ministries. I have tried to explore some of the facets of it here for your rumination. It is my contention that wholeness is the key to effectiveness and faithfulness in ministry. Ultimately, integrity is God's gift to us. We are whole because he creates us whole. Our sinfulness fractures that wholeness and only by his grace do we ever regain it. Our challenge then becomes to live out of, or walk in, that wholeness in our daily walks. Like an internal gyroscope, integrity guides our days and allows us to offer to the night our peaceful spirits.

Notes

1. Speed Leas, *Time Management* (Nashville: Abingdon, 1978), p. 15.

2. John C. Harris, *Stress, Power, and Ministry* (Washington: The Alban Institute Inc., 1977), p. 137.

3. Jay C. Rochelle, "Paying Attention to the Center," *Lutheran Partners* (September/October 1988), p. 10.

4. William E. Hulme, et al., *Pastors in Ministry* (Minneapolis: Augsburg, 1985), p. 101.

5. Ibid., p. 103.

6. Daniel V. Biles, *Pursuing Excellence in Ministry* (Washington: The Alban Institute Inc., 1988), p. 8.

7. Ibid., p. 9.

8. Harris, pp. 56–57.

9. Biles, p. 34.

10. Chris Argyris, *Intervention, Theory and Method* (Reading: Addison Wesley, 1970), p. 39.

11. Gary L. Harbaugh, *Pastor as Person* (Minneapolis: Augsburg, 1984), p. 125.

12. Ibid., pp. 125–126.

13. Hulme, p. 97.

14. C. Neil Strait, "What To Ignore in the Ministry," *Pulpit Digest* (September/October 1988), pp. 33–34.

15. Harris, p. 74.

16. Hulme et al., pp. 98–99.

17. Leas, p. 21.

Robert J. McAllister, Ph.D., M.D.

Anger and Guilt

Dom Vernon Moore wrote one of the early textbooks in psychology and entitled it *The Driving Forces of Human Nature*. The same author had a companion volume, *Cognitive Psychology*. These two titles maintained a rather artificial distinction between cognitive processes and emotional processes. However, in choosing the first title, the author succinctly made an important statement regarding emotions, namely, they represent the driving forces of our lives.

Anger is frequently regarded as a negative emotion, and in addition, is often associated with sinfulness. This pejorative view of anger transforms it from being a healthy component of human response, to being an unhealthy aspect of the human condition. Characteristically, religion has contributed to this harsh view of anger with the position that if anger drives humans anywhere it drives them to violence in a variety of sinful ways including the verbal violence of voiced rage, gossip, calumny and detraction, the physical violence of war, wife beating, child abuse, rape, and the social violence of poverty and prejudice. Because traffic accidents result in permanent injuries, destruction of property, and loss of life, this is not reason enough to do away with automobiles on the grounds that they are evil. Because anger produces evil results is not reason enough to call anger evil. Sexual drives certainly result in wrongdoing, but religion has distinguished between sexual drives and expressions that are healthy and sexual drives and expressions that are unhealthy. Various religions may argue the latitude permitted on the healthy side, but there is common agreement that there is a healthy component in sexual matters. The same may be said about the hunger drive, with greater latitude for the healthy expressions of hunger. This drive too has an unhealthy expression when the level of nutritional intake becomes a distinct hazard to an individual's physical and emotional well-being.

Anger often does not fare as well as other driving forces do when viewed by organized religion. Some religions declare that anger is sinful and has no place in human responses. "Anger is mine, saith the

Lord." This rigid interdict regarding anger ties guilt to any infraction. Any angry response, calculated and deliberate, or spontaneous and impulsive, shares equal guilt. The slammed door, the abrupt departure, the failed enthusiasm, announce to the individual, if not to the world, that the religious code has been violated. If the individual gains control over these outward manifestations of irritability, there remains an accounting for the internal stirrings that cause such external responses. What does one do about that inner irritability, that non-verbal feeling that makes its way into some kind of unspoken phraseology, "Get off my back. Go to hell. Leave me alone. I hate you. Drop dead." The rigid religious person must account for these sentiments, although they may never be formulated clearly but only take the illusive form of inner inclinations that put words to feelings and make them appear to be well-thought-out ideas with decision goals.

Although many religious systems do not denounce so definitively anything that has to do with anger, the kind of attitudes outlined above permeate much of the religion professional's thinking about anger. Although his or her theological background may permit some distinctions in regard to anger the religion professional's personal adherence to a "higher standard" may not allow for such latitude. This further limitation of the minister's anger is usually supported by the congregation he or she may serve. It is permissible for the reverend to engage in sexual intercourse with spouse, although church members would probably prefer not to think about it. It is probably not permissible for the religion professional to feel sexually attracted to anyone other than the spouse. Congregations may permit some display of wrath in relation to just causes, a kind of righteous anger, a spiritual alignment with the Almighty. Such display of homiletic ire is seen as an intellectual stand intended to stir others to right conscience and good deeds. It is, after all, non-personal. But what if the pastor berates the paper boy for not putting the paper well under the porch out of the rain? Or what if the pastor shouts angrily at her or his children for not coming in the house when first called? And if the pastor learns of some grapevine gossip maligning a family member, should the pastor not respond in anger?

Unfortunately many religion professionals find themselves so constrained by their own lofty ideals and by the narrow expectations of their congregants that they avoid the natural and healthy outward manifestations of anger. This avoidance leads to emotional impairment in one of two ways. The person who denies the expression of anger may reach a point where the feelings of anger are also denied and eventually unrecognized. Or the person who denies the outward expression may store inside a backlog of anger that does not dissipate but builds to an explosive level of fettered fury. Either situation is less than wholesome.

Anger, like most powerful emotions, has three basic components. It is important to understand these clearly. First, there is the immediate response to the stimulus causing the anger. This can best be conceived of as psychological hurt or emotional pain. The stimulus may be a slap in the face, a verbal attack, a social put-down. The immediate response is a feeling of being hurt, wounded, damaged. Somehow emotional pain has a way of spreading throughout the individual. If someone kicks a person in the shin, the physical pain remains localized. But emotional hurt spreads like a systemic infection throughout the self. This creates two additional components of the anger response. The second component is the physiological response to the psychological wound, and the third component is the mental response.

The autonomic nervous system controls body functions that are not normally under voluntary control. Blood pressure, respiration, circulation, cardiac hemodynamics, gastrointestinal function, and endocrine secretion are to a great extent regulated through the sympathetic and parasympathetic chains of the autonomic nervous system. When someone is angry, gastrointestinal motility, absorption, and digestion are slowed. Cardiac output and respiratory rate increase. Oxygenation is enhanced to the central nervous system providing greater alertness and a sense of power. Blood flow to the skeletal and voluntary musculature increases, simultaneously decreasing blood flow to the viscera. The third component of anger which occurs simultaneously with the second component is the mental component. Persons are most conscious of this component, and it is precisely here that guilt arises most prominently. The mental component seems so intellectual, so voluntary, so involved with judgment and decision. Just as the psychological pain spreads throughout the body functions, so it permeates mental functions. And minds work in words and mental pictures. So angry minds are full of harsh words of retaliation and hurtful pictures of revenge. These cause pangs of guilt in the person who fails to distinguish the great distance between angry inner-mind words and the same words spoken or the violent inner-mind pictures and those pictures acted upon.

These three components are natural, integral parts of anger.

They are part of the stimulus-response pattern with which we are created. These components are as morally neutral as are our component responses to the pain of touching a hot stove or breaking a leg skiing. There is the local pain, the autonomic physiologic reactions, and a variety of associated mental pictures, all of which have nothing to do with right or wrong.

There is a fourth component of anger which appears in a variety of ways and with a great range of intensity. This component might be called the secondary phase of anger as opposed to the three integral components mentioned above which might be called the primary phase. The secondary phase of anger includes the more reasoned and deliberate prolongation of the mental words and pictures which occur spontaneously and naturally in anger, as well as the external manifestation of those inner-mind events associated with anger. Moral concerns rightfully enter at this juncture. How one expresses anger externally, how one harbors and nurses internal angry feelings and thoughts and plans, this component of anger is the rightful province of the moral theologian. However, even here some distinctions are obvious. The sudden, brief, spontaneous response represents one end of the spectrum. The slammed door, the muttered retort, even the broken dish, leave little or no damage to anyone. On the other hand, physical attack, verbal abuse, or sexual violence may cause irrevocable injury to another and destroy a relationship.

Religion professionals need to know for their own sakes as well as in their ministry to others that some components of anger do not come under a moral rubric and have no rightful association with guilt. It is unhealthy to attempt to suppress the natural components of anger through the use of guilt, but early child rearing practices often do precisely that. The fourth commandment is sometimes used by parents and religion professionals to curtail and control anger in a child. Children have much to be angry about, for they often perceive the restrictions of the adult world as unfair, arbitrary, and discriminatory—precisely the ingredients of life that so often make adults angry. When they become angry, they may be told by the adults in authority that anger is at worst sinful and at best unacceptable. Thus the stage is set for later guilt feelings when they experience anger. We encourage children to feel and express other emotions—love, sadness, delight, fear. It is curious that adults can rarely tolerate, much less approve of, their angry feelings.

When anger is suppressed in childhood and repressed in adulthood it really is not obliterated. The conscious components, that is, the sense of hurt and the mental word-pictures, disappear. But the autonomic nervous system is not controlled by "conscious," so the physiological reactions continue, resulting in a variety of body adjustments that prepare one to respond to anger provoking stimuli, but which in the absence of angry feelings and angry responses resemble a racing motor that never gets put in gear. The anger, now unconscious, fuels the physiology but there is no place to expend the generated energy. Various results ensue: physical tension, skeletal muscle aches, tremulousness, poor digestion and a variety of gastrointestinal complaints, hypertension, tachycardia, flushed face, shortness of breath, and hypervigilance. Psychosomatic illnesses develop in persons who dissociate the feeling components of emotion from the physiological components of emotion. Their physical symptoms result from the physiology of their emotions, even though their verbal reports indicate that their emotional life is peaceful. Psychosomatic disorders result from unrecognized emotional reactions. Perhaps unacknowledged anger is the most common of these emotional reactions.

There is an additional hazard in the denial of angry feelings. One needs to keep a current inventory in this area. The biblical admonition "Let not the sun go down upon your anger" is a healthy principle, if it suggests "Be angry, get it out, have it over with." We cannot afford to stock our emotional shelves with angry feelings, conscious or unconscious. If the shelves are full of angry feelings there will be no room for other feelings, and we may miss the rewards of love and intimacy and the values of grief and fear. As an individual fills with anger, conscious or unconscious, love is tainted, intimacy is suspect, grief is avoided, and fear is lost. The result is loneliness, isolation, impulsivity and imprudence. Not only does cultivated anger contaminate other emotional responses, it may also lead to unexpected precipitous destructive behaviors. The repression of anger does not successfully quiet the physiological response of anger nor does it often prevent the external manifestations of anger. Repression only obliterates the conscious components of anger. Although the extended nurturing of angry feelings and the external manifestations of anger are both usually conscious elements of anger, they can operate unconsciously. Then we have a person made angry by some outward stimulus, who is not aware of being angry but who has the physiology of anger in motion, and who acts in ways that are hurtful to others at the same time claiming that this is not so.

Case Study

Tim grew up in a rigid and religious home environment. His father was a stern man who punished infractions of his authority "swiftly and fairly" as he always said. Tim's father often commented to others that he had "never punished in anger," but Tim knew that the whippings he received were too severe and too alienating for his minor infractions. Tim's mother read the Bible daily and often quoted those stories of God's firm justice and the punishment of the disobedient. These stories were used to respond to the wickedness Tim's parents saw in the world around them and seemed to Tim to suggest that God would avenge the probity of his parents in due time. Had he been more psychologically astute he might have realized that his mother's wrath was somehow displaced to God who served her need for vengeance. Duty was the family watchword, and grim was the family outlook. Superficially Tim's home was peaceful although there was a high level of unconscious anger and some violence disguised as righteous parental and divine punishment. Tim had no modeling of healthy anger and no outlet for his angry feelings. He went through a lengthy period of having nightmares filled with people chasing and stabbing and shooting and beating one another. About the time the nightmares stopped, he developed a skin problem which was finally diagnosed as psoriasis. In college he was treated for stomach ulcers.

Tim completed college and then went on to divinity school. He married shortly before he was ordained. Fifteen years later Tim was a successful pastor of a large city parish. He was considered friendly, mild mannered, and "always available" by his congregants. No one ever saw Tim angry except in those fiery sermons he preached in which he called down the wrath of God on "all evildoers and those who carry evil in their hearts." His wife and two children could not call him an angry man, nor did Tim see any of the "evil of anger" in his heart. On the other hand, Tim never confided in his wife and frequently admonished her "not to put her nose into any church matters." Their marriage grew cold very early, and after the younger child was born ten years earlier they had ceased being sexual partners. Tim spent unusual amounts of time with the church secretary and shared a great deal of emotional intimacy with her. In every church he had served, there had always been a female member of the congregation with whom he had had a similar relationship. Although there were occasional sexual indiscretions, these seemed not to be of major importance. His older child described her father as a "non-being" in her life and by age fourteen she was beginning to engage in various delinquent behaviors to retaliate for her father's emotional neglect. At age forty, Tim had developed hypertension, severe obesity, chronic ulcerative colitis, and mild diabetes. He entered therapy when he found that he was suddenly and unexplainably unable to continue his Sunday service. With considerable embarrassment he had abruptly lost his ability to concentrate on what he was doing and in a clumsy manner he mumbled excuses and left the pulpit.

Therapy was a prolonged and arduous experience. Tim was full of rage dating back to his childhood, rage which he had totally denied, and about which he now felt terrible guilt as it surfaced into his consciousness. Rage toward his father for the whippings and even greater rage for the cold, stern, forbidding posture of a parent. Rage toward his mother for her judgment of others and her perpetual invocation of God's wrath on their heads and even greater rage for her giving priority to church affairs over her attendance at his school functions. Rage toward his wife who turned her attention from him to their baby when they had only been married fifteen months. Rage at their children for taking his wife, who had the potential to become his first true friend, from him. And rage at God who gave him life but made it unbearably difficult, who gave him other people but set up barriers between him and them, who gave him feelings and punished him for having them.

Anger must be looked at honestly and dealt with responsibly. It is a motivating force of human nature. It results from the friction of living and is caused by the rough edges that are permanent contours of human beings. Anger can move us to effect change, sometimes in ourselves, sometimes in situations, and sometimes in our interactions with others. In judging the expression of anger, two different criteria can be used; one is the age appropriateness of the expression, and the other is the morality of the expression. Temper tantrums are not inappropriate for a baby, and for two or three year olds they may be tolerated briefly; they are inappropriate for a thirty year old. The unit of measurement in these instances is not related to rightness or wrongness. It must also be acknowledged that anger often makes people behave in ways that are more immature than are their usual patterns of behavior.

There is no precise pattern for the adult expression of anger. The prerequisite is of course the acknowledgment of one's angry feelings. What one does about them can vary considerably and should depend on how important the situation is. It is not necessary to go through life demanding to see the manager in order to ventilate one's hostility. Some angry feelings may dissipate quite readily without our doing anything. By the count of ten some angry feelings do pass. Others require some outward action. Expressing the anger verbally or in action may be necessary, but along with the expression there should be some sense of whether the words or actions are just the boiling over of the kettle or whether they are designed to change a situation or to hurt someone else. Anger is not counter-productive if it is simply the non-hurtful outward expression of angry feelings. Anger that is suitably confrontive, that is sufficiently controlled and directed, is a productive force in dealing with life issues and interrelational conflicts. Anger that is designed to hurt others may be very counter-productive and requires some evaluation by the second criteria of rightness or wrongness.

Many persons view anger as always being hurtful, and they typically feel hurt by any anger in the vicinity. They are prone to associate any angry feelings with a sense of guilt. They even feel guilty when other people get angry. Angry words or gestures that are truly not meant to be hurtful by the angry person should not be interpreted as hurtful by others. The angry person may make unreasonable statements that hurt another, but the other, who is presumably more reasonable and calmer, should attempt to sort out what is the intent of the angry person. On the other hand, there is anger that intends hurt, that plans revenge, that organizes retaliation. This anger must be evaluated according to moral standards. People need to have a sense of responsibility for the harm their anger causes. Anger that is brief, explosive, and non-hurtful to others is a momentary disturbance on life's scene. But anger that smolders for long periods, anger that rants endlessly at life's injustices, and anger that plans revenge at some future time contribute to the violence and hate that are part of the world's darkness. Some people vent their anger indiscriminately by attacking anyone who crosses their path or by complaining about their spouses, their employers, their government, or their church to anyone who will listen. If lighting one candle contributes something to alleviating the world's darkness, and if small acts of kindness contribute to the pool of love in the world, then throwing Molotov cocktails of anger indiscriminately (no matter how small) contributes to the world's violence and abyss of hate.

Popular literature encourages people to become aware of and comfortable with their feelings of affection, as manifested in intimacy needs and in sexual expressions. It is also important for persons to become aware of and comfortable with their angry feelings. Most of the components of anger that have been examined are amoral. There is no reason for guilt to be associated with them. A healthy and holy perspective on anger allows for its presence as part of human emotion, permits its expression in a variety of non-hurtful ways, and demands personal responsibility for making any contributions through one's anger to the evils of hate and violence.

Joseph W. Ciarrocchi, Ph.D.

Personality Disorders in the Religion Professional

To appreciate the role of personality disorders in religion professionals we must first examine the concept of a personality disorder itself. Personality traits usually describe enduring patterns of behavior, perceptions, and cognitions which people demonstrate across multiple situations. From the standpoint of psychopathology these traits become dysfunctional under several conditions (Millon, 1986). First, if patterns are inflexible, then solutions to complicated life problems simply do not work. Second, inflexible patterns in and of themselves create vicious cycles. For example, if a preoccupation with minutiae occurs when novel solutions are required, the individual has generated a self-perpetuating loop. Third, if stress easily overwhelms an individual in his or her coping skills, it is unlikely that adaptive problem solving strategies will be applied even though the strategies would work in principle.

Personality occurs on a continuum and all people at times experience dysfunction due to their personality repertoire. However, the concept of a personality disorder implies that such individuals have enduring patterns which either generate significant personal distress or render them environmentally dysfunctional. Such individuals are not ill or sick in the sense that we use this word for psychosis, severe anxiety, or depression. Rather their behavioral styles create problems in living. They are often isolated and withdrawn, experience low levels of stimulation, and tend to be emotionally impoverished. Frequently their odd, eccentric, or insensitive interpersonal styles lead to social isolation, confusion, and the loss of pleasurable interpersonal experiences.

Such patterns may generate their own primary emotional difficulties. Anxiety is common when the individual begins to focus on what people think about his or her performance. Similarly, depression is often the result of social isolation, whether the isolation is self-imposed due to fear or is a result of others avoiding the person with an obnoxious personality style.

In all of the above situations personality disorders are experienced as subjective stress to the individual. However, there is a flip side to this experience where personality disorders are experienced as stressors to the community. Some personality disorders involve self-absorption, insensitivity, boorishness and lack of cooperation, and these qualities generate interpersonal conflicts. Such behavior often evokes confrontation, arguments, and splitting. Tension increases as the communication patterns become more indirect and community members avoid each other. Within the person these reciprocal interaction patterns usually provoke defensiveness with an exaggeration of a "we–they" mentality. As this pattern unfolds I have often observed the development of a defensive grandiosity, particularly in the religious professional, which takes the form of a "vision" of either church or congregation that lesser mortals simply cannot appreciate. This pattern causes such diviseness that I refer to personality disorders as "saboteurs of community."

At this point a totally self-defeating cycle is in place—a loop which appears impenetrable and enduring. The resulting atmosphere is fraught with tension, avoidance of serious issues, and periodic anger outbursts from all concerned. Anxiety and depression are not uncommon in this situation as well, although one often sees these emotions in colleagues more than in the person with the personality disorder.

Common Types

The official diagnostic code book of the American Psychiatric Association (Author, 1987) lists thirteen personality disorders, and certainly religion professionals experience all these patterns. Space permits discussion of only the most pertinent disorders relevant to religion professionals seeking help. The three more severe types—paranoid, schizotypal and borderline—are not as commonly found as others, and they present clinical issues that are beyond the scope of this brief chapter (for further information please see Davison and Neale, 1986).

In religion professionals the following types are quite common. *Self-Defeating Personality Disorder:* This represents a diminished capacity to experience pleasure along with passive acceptance of pain. *Avoidant Personality Disorder:* These persons are hypersensitive to the pain of rejection, yet do not feel a particular sense of pleasure when others give them approval. *Dependent Personality Disorder:* With this personality style the source of gratification depends excessively on others, yet the individual acts in a passive manner to obtain this gratification. *Passive/Aggressive Personality Disorder:* These individuals are ambivalent over the source of their gratification—vacillating between the self and others. One minute they may eagerly seek approval and appear cooperative, yet the next minute they are stubbornly resistant and withholding. *Compulsive Personality Disorder:* These individuals are also ambivalent regarding seeking gratification from the self or others. However, they are more likely to present a steady pattern of compliance with a rigid work schedule (even to the point of workaholism). Their work style tends to fall in the category of applying rules and regulations in a rigid fashion. Their ambivalence is characterized by rebellious wishes which they usually experience as an inner tension, often physical in nature. *Histrionic Personality Disorder:* These individuals also seek gratification excessively from others, yet they attempt to achieve this by manipulative, attention-seeking behavior.

My own clinical impression suggests that these are the commonly found types in religion professionals presenting themselves for counseling or evaluation. I am also currently studying a large sample of religion professionals seeking psychiatric evaluation to determine the empirical validity of these clinical impressions.

Cultural Barriers to Growth

Many aspects of the religion professional's milieu allow for personality disorders to fade chameleon-like into the background. The milieu of ministry unwittingly supports certain aspects of these disorders. This results in a "slow reaction time" for self-honesty which fosters denial and actually reinforces the maladaptive behaviors. Generally religion professionals with personality disorders seek treatment for the anxiety and depression which are the products of a personality disorder rather than for the maladaptive behavior pattern itself. These comments are not meant as an indictment of the milieu of ministry. For example, an aggressive personality disorder is more probable in the business world than a dependent type, yet the business world is a legitimate social structure. To the extent that any milieu creates barriers to growth it is incumbent upon participants to alert themselves to the excesses hindering growth and to respond appropriately. Indeed, it appears that several principles, operating either formally or informally, allow for the masking of personality disorders in the religion professional.

The religion professional is a servant to others. The theology of service in ministry is well formulated in various religious traditions. Personality disorders corrupt this principle in several ways. The compulsive personality disorder seeks gratification through work to the exclusion of other dimensions. The world of feelings is ignored or denied for fear that the inner tension and resentment from being a slave rather than a servant will emerge. The dependent personality disorder craves approval and becomes comfortable with service as the means to achieve this. Such individuals are quite content to give themselves totally to others and thereby forego personal time, needs, and goals. Such behavior patterns often result in mild to moderate depression as the person's own needs go unfulfilled. They also find themselves quite vulnerable in work settings devoid of regular affirmation. One could also wonder how well such persons could challenge their flocks with the many "hard sayings" of faith since their need for approval is so paramount.

The histrionic personality disorder also seeks others' attention and approval, but in religion professionals their patterns tend to at least raise eyebrows if not blatantly conflict with social customs. The religion professional who overdramatizes, seduces, and manipulates others in the name of service can easily mask an excessive dependency on others. Many colleagues and lay persons are initially drawn to the aura of excitement that surrounds histrionic clergy and this often passes as "charisma." These individuals run into difficulty if their attention-seeking maneuvers go beyond socially or morally acceptable behavior. Anxiety and depression often follow as congregations eventually catch on to what is essentially a superficial side show and begin to abandon this minister.

The minister as ascetic. Most religious traditions expect some degree of asceticism or self-abnegation in their leaders. Most, if not all, spiritual traditions devalue self-indulgence and describe various levels of self-discipline as freeing the person for spiritual growth. This norm may also mask maladaptive behavioral patterns in the religion professional. In its extreme expression some believe that any care of self is identical with self-absorption. The self-defeating personality disorder reverses the reinforcing aspects of pain and pleasure. Some religion professionals are stoic to the extreme and the ascetical tradition can be used to justify the self-denying component. Ironically, ascetism only makes spiritual sense for those who have a rich capacity for pleasure. This distinction, however, is lost on the masochistic person.

The avoidant type has diminished capacity to experience pleasure yet is quite sensitive to pain. These religion professionals usually develop a "martyr complex," expecting the worst of people and events while wearing their rejections as badges of election. They scan the social environment, constantly reading into other people's neutral behavior the signs of their own abandonment.

The minister as model of charity. The tenet to love others as we would desire to be loved is a guiding principle for many major world religions. It is safe to say that most religion professionals strive to exemplify this value in their own lives. Some personality types, however, stand this principle on its head and tend to make unassertiveness a commandment. These types consider any direct expression to others of their own self-interest as egotistical heresy. While direct expressions of *positive* feeling are allowed and valued, expression of *negative* feeling is considered uncharitable, hurtful or unkind. If negative expressions must be communicated, the first choice is to do so in as indirect a manner as possible. They hope the other person will figure out the message and change. If this strategy fails, then the message will be communicated in an impersonal manner (e.g. written message, memorandum, through a third party, etc.). While this process gives the appearance of adhering to the golden rule, nothing could be farther from the truth. For passive/aggressive individuals this process is used to deal with their anger indirectly, while for dependent personalities this strategy helps them avoid dealing with the possibility of rejection.

A Model for Change

Briefly, personality disorders can be experienced as both stress and stressors. For those experiencing their behavior patterns as subjective stress there are a variety of effective treatments. For those who are excessively dependent on others for their source of meaning and gratification several strategies are useful. Counseling may alter a belief and emotional system which relies excessively on others for approval and affection. Guided action strategies encourage the religion professional to try new ways of relating which are self-authentic and which run the risk of generating disapproval, at least the disapproval of some. For persons who are excessively self-denying, emotion-focused therapy explores the low self-esteem which usually buttresses self-abnegation. Guided action strategies are devised to "test the waters" of self-care. The religion professional develops plans to alter a lifestyle imbalance, and this often has the effect of improving mood.

For types who struggle with setting limits, emotion-focused and cognitive strategies help motivate the religion professional to appreciate the importance of limit setting both in themselves and in relationships to others. They are helped to appreciate the psychological law of diminishing returns when attempting to be all things to all people in non-stop fashion. Assertiveness training may help them to learn the mechanics of saying no graciously. This skill allows the minister to protect his or her private domain so that ministry may eventually be refueled.

Guidelines for Referral

Helping individuals with personality disorders bears some resemblance to addiction intervention. Denial in the individual is often rampant, and authority, friends, or family frequently need to point out the self-defeating patterns to the minister and suggest help. Occasionally an authority figure must insist on counseling since, contrary to popular wisdom, this "constructive coercion" is not always counter-productive. For the person whose personality disorder is experienced as stress such a recommendation often comes as a relief.

For those individuals whose personality disorders often appear to be more stressful to others than to themselves, constructive coercion is often essential. However, the expectations of the referring party should be kept realistic. Often the only process that is adhered to is the evaluation component. At times the self-centeredness, sense of entitlement, grandiosity or suspiciousness is so pervasive that there is no openness at all to counseling. If counseling works in these instances it is mostly the skills of the therapist reaching some desire for growth not totally smothered. But this outcome can almost never be predicted in advance.

Authorities have to accept the limits of counseling with those personality disordered individuals whose subjective experience of stress is minimal. When therapy works in these situations it generally is lengthy. More often than not communities and congregations must simply deal with such an individual charitably but firmly, using various external regulations to influence appropriate behavior. When these methods are ineffective the community must sometimes "let go" of the religion professional who needs to discover some ministry in a setting removed from his primary community. Authorities must weigh the good of the total community against the wishes of the individual in such instances and decide accordingly.

My own clinical approach in working with religion professionals who have limited insight as to the degree of stress their interpersonal style generates is to employ gentle confrontation. Once I have assessed the individuals' personal styles I will give them the task of observing the impact of their behavior on others. They are requested to speak with a variety of trusted individuals in their congregation or community and request objective feedback. Since the feedback they receive is quite often negative, a non-judgmental stance is essential. For the religion professional to change he or she must objectively comprehend the impact of his or her behavior, yet not feel blamed. Once the problem behaviors are identified, we then work together to develop a change plan to address the problem behaviors. If, for example, self-centeredness is identified, we discuss concrete ways to implement other-directed behavior.

In referring such people for counseling, referring individuals may note that many therapies are symptom focused and quite helpful in providing relief from the anxiety and depression that accompanies personality disorders. The difficult part begins when the anxiety and depression improve and the personality disorder is revealed as the antecedent. Even therapists who practice structured, brief psychotherapy find that the treatment of personality disorders procedes slowly if it is to be effective. Most therapists also discover that insight oriented psychotherapy alone is limited. Focused change strategies are also required to alter the maladaptive behavior patterns.

In summary, a personality disorder in a religion professional both generates significant stress for the person and disrupts the adjoining community or congregation. The behavior patterns tend to be enduring, and while they generate anxiety and depression they exist far beyond the emotion of the moment. Furthermore, the milieu of congregation or community frequently fosters the religion professional's lack of self-confrontation and can even present barriers to treatment. The nature of personality disorders may require direct intervention by the community or congregation at least at the evaluation stage. Personality types in the religion professional which center around excessive dependency on others or unassertiveness can be effectively treated with a variety of counseling strategies which focus on self-awareness and behavioral change. Personality types which generate stress in the community due to narcissistic features in the religion professional may require direct confrontation and constructive coercion in seeking psychological evaluation. However, in these instances the religion professional often does not continue in counseling and congregations may need to resort to external regulatory structures to assist these religion professionals in maintaining appropriate boundaries in their ministry. Many therapists can attest that change and growth are possible for those seeking help, yet these same therapists would probably acknowledge that the treatment process is slow and complicated as various levels of the person's behavioral patterns are uncovered. For those open to change improvement is possible, but growth involves a strong commitment from both the individual and his or her congregation.

Kay C. Smith, B.S.
Virginia Carson, M.S., C.T.R.S.

Thou Shalt Not Play

The leisure life of religion professionals is in critical jeopardy. External demands of church, family and community as well as internal expectations of dedication and service combine to upstage well intentioned plans and efforts to take care of individual needs to recreate and re-create. The daily lifestyle of religion professionals has increasingly become a difficult, if not impossible, struggle to balance the competing needs of congregants, family, self, and the ever changing demands of the church. Often the easiest of these needs to forego is self, and the piece of self most often left ill attended is the individual need and desire to play and recreate.

It is generally accepted that leisure and recreation contribute significantly to the social, psychological, physical, and creative well-being of humankind.[1] In the United States, many of our educational goals and spiritual values reinforce and support aspects of the recreational experience. Recreation is seldom viewed as sinful, a concept imported to these shores by some Calvinist and orthodox forebears. In fact, many modern religious leaders believe that the church is responsible for providing some leisure opportunities for congregants.

The Reverend Warren Ost makes an impassioned argument for the value of leisure within the religious experience when he writes:

> Leisure and recreation opportunities and guidance are no longer identified with class, education or training. It is the concern of every community agency including the Church to help people make the creative and restoring use of leisure and recreation. How can the Church talk about eternal life when most people don't know what to do with next weekend?[2]

Stress and burnout in religion professionals has been widely studied and reported. Many recommended solutions suggest the need for a more balanced lifestyle and more effective time management prioritization. But the often overlooked and understudied component of the stress and burnout picture is the leisure time of clergy. Many questions remain unanswered or even unasked. Do clergy truly value leisure? How much leisure time do they actually have? How do they spend it? Do they feel they have control over how much leisure time they have? What barriers exist to inhibit their leisure time use? Are men and women clergy alike or different in their leisure practices and attitudes?

Historical Overview

To understand and discuss the role and value of leisure in the lives of religion professionals today it is useful to trace the development of leisure.[3] For our primitive ancestors, daily life was a constant struggle for survival and there was no delineation between work and leisure. Many of life's survival tasks such as hunting, food gathering, tool making and weaving were the forerunners of today's leisure and sports recreation.

The golden age of Pericles in ancient Greece saw leisure emerge as an important and distinct part of daily life. Games and sports competition flourished and were a component of religious festivals. Intellectual accomplishments and the pursuit of excellence in all aspects of life were encouraged and recreation and play had inherent value in Greek life.

The Romans glorified the ultimate expression of leisure as the absence of work and enhanced the concept of spectatorism as a component of leisure. They championed athleticism but emphasized the competitive aspect of sport, often to the level of the gruesome. A class distinction emerged as these ceremonial celebrations were often designed as entertainment for the wealthy and performed by the enslaved for the diversion of the masses.

By the middle ages, often viewed as a time of ignorance and suspicion, a well-defined schism between the social classes was evident in the type of leisure activities pursued. Wealthy men were spectators or competitors in archery and jousting tournaments and in organized hunting and war games. Women entertained, played board games, and enjoyed dancing. Peasants and serfs toiled long hours and relieved life's tedium with practical jokes and bawdy off-color songs.

The beginning of organized sports emerged, and variations of tennis, soccer, and badminton were played by peasants at holiday celebrations.

In the far east, a rigid class structure defined the role of leisure in one's life. The poor and low-born served and often entertained a master. They staged performances that included acrobatics, musical and dance demonstrations, story-telling, sword fighting and elaborate war tournaments. In Europe, the Renaissance brought a rebirth of the value of arts and literature for the masses and instruction of play entered the educational curriculum. Religious reformation during the 1500s gave birth to Protestantism and spawned repressive attitudes toward recreation and leisure. Some viewed entertainment as sinful. Play went underground.

Colonial Americans brought with them leisure values and attitudes as varied as the ethnic, cultural and religious heritages they had left. Titled wealthy, working class, slave, landowner, Calvinist, Anglican, and American Indian each contributed specific leisure values and practices. Leisure eventually flourished in this melting pot atmosphere but not without the predictable clash of divergent backgrounds and beliefs. The industrial revolution gradually resulted in increased individual wealth, and as machines made daily life easier, people had more time for leisure.

Nineteenth century America saw the establishment of national and state parks and playgrounds in the inner city as well as the birth of voluntary recreational organizations such as the YMCA. World War I and encamped soldiers in training triggered the growth of commercial recreation. The federally sponsored Civilian Conservation Corps developed hiking trails and camping opportunities nationwide.

The advent of the age of technology has elevated leisure concepts to never before dreamed of levels of sophistication. Commercial recreation is at its zenith. The arts flourish and sports are a national obsession. But now spectatorism, once the function and privilege of the wealthy, threatens our collective health and fitness.

The family and community as we once knew them are under constant assault. Two wage-earner families and single parent families, each present unique challenges to leisure time use. In increasingly urbanized America, recreation outside the home is frequently organized, scheduled and must be paid for while leisure at home is increasingly high-tech, solitary, and spectator-oriented. The average wage earner works 37.6 hours and has 41.7 hours per week for leisure,[4] but, in an inversion of our European class distinction heritage, it is the working class who more typically experience this largesse of leisure time. Successful professionals and business executives work long hours, take work home, and assume many community civic responsibilities.

Leisure and the Clergy

It is useful then to ask where, in this overall picture of society and leisure, religion professionals, and in particular Protestant clergy, fit. It is our premise that while clergy face some unique challenges inherent in their vocation, they, like other professionals, work excessively long hours and find limited time for leisure.[5] It is expected that financial constraints and difficulty in prioritizing self before expectations of the vocation are the primary barriers to greater leisure time use. Further, we speculate that women clergy feel the additional burden of family responsibilities in addition to vocational responsibilities.

To test these hypotheses we designed a Leisure Needs Assessment consisting of twenty-five questions to explore the following areas: time spent on work and leisure; leisure preferences, practices, and values; and barriers to leisure time use. The Leisure Needs Assessment can be found at the end of this chapter. We mailed the questionnaire to 220 Lutheran ministers currently serving congregations in the Middle Atlantic region. We did not follow up our initial mailing in any way. We received a total of 80 responses—72 males and 8 females—a 36% return rate of the completed questionnaire. From all the responses, we have compiled the most frequently reported ones into a profile of the typical respondent, male and female presented separately. Our sample is admittedly small, particularly the female group. It is also speculative to infer from this sample any attribution of the summarized results to clergy of other religious denominations. The need for additional cross-denominational studies will be addressed in a later section. Nonetheless, we believe it is a ground-breaking effort to begin to examine an important and overlooked component of the life experience of religion professionals, namely their beliefs and attitudes toward leisure. We invite critical review and encourage others in the field of leisure education and religion to continue exploration of this population and subject.

Male Profile—Don is a 46 year old, married pastor with two children, serving a Lutheran congregation in the urban Mid-Atlantic region. He works at least 59 hours each week on congregational matters, and works additional time responding to emergencies which frequently arise. Recreation and leisure activities account for seven hours or less of his time each week (Table 1). He strongly feels he would like more time for leisure, yet he also feels he has control over the amount of time he has for leisure. Though he has many leisure interests, his most frequently stated free time pursuits are reading, being with family, home maintenance activities, and watching television. His preference is to spend his leisure time with others in planned activities (Table 2). Don emphatically pinpoints work obligations, including the unpredictable emergencies, as the single largest barrier preventing him from participating in more leisure. He also names family responsibilities and finances as barriers to leisure and the impact of aging as a limitation. He spends more on leisure than his female peer, but still less than $20.00 per week. Don states that leisure brings the following benefits to his life: escape from work, physical fitness, opportunity to get recharged, fun, friendship, and creative growth. He relies primarily on himself to decide what values he receives from leisure.

Female Profile—Joanne is also a Lutheran minister actively serving a congregation in the Mid-Atlantic region. She is married, has no children, and is 38 years old. She spends only 6.3 (Table 3) hours and less than $10.00 per week on leisure. As a minister, she works an average of 57 hours per week, not counting emergencies. Joanne is dissatisfied with the amount of time she has for leisure, but less so than her male counterpart. She has a wide variety of leisure interests, but the most frequent leisure activity she participates in is reading, followed by spending time with family, watching television, and sleep. Like her male peer, Joanne believes that her work, including the unplanned emergencies, is the largest impediment to leisure. Other barriers to her free time use are finances and family responsibilities, which seem more problematic to her than her male peers. She has extensive cognitive awareness of the broad benefits arising from leisure participation which she describes as getting unhooked from work, a calming re-creative effect, connecting with family and friends, broadening horizons, and tension relief. She has no strong preference whether leisure opportunities are spontaneous or planned (Table 2) and also equally enjoys solitary activities and leisure with others.

In the following discussion, we present a more detailed look at the data received from the completed questionnaires which helped us

Table 1:
Male Clergy's Use of Free Time

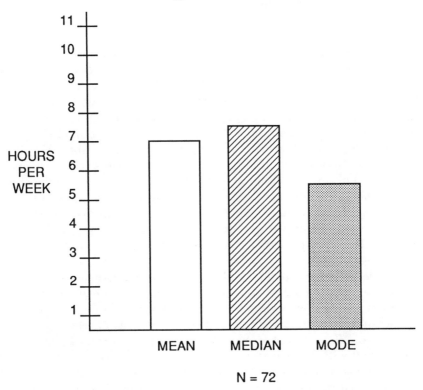

N = 72

compile these profiles. An attempt will be made to compare and contrast male and female responses, explore seeming contradictions, and propose areas needing further study.

Do Clergy Understand the Value of
Leisure in a Balanced Lifestyle?

Yes! Both male and female clergy in the sample were very knowledgeable about the importance of leisure. Each stated multiple reasons for the value of leisure in his or her life, describing in a variety of ways the physical, social, psychological, spiritual, and creative expression benefits. However, it seems clear from other responses, namely hours of leisure actually practiced each week as well as hours

Table 2:
Preference of Clergy Engaged in Planned or
Spontaneous Leisure Pursuits
by Sex

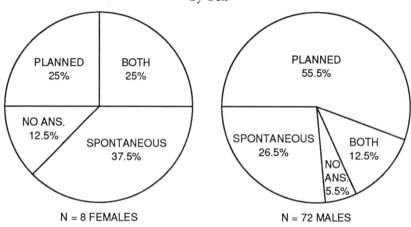

N = 8 FEMALES   N = 72 MALES

per week worked, that these same clergy, despite intellectually valuing leisure, didn't practice what they knew to be true and believed to be important.

Source of Leisure Values

Question 13 in the Leisure Needs Assessment asked clergy, "How did you acquire your leisure values?" Though asked to indicate the *single* most important influence, many clergy named several sources of influence as the most important. Thus, the following reported percentages total more than 100%. Eighty-one percent of the clergy in our sample (Table 2) reported that the most important influence on their acquisition of leisure values was "self." Friends and spouses were the second (25%) and third (22.5%) most important influences named by the sample group. Notably, the Bible was rated the least influential (10%) by this group of clergy. One wonders what impact biblical teachings might have on leisure values of clergy of other denominations. Further studies are needed.

When we looked at the answers of male and female clergy persons separately we noted a significant difference in how each rely on spouses for leisure value acquisitions. Twenty-five percent of the

Table 3:
Female Clergy's Free Time

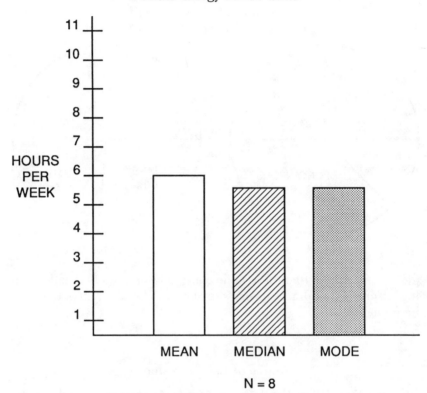

N = 8

male pastors (18 responses) reported that their spouses had an important impact on their leisure values whereas not one female pastor (0%) rated spousal impact as most important. We need additional studies to verify if this phenomenon occurs when greater numbers of women ministers are surveyed and also to explore possible explanations for such a difference from male pastoral responses.

Is Seven Hours a Week Enough Leisure?

A comparison of the responses of clergy in our survey, and the national averages for work and leisure per week, reveal that clergy work 21 hours longer (59 vs. 38) and recreate 35 hours fewer (7 vs. 42) than the average American! In this pattern of long work hours and minimal time for leisure, clergy have turned back the clock to the early 1900s when a 60 hour work week was the norm for working people. Based on a real-life schedule the mean number of hours per week spent on leisure reported by our sample (males = 7; females = 6.3) result in an average of less than one hour per day of leisure activity. This one hour each day would necessarily encompass all the regular daily leisure activities such as reading the newspaper, interacting socially with family members, and even routine leisure pursuits such as watching the evening news on television. Additionally, it would also include any scheduled fitness activities, cultural events or creative and hobby activities. If on some days leisure activities were several hours longer than the average one hour, the minister would have to abstain from all leisure on a number of other days that week. He or she would then have no leisure—planned or spontaneous—for several entire days and evenings. Envisioning this pattern as a lifestyle to be followed week in and week out sounds more like institutional regimentation than a lifestyle of choice and enjoyment. Do clergy really live like this? Our survey sample suggests they do.

How Do Clergy Spend Their Free Time?

For both male and female clergy, the most frequently reported use of free time was reading followed by spending time with family members. For male ministers, home maintenance activities and television watching ranked as third and fourth in free time use while female pastors listed watching television and sleeping as third and fourth.

It is obvious that many aspects of these free time activities are not leisure. It appears that when ministers had free time they often filled it with parenting and family responsibilities. Chosen leisure activities became those that could easily and spontaneously be accomplished at home.

An important question surfaces regarding the mention of reading as a leisure activity. Is all of this reading recreational reading, i.e. fun or diversional, or is it work related reading carrying expectations of comprehension and retention? Future studies would benefit from follow-up questions to clarify the exact nature of reading when it is listed as a leisure activity. Our conjecture is that at least some of reported leisure reading is probably work related reading. If this is so, then ministers are spending even fewer than seven hours per week in leisure!

Table 4:
How the Majority of Free Time Is Spent per Week by Sex Differentiation

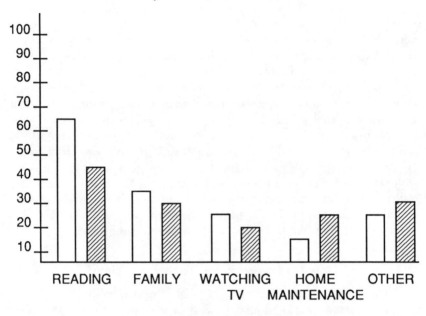

N = 8 FEMALES ☐

N = 72 MALES ▨

A majority of male clergy reported preferring to spend their free time with others over being alone. Yet their most frequently reported free time activity was reading, a solitary activity. Moreover, of their next three predominant activities, spending time with family, home maintenance, and watching television, the only likely others are family members. Is this what male clergy meant when they answered others to Question #5 or do they experience enforced limited social contact outside of work and family as a result of their difficulty with scheduling leisure time for personal use?

The female clergy in the study named watching television and sleep, which are passive and restful activities, as their third and fourth most frequent free time activities. In rating sleep as a preferential use of free time, are women clergy affirming the heavy burden they feel juggling multiple roles? It is also notable that more than half of the clergy women responding had no children or no children living at home. Does this suggest that these women are excessively tired from balancing only two roles, minister and wife? This issue requires further attention in future studies with a greater number.

Lastly, some would question the appropriateness of comparing statistical norms of clergy with those of the average American. They might suggest that the clergy lifestyle more typically resembles that of the doctor who also has a heavy schedule and frequent emergencies. Such a suggestion may have some validity in comparing lifestyles, but does not address whether such a lifestyle is either healthy or desirable for either group. Eighty percent of our total sample stated that their present amount of leisure time was *undesirable* and that they wanted more. The obvious question is, "If clergy want more leisure, what prevents them from having more leisure?" To begin to answer this we must look at what clergy define as barriers to their leisure time use.

Barriers: Why Don't Clergy Play?

Both men and women clergy in our study believe work duties are the primary barrier keeping them from greater leisure time. They particularly target the emergency aspects of their ministerial duties as time-consuming and interfering with plans to fulfill personal needs. It appears that because parishioner needs arise unpredictably, the time needed to respond to them is typically added onto an already full work week, which thus balloons way beyond forty hours per week. Most clergy apparently do not conceptualize this extra time worked as "compensatory time" to be taken as time-off at a later date. In our study, only one person in the entire sample reported a work week of 40 hours per week. The range was 40+ to 120 hours, with the mean for male clergy 59.3 and for female ministers 57.1 hours per week (Table 5).

If clergy determine their own schedules, it is thus the minister himself or herself who is ultimately the barrier preventing greater personal leisure time use. There is an internal belief system that seems to override their acknowledged desire for more personal time. It appears that many clergy struggle with and succumb to a learned expectation that work comes before self. Knowingly or not, internal control over prioritization of time use is thus relinquished; time and work responsibilities instead of self are then identified as the culprits. Thus, if control over time use is externalized, empowerment to change this unsatisfactory aspect of one's life is surrendered.

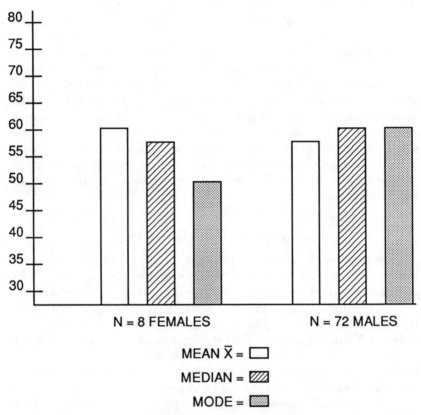

Table 5:
Bar Graph Representing Number of Work Hours per Week by Sex

N = 8 FEMALES   N = 72 MALES

MEAN X̄ = ☐
MEDIAN = ▨
MODE = ▦

Control of Leisure Time Use:
Who or What Decides?

Several questions in the survey explored the area of locus of control over scheduling of leisure time.[6] Answers produced some curious and mixed results. Remember that 80% of our total sample stated a desire for more leisure. Yet, 31% of them didn't believe they had control over the amount of their leisure time. Stated another way, the ministers in our survey believe that external conditions and issues determined or controlled their use of time. One clergy, when asked to explain why he felt no control, cited "demands of the job and need to juggle family schedules." This was a fairly typical answer and demonstrates the belief that determination of one's use of time is outside one's individual control. These clergy ascribe leisure to an external locus of control.

The internal locus of control belief is astutely stated by one clergy in the study who explained, "I am responsible for planning my own time use. If I don't set aside (time for) more leisure, it is my own decision." There is no doubt that it is a constant struggle for clergy to juggle the often competing demands of parish responsibilities, family, and personal needs. Yet, it is our belief that within each of us rests the ultimate control over what we choose to prioritize in our daily life. Sixty percent of our sample ascribe allegiance to a belief in internal locus of control over time use.

We decided to look at this subgroup of clergy in the study who did indeed feel they had control over leisure time scheduling to see what they actually *did* with their time use. This subgroup consisted of 48% of the total 80 responses, 46 males and 2 females, all of whom responded yes to Question 22 in the Leisure Needs Assessment Questionnaire (Do you feel you have control over how much time you spend in leisure pursuits?). We also looked at this subgroup's responses to Question 3 (How many hours per week do you work?), Question 4 (How much time per week do you spend engaging in leisure activities?), and Question 21 (Would you like to have more time to spend on leisure?).

What we found is best summed up in one clergy's response when he states, "I don't always exercise the control I have." This is an honest and insightful man! He represents 77% of the subgroup who reported that while they believed they had control over the amount of leisure time, they still desired more. This group of clergy accepts the fact that the ultimate responsibility for prioritizing time use rests within, but they also know that they aren't fully exercising it! How right they are! In fact, 58% of the subgroup recreated fewer than seven hours per week, less than one hour per day; 65% of the subgroup worked more than 50 hours per week. Percentages total more than 100 because some clergy fit into both categories; 40% of the subgroup both work over 50 hours weekly and recreate fewer than 7 hours per week. Considering either factor, 83% of these clergy in the subgroup who believe they exercise control over leisure time use really either work too long or recreate too few hours each week. Most importantly, we remember that clergy themselves say they want more time for leisure, but many have yet to discover how to change present work/play patterns. One clergy in our survey accepted his ability to effect this change when he said, "I'm getting better at taking

charge of this (leisure time use)." Empowerment to change lies
within each individual's increased utilization of his or her internal
locus of control. In other words, if you want more play time, you have
to make it happen by valuing your need to recreate at least as strongly
as your desire to serve others.

Summary

This concludes a brief historical review of leisure, and an in-
depth focus on views about and use of leisure of the clergy from one
denomination. We remember that during some periods of history
only the wealthy had access to recreational opportunity. In other eras
play was viewed as sinful. Leisure in America has evolved from these
and from other influences, including the changes wrought by the
industrial revolution and the more recent and still present revolution
in technology. In their leisure values and practices, clergy, like the
rest of us, are a product of individual life experience previously
shaped by familial, cultural, and religious heritage. Recent forces of
change in sex role expectations and economic considerations provide
still greater challenges to leisure time use by clergy. Our survey focused on Lutheran ministers and their leisure time practices and attitudes. We hypothesized that they, like other vocational groups designated as professionals, would be found to work long hours at the cost
of personal leisure time use. Our findings support this hypothesis.
The mean score for work hours per week for our clergy was 58.24
hours and 6.85 hours for leisure. Nationwide the American averages
per week are considerably lower for work and significantly higher for
leisure. Of the clergy we studied, work duties ranked as the single
greatest impediment to leisure. Female clergy named financial constraints second as a barrier followed by family responsibilities. Male
clergy ranked family responsibilities and financial constraints respec-
tively as the next two biggest barriers to leisure.

Our expectation that ministers would state difficulty in prioritizing self before work duties was in fact borne out as the greatest
barrier to leisure. The Protestant work ethic seems alive and well in
Lutheran clergy! Clergy overwhelmingly want more leisure. Clergy
in our sample also value leisure for the many and varied benefits it
brings to life experience, and they no longer seem to view play as
sinful as some of their ministerial ancestors did. Some responses
seemed to reveal contradictory information. Clergy felt they have

control over how much time they have for leisure (60%) while con-
versely reporting they want more time for leisure. Of clergy reporting they have control over leisure time use 83% either work excessively or recreate minimally. The majority of the clergy in our study
stated they preferred leisure with others, yet their four most frequent
usages of free time are in solitary or family activities.

Implications for Further Studies

This study stimulated many questions and ideas for further study.
With only eight women clergy in our sample, we can make only a
limited attribution of our results to women clergy as a group. Future
surveys with a larger female sample are needed. Studies might also
explore in greater depth the impact of multiple roles of minister, wife
and mother on leisure use patterns. Further inquiry is also indicated
to substantiate the curious phenomenon in our results wherein 25%
of our male sample reported they relied on their wives for acquisition
of their leisure values but 0% of the female sample stated they relied
on their spouses for acquiring leisure values.

Cross-denominational studies are essential to determine the impact of theological differences on leisure attitudes and practices. Is
limited leisure time use a hazard to all clergy professionals or does the
Bible have a greater influence on leisure value acquisition of clergy of
some denominations than it did for Lutheran ministers? In our study,
reading was reported as the number one leisure activity by both male
and female clergy, yet we question whether all this reading was recreational. Future studies with follow-up questions could differentiate
between recreational and work-related reading. One area we did not
examine was the impact of seminary training on leisure value acquisition, leisure time use, and the importance of leisure in a healthy balanced lifestyle. Are these issues addressed in seminary curriculum?
How? If not, do they need to be?

Conclusion

It is our contention that understanding and valuing the importance of leisure as a regular and significant component of daily life is
central to the maintenance of health and well-being. Clergy, it seems,
do recognize this. But recognizing and valuing leisure are not
enough, for each of us must practice what believe. Work then leisure,

or leisure then work—the choice is ours. As one Lutheran minister puts it, "time is there for the taking." Will we or will we not?

Notes

1. Richard G. Kraus, *Recreation and Leisure in Modern Society* (Santa Monica: Goodyear Publishing Company, Inc., 1978).

2. Richard G. Kraus, *Recreation Today: Program Planning and Leadership* (Santa Monica: Goodyear Publishing Company, Inc., 1977).

3. Richard G. Kraus, *Recreation and Leisure in Modern Society.*

4. Richard G. Kraus, *Recreation Today: Program Planning and Leadership*, p. 7.

5. Robert Neale, *In Praise of Play: Toward a Psychology of Religion* (New York: Harper and Row, 1969).

6. Wayne Stormann, *Work: True Leisure's Home?* (Leisure Studies, Vol. 8, No. 1, 1989).

Needs Assessment Questionnaire

DEMOGRAPHIC INFORMATION

Please complete the following information:
1. Sex: Male   Female
2. Age:
3. Marital Status:
   Single (Never Been Married)   Separated   Married
   Divorced   Widowed   Remarried   (Circle One)
4. Children/stepchildren at home; give ages.

_____

5. Children living elsewhere (specify ages and situation).

_____

LEISURE NEEDS ASSESSMENT

1. Do you currently participate in leisure activities:
   Yes   No   (Circle one)
2. In what type of leisure activities do you participate? Be specific.

_____

3. How many hours per week do you work? _____
4. How much time per week do you spend engaging in leisure activities?

   0–3 hours   4–7 hours   8–11 hours
   12+ hours   (Circle one)
5. Do you prefer to spend your leisure time:
   alone? with others? (Circle one)
6. How much money do you spend on the average per week on leisure activities? _____
7. What prevents you from participating in leisure activities? Be specific.

_____

_____

8. Do you have limitations that affect your participation in leisure activities?   Yes   No   Please list _____

_____

9. How do you spend the majority of your free time?

_____

_____

10. What benefits do you feel you get from participating in leisure activities? Please list.

_____

_____

11. Do you prefer to participate in leisure activities that are:
Planned   Spontaneous   (Circle one)
Explain: _____

_____

12. What makes you happy? _____

_____

13. How did you acquire your leisure values? (Circle the most important)
Self   Parents   Bible   Spouse   Friends   Other
Explain: _____

14. Have your leisure values changed since your youth?
Yes   No   (Circle one)
If yes, how? _____

15. Do you incorporate leisure values into your sermons?
Yes   No   (Circle one)
If yes, how do you accomplish this? _____

_____

_____

16. What do you consider to be your best asset? _____

_____

17. In what area would you like to improve yourself?

_____

18. What area of leisure do you enjoy the most? (Circle one)

Social Interaction   Spectator Appreciation
Creative Expression   Physical Exercise
Intellectual Stimulation   Solitary Relaxation

19. Please rate each activity:
    1. Not a part of your lifestyle
    2. An occasional part of your lifestyle
    3. Regular part of your lifestyle
    4. Major part of your lifestyle
    5. Most important part of your lifestyle

    Games ( )
    Sports ( )
    Nature Activities ( )
    Collection Activities ( )
    Art and Music Activities ( )
    Craft Activities ( )
    Volunteer Activities ( )
    Organizational Activities ( )
    Educational and Cultural Activities ( )
    Romance and Sex ( )
    Drugs and/or Alcohol ( )
    Gambling ( )

20. How much vacation time did you take in 1988?

    _____

21. Would you like to have more time to spend on leisure?
    Yes   No   (Circle one)

22. Do you feel you have control over how much time you spend
    in leisure pursuits?
    Yes   No   Explain: _____

    _____

23. What skills or competencies would you like to learn or master
    that relate to leisure activities? Please list and/or explain.

    _____

    _____

24. What do you find that satisfies you most in life?

    _____

    _____

25. Additional comments:

    _____

    _____

    _____

    _____

Mary Ellen Merrick, I.H.M., M.S.

Addicted . . . Who, Me?

Individual women and men come to a decision about becoming a religion professional from a broad variety of backgrounds and experiences. For some the idea of dedicating one's life to the service of God's people has been a long-standing one; others have been aware of a more gradual inclination, and, for a few, the thought has felt like a surprise with a mixture of "Who? Me?" and the disruption of a more carefully planned direction. However, when a person comes to ministry there is seldom any conscious thought of the service becoming self or other destructive due to the disease process of addiction, chemical or otherwise.

There are many areas in the understanding of addiction that have not yet been researched well enough to have definitive answers to the complexities involved. One fact that is clear is that few groups can consider themselves exempt from the potential hazards of the disease process. As a "group" women and men in ministry have no guarantee that dedicated service provides insurance against a primary, progressive, chronic and potentially fatal process.

Addiction is defined more frequently as an unblinking attraction to a substance and/or behavior that causes a violation of one's belief or value system resulting in disruption in one or more critical areas of an individual's life. At first glance this definition may appear easy to apply and many people "compare themselves out" by thinking that the signs and symptoms are fairly obvious. What is missed in this kind of approach is how subtle the process usually is. Also missed are the clever and baffling lengths that people will develop to keep the process hidden. What is sad is that the person who is expending the time, energy and creativity needed to hide the true situation is also deluded into believing that the facade is real.

A delightful story by Penny Jones appropriately entitled *The Brown Bottle* describes the lure that a bright shiny object held for a young caterpillar named Charlie. The story goes like this:

Once there was a caterpillar named Charlie who lived in the Valley of Promises. There was nothing observably special about Charlie. He was an average looking caterpillar amidst thousands of others. Like them, he spent the majority of his time crawling from leaf to leaf, eating as much as he pleased, and dozing in the warm sunlight. Life was good and Charlie was happy. As you know, there is something very special about caterpillars. From the time they are born, they are aware that something beautiful beyond imagination will one day occur. It is called The Promise.

Charlie was a believer. For as long as he could remember, he had loved The Promise. Its mystery filled his days and nights with dreams of anticipation.

In this way, Charlie was special, for his love of The Promise by far exceeded that of any normal caterpillar. He grew more and more impatient in his intense desire to receive its gift.

One day, as Charlie was exploring the valley, he was attracted by a bright, shiny object lying in the meadow. It was a brown bottle. The sun's rays danced on the glass and gave it an aura of golden splendor. It seemed to beckon Charlie. Filled with excitement, he hurried as fast as he could go.

Charlie was a bit scared when he reached the bottle, for it was something entirely new and frightening. As he explored it, curiosity soon overcame his fear. He traveled its surface from end to end and top to bottom.

When Charlie entered the bottle, something magical seemed to happen. A soft mellow glow enveloped him in the warmth of a false utopia. After a time, he was lulled to sleep by the gentle voice of the bottle whispering of pleasures yet to come.

At first, Charlie spent most of his time leading the normal life of a caterpillar with only occasional trips into the brown bottle. But as the days passed, he longed more and more for the mellow glow it offered and his trips became more frequent.

He began to venture deeper and deeper into the bottle to find the utopia he sought.

Sometimes Charlie's friends came to visit while he was in the bottle. As he moved about within its glass walls, he appeared to be different than he really was. Pleased with all the attention he received, he would do silly things to make his friends laugh. Charlie loved being the center of attention and his friends' laughter made him feel important. Then, the bottle seemed to whisper, "Charlie, when you are with me, you are a very, very special caterpillar." And Charlie felt that, indeed, what the bottle had said was true.

By the end of the summer, Charlie seldom left the bottle. It had become more important to him than the warmth of the sunlight, more important than the companionship of his friends, even more important than the Valley of Promises itself. He began to depend on the bottle for all of his needs. It had become his home.

With the coming of fall, the world outside bottle began to change. Cold winds swept down from the north. Green plants turned brown and died. There was a rush of activity among the caterpillars for they knew that they, too, must change with the seasons and prepare for the winter to come.

On the final day of preparation, Charlie's friends went to the bottle and called to him, "Charlie, please come out before it is too late. We must get ready to receive The Promise."

Surrounded by the warm glow, Charlie gazed out upon the barren valley. "I would be foolish to leave this warm, safe place and go out into the cold with you. I could leave if I wanted to, but I would rather stay here." Laden with sorrow, Charlie's friends turned away from him in hopelessness and returned to their tasks.

One day, as Charlie gazed out upon the snow covered valley, the bottle again spoke to him, "Charlie, you have seen your friends suffer from the cold in their quest for The Promise while you remained here, warm and safe, with me. Surely by now, you know that I am better for you than an empty promise."

And Charlie knew that, indeed, what the bottle had said was true. On that day, Charlie deserted his belief in The Promise, and surrendered his dreams to the control of the brown bottle.

Winter passed slowly and Charlie lived in a hazy world within his glass confines. During his long stay, he had not eaten or taken care of himself. He began to grow frail and thin. The warm glow was slowly fading. The bottle's walls were becoming cold and uncaring. On occasion, Charlie tried to reach the bottle's opening in an attempt to again find the outside world. But now the voice of the bottle was cruel and commanding, "Charlie, you cannot leave." Weak from hunger, and filled with despair, Charlie would slide feebly back into the depths of the bottle. At these times, he would utter quietly to himself, "I could leave if I wanted to, but I would rather stay here."

The mellow glow was completely gone now and there was nothing special about Charlie anymore. His good feelings about himself had gradually been replaced with guilt and hatred. He had become nothing more than a sad, frightened little caterpillar, trapped in a brown bottle. Spring came. The valley was filled with beauty beyond compare. The sky was a rainbow of color as thousands of butterflies tested their wings for the first time in a never ending flight of freedom.

. . . . THE PROMISE HAD BEEN FULFILLED. . . .
On the day of Promise,
Charlie died.
Alone,
in silent desperation.
No one knew.
No one cared.
Least of all, the brown bottle.[1]

Charlie never had the opportunity to experience the wonder and beauty of The Promise. The necessary metamorphosis that would have produced a creature of incredible beauty was exchanged for a shallow and empty lure. This little story points out one of the key concepts about any addiction. Like a swiftly flowing stream that gradually gathers speed and power, the disease process carries the individual along in its current. The person truly believes that he or she can climb out of the torrent any time. The truth that becomes painfully clear is that, even if the person recognized the destructive process himself/herself, it is usually quite rare that the process can simply be stopped.

Long before help arrives, a dual pronged force begins to haunt the minute by minute existence of the person who has become enslaved in the addictive process. Treatment professionals expect a certain amount of shame and guilt to be present when someone enters treatment. The guilt is often easier to address for it centers in behaviors that are outside of the self. To say "easier" does not mean that work and serious effort to change destructive patterns are not required. "Easier" simply means by comparison with shame. All too often guilt is worked through but the deep shame is not brought to light.

Shame has to do with the vulnerable inner self, the core of who each person is. At all costs this part of the person does not want to be exposed when it is held captive by a "shame-based" dynamic. Shame will disguise itself with clever defenses such as anger, apathy, control, depression, obsessive use of people, places, or things and the need to escape.

When a religion professional begins to use a chemical substance, a behavior or a food in an abusive manner, he/she develops a relationship with this "other" and gradually this relationship becomes primary. This happens with most people who suffer from active addiction, but it seems to be deeper for the religion professional. How can a person who stands before others and tries to help them develop a deeper understanding of their God not feel intolerable shame once the addiction has taken over? The defense of denial certainly contributes greatly to maintaining the facade of "looking good." Religion professionals are typically bright, creative and highly functional. The presenting picture, even after some deterioration has set in, conveys the image that all is well. Most religion professionals, aware of their position in the community, will not begin their usual pattern of abuse until the responsibilities of the day have been completed. The pattern has the flavor of "relaxing after a day's work." What is not apparent is the relational quality that some individuals will begin to establish with a process that eventually will be self and other destructive.

There will be less and less congruence between the person's inner and outer worlds.

An example of this conflict was voiced one day in a treatment group by a woman who was a member of a religious community. This woman was a teacher in the parish school and, at the beginning of her treatment, had felt comfort in believing that her "drinking had not caused damage to anyone but herself." As time and treatment began to take effect, this woman had to face the reality that being physically present in her classroom each day did not mean she was teaching. Despite any outward appearances, there were days when this woman felt so apathetic from mild withdrawal (hangover) that she would assign her students a period or two of "independent study." This tactic would allow time for the toxic substance, alcohol, to be eliminated from her system sufficiently for her to teach the rest of the day. Neither this woman nor anyone else on that faculty questioned the fact that the "independent study" was not a planned activity for the students. It was inserted because of a need to stabilize a body that was in torment due to consuming an overdose of alcohol.

Facing the reality that alcohol had become more important to her than her students, her co-workers, and even her God was a moment of searing truth. The powerful defenses of denial and rationalization had kept the disease process moving steadily downward. This woman smiled, appeared competent and trustworthy, and was hiding a terrible secret. Until she could confront what was holding her bound, she could not experience any real freedom. With the support of staff and other patients, this woman took the first tiny steps toward sobriety.

Another example of the effect of this cunning, powerful and baffling disease was a minister who lived in one of the southwestern states. From time to time he would take short excursions to Mexico. His mission was to secure Darvon from as many pharmacies as he could manage to visit in an afternoon. This man knew almost no Spanish, but he did know the Spanish word for more which is "mas." He would show one capsule to the person behind the counter (prescriptions are not needed in Mexico) and as this individual poured the medicine on the glass top, the minister would urge, "Mas, mas." This ritual would continue from pharmacy to pharmacy until the minister felt he had enough for a few weeks.

To elude customs officials the minister would purchase cheap Mexican pottery and some liquor and hide the Darvon in a compartment he had designed in the back seat of his car. With his clerical garb and a ready smile, he would slip through customs paying only a minor duty on his "Mexican souvenirs." This pattern continued for several years until he began to need more of the drug to achieve the desired effect. He found that if he combined the Darvon with Scotch, he could feel the way he wanted. This behavior eventually resulted in a series of DWI's (Driving While Intoxicated) which brought him to the attention of his bishop. The bishop acted quickly and the minister went for treatment of his polysubstance abuse. It was discovered that although the minister used Darvon as his drug of choice, he was abusing several chemicals in the same class. This minister had a fine record in his area and his "secret" was something that many people in his life were willing to ignore.

There are many examples like the two described above. The point is that the disease process hides well in highly functioning people. It is not until the later stages when it becomes more entrenched that the individual exhibits clearer signs of deterioration. Even then adequate assistance may not be forthcoming.

Giving and receiving help for any addiction is difficult. Although described as primary, progressive, chronic, and potentially fatal if not arrested, the power of the created relationship between the person and the focus of the obsessive compulsive behavior is enormous.

It seems that breaking this relationship for most people is one of the greatest challenges they will ever encounter. For well-educated, professional people like doctors, lawyers and religion professionals it seems worse. There is a sense of "This happens to other kinds of people—not me!"

What people begin to learn is that addiction is an equal opportunity disease and does not exempt anyone if the person's biochemical makeup will serve as a host environment. Since individuals do not plan to become addicted, there is disbelief when it does happen in the course of a person's life.

Other variables help to keep the reality of addiction out of awareness. The stereotype image of the skid row derelict still rushes to people's minds despite the fact that this population comprises only three to four percent of addicted individuals. What people fail to grasp is that a gutter or grate can be in a person's heart and mind. Because it can't be seen, it is denied.

The role of a religion professional still carries quite a few automatic assumptions. This group is entrusted with the joys and sorrows of other human beings and, much like therapists, they have many projections thrust upon them of how they should or should not be. This can become a heavy burden and the individual's identity may become fused with the role. This is clear to treatment personnel when a newcomer can only describe *what* he/she does rather than *who* he/she is.

It is not unusual for the religion professional to have difficulty "getting into treatment." This is most evident in an in-patient setting where other patients and, at times, even staff may unconsciously collude in helping the religion professional remain in the role of helper. There is something about the titles of Father, Reverend, Rabbi, Sister and Pastor that elicit a trusting positive response from many people. "Instant counseling" sessions occur in treatment settings among the patients until the religion professional is able to grasp his/her own need to put this important aspect of active ministry aside for personal time and space. What seems to grow dull with the passing of many years of service is the human need to have one's own feet washed. It is a moment of real surrender when a religion professional engages in the therapeutic process and allows others to *do* for him/her. This is a reversal of life lived in the real world and feels awkward. It takes a while to tease out if the role is learned behavior or defense. Many times it is not one or the other but part of each. The crucial factor is that the role be set aside until it can be assumed more freely. The difference may not be distinguishable externally by outside observers but the religion professional who no longer needs to serve but *chooses* to serve is an internally freer person who has begun to learn about healthy interdependence.

Another roadblock for the religion professional may be the fact that many formation programs in the past concentrated on academic pursuits that readied religion professionals "from the neck up." Until the recent past not much attention was given to a person's affective life. Feelings are like an unexplored region of a newly discovered planet. They are alien to the person. Vocabulary that is typically extensive becomes restricted. Feeling words are reduced to "good," "bad," or "upset." There is little ability to nuance different levels of feeling, and certainly no self-respecting religion professional ever feels angry!

It takes some hard work and effort to integrate the head with the heart. Until this journey is taken and this connection made, the religion professional can become deluded by convincing himself/herself that everything can be "figured out, understood and resolved" with speed that resembles a flashing bullet. Patterns that have helped to create the skills for the addictive process do not disappear with just good insight. The intent to change becomes no more potent than a New Year's Eve resolution unless some concrete action accompanies it. Addicted religion professionals make the same promises, the same pleas, repeat the same painful experiences as other people in other groups do until they decide they have hurt enough.

Perhaps the most poignant aspect of the religion professional's struggle in the addictive process is to be present as each one reflects on a personal experience of God. More often than not it is a powerful moment when the person can discuss honestly and freely the reality that a personal relationship with God is something that feels strangely absent. It is difficult for someone who spends many hours a day over years and years trying to help other people with their spiritual concerns to admit that his/her own interior life is not what he/she wants it to be. Although painful, if the religion professional will ride the storm through, the force of this issue of intimacy will lessen over time. The religion professional has a new opportunity to approach the God of his/her understanding and begin a relationship that can be free of developmental baggage from the past. One priest who had directed retreat experiences for other people for over fifteen years came to the point of being able to state that he "feels like a novice in the area of my own relationship with the Lord and that feels O.K." This man was able to wrestle with the fact that he had not spent quality time in developing his own spiritual life. He believed that the ministry he did with other people would satisfy his own needs. He put it well one day when he said, "I never thought that what I suggested that other people try to help with their relationship with God was applicable in my own life as well. It was as if I held myself exempt and expected the relationship to come with the package of priesthood." This man was able to confront his own myths and attitudes and find himself in a newer and more human place.

Ministry has moments of great happiness and great sorrow. If a minister, man or woman, encounters a struggle with addiction of any kind it could very well be an invitation to "come apart and pause a while with me" and assess where the path of life has brought that person. What initially may be viewed as a shameful burden may become a gift that allows a person to look at his/her vulnerable self and to incorporate that important part of a human life into an expression of ministry that gives evidence of God's compassionate and unwavering love for creation.

Notes

1. Penny Jones, *The Brown Bottle* (Hazelton: Hazelton Foundation, 1983).

Robert R. Lutz, M.Div., D.P.C.

Approval and Achievement:
Blessings or False Gods?

As I think about my life early in parish ministry, a typical day unfolded something like this. I arose with my wife at 6:00 a.m. She went off to work while I struggled to stay awake and pour over theological journals, the denominational magazine and all the other things I "should read" to stay current and informed. They always seemed to accumulate faster than I could read them, and rarely did they contribute directly to my ministry. No matter. I may have been sleepy, but I was staying informed!

By 8:00 a.m. my son was awake and my attention focused on getting him off to kindergarten. Then it was on to the office for administrative chores, sermon preparation, and, on occasion, a morning meeting. After lunch I made hospital calls, home visits, canvassed the neighborhood for new members, and for a time drove a school bus to help make financial ends meet. A vague feeling of guilt followed me most of the day. In the office I felt I "should" be out making calls. Out in the community I felt I "should" be in the office fashioning the next sermon which had to be informative, relevant and, of course, entertaining.

The evening was occupied with home visits to those away during the day, board meetings and Bible classes. I'd get home between 10:00 and 11:00 p.m. The schedule was not so much the problem. The pressure to produce, like being on a treadmill which kept moving a little more rapidly than I could run, was the killer.

Looking back, I am acutely aware that an inordinate need for approval and a drive to achieve, two pathological forces, were very much operative in my life. As I examine my appointment book today, I am reminded painfully that these two culprits are still impacting on my life and, at times, on my emotional health. Struggling with approval and achievement needs is a lifelong process for me. The difference between then and now is that now I have some awareness of what fuels those unhealthy fires—the passion to produce and the preoccupation to please—and I've taken active steps to remove some of the fuel. Like the raging forest fires of the great northwest, these unhealthy drives may tend to die down with age. However, for those not content to wait and tolerate the damage, there is much that can be done right now.

With this chapter, I'd like to share some of the insights and strategies I've found useful. Seeing approval and achievement in their extremes as false gods will serve as a way to frame what I have to say. The predicament of the Israelites in Exodus 32 comes immediately to mind as a starting place.

> When the people saw that Moses had not come down from the mountain but was staying there a long time, they gathered around Aaron and said to him, "We do not know what has happened to this man Moses, who led us out of Egypt; so make us a god to lead us. . . . So all the people took off their gold earrings and brought them to Aaron. He took the earrings, melted them, poured the gold into a mold, and made a gold bull-calf. The people said, "This is our god . . ." (Ex 32:1,3–4, Good News Bible).

It is not difficult for me to understand why the children of Israel made a false god. They were alone in the desert. The emotional dust was still settling from the pursuing Egyptian chariots. Moses was off receiving instructions from God, a God they had never seen. Time passed—ten days, twenty days, then thirty, then forty. I think the children of Israel were getting nervous, feeling anxious and insecure. Finally, when they could stand it no longer, they said to Aaron, ". . . make us a god to lead us." So he made a gold bull-calf, a god they could see and touch. And they felt better for a little while. It was not long, however, before their false god let them down. The dynamic process in this familiar Bible story affects me as it affects us all. An infant feels anxious and insecure when mother is away. Certain traditional "false gods" help during such times: a security blanket, a bottle, or maybe a pacifier, but only for a while. As the child individuates from mother and the ego matures, blankets and pacifiers are no longer as helpful. The child's sense of security and well-being begins to come from within. But parents do not parent perfectly and children do not grow emotionally and developmentally without flaw. Thus we move into adulthood with our own unique areas of vulnerability, our own healthy and unhealthy emotional needs which impact upon the direction and style of our daily lives. As an adult child of God called into ministry, I preach and teach about the God who brought the Israelites out of Egypt and from whom they awaited word, growing anxious as the days passed. And I, too, have my anxieties. Some anxiety is left from unresolved childhood conflicts. Some, called existential anxiety, simply accompanies being human. Theologian Martin J. Heinecken describes sin as a nameless anxiety or dread resulting from the possibility of being able to act in freedom without being completely free. He contends that there are only two possibilities for the absence of this anxiety. One is to be God who is absolutely free, without limitation and fully in charge. The other is to be in the womb with no freedom, where all wants are supplied and no decisions are made. These alternatives being impossible, anxiety or dread comes from living in the in-between state of limited freedom. Acting creatively in freedom, we simultaneously overreach ourselves. It seems to me that this is the condition of sin in which all persons live, even those of us who minister.[1]

In this state of creative tension, I need some word from the Lord that I am "O.K." I need something to bolster my sense of security, to loosen the knot in my stomach that continually asks "How am I doing?" Claimed by God in the waters of baptism, renewed and strengthened by word and sacrament, I should know the source of my security and self-confidence. Yet, often the jagged edges of my life experience keep me uncomfortable and anxious. This phenomenon is not unique to me alone. It is not uncommon to seek the fulfillment of unmet security needs outside ourselves and apart from God-in-us. The more things outside the self form the basis of our ego strength, the greater the potential for them to become like false gods in our lives. Therein lies the pitfall. False gods will, like the bull-calf, always let us down. The approval of others and the need to achieve can become such false gods.

Perhaps addressing these issues could be seen as a kind of repenting process. I use the term repentance as a process of assessing aspects of life which are unhealthy and deciding to make constructive changes. In both the Hebrew of the Old Testament and the Greek of the New Testament, repentance means the reorienting of life and personality.[2] As I become aware of their hollowness, I can turn away from the false god of approval or the false god of achievement and orient myself toward healthier ways of meeting the security needs they represent.

Some of the illustrations I use in talking about approval and achievement are from my own life. Some are from the lives of ministers who have sought me out for counseling, and some are situations I have observed. The names and details have been changed to protect confidentiality, but the dynamics are genuine.

Approval:
Source of Motivation or Golden Calf?

Reverend Bill was the pastor of Peace Church, a large, growing suburban congregation. He was loved by many people. Going out of his way not to offend anyone but to be accommodating, all things to all people, always available, Reverend Bill worked hard at being a people-pleaser. It was not uncommon for him to agree to weddings and their attendant rehearsals and receptions in the midst of vacation or in close proximity to busy and stressful times like the Christmas or Easter seasons. His denomination was urging parishes to celebrate communion more frequently. Reverend Bill supported this idea theologically, but would never raise it as an issue with his members lest it be offensive to some who might consider it "too Catholic." The chancel was being renovated, and this too was emotionally trying for Reverend Bill. Making major changes in design and decor involved disturbing some of the memorial furnishings and appointments given by members to remember loved ones, and Reverend Bill did not want to hurt anyone's feelings.

At an annual meeting the congregation became split over the controversial issue of redesigning the chancel. Each side had faithful members with valid points backed by sound reasoning and much emotion. By the time it reached the boiling point, there was no turning back. The congregation had to go one way or the other and hurt feelings were inevitable. Reverend Bill, now under tremendous stress, could no longer remain neutral. He took a stand, but in the process alienated some loyal members, a few of whom were also friends. It was around this time that Reverend Bill began feeling noticeably anxious. He experienced a loss of energy and enthusiasm and began to have difficulty sleeping. When the anxiety turned into full-blown panic attacks, he sought professional help. Since he had based much of his sense of security on the approval of the people he served, approval had become like a false god which finally let him down. With his sense of well-being severely shaken, his stress level dangerously high, Reverend Bill developed a major depressive episode.

First, it needs to be said that nothing in creation is inherently evil. Approval can be a source of rich blessing, a means through which

God works. Approval feels good, while disapproval and rejection are usually painful. It is natural and human to want to feel good. A few positive comments about a sermon tell me that it was heard and appreciated. A letter of thanks following months of visiting a hospitalized parishioner is a validation of that effort to be present to the member in time of difficulty. Words of support and encouragement help me to endure when I feel my efforts are of little consequence, to keep going when ministry seems like rowing upstream against a strong current. Approval is basically a good thing, a gift from God.

When the approval of others becomes the main indicator of self-worth, however, it has slipped into the role of a false god. On Sundays when affirmation about the service are not readily forthcoming, I may wonder what I did wrong. I may be tempted to discard an excellently timed, pointedly relevant sermon as inferior if no one tells me how good it was. The prophetic role of ministry, bringing God's word of judgment to bear on a situation, will be especially difficult and stressful because prophets usually are not popular. Prophetic messages, often desperately needed, are frequently seen as trouble-making, boat-rocking and threatening to the status quo. The Old Testament prophets were beaten, stoned, thrown down wells and run out of town. No approval there! Yet sometimes we are called to speak the word as prophets. More generally, leading a congregation into any kind of change may be a source of unhealthy stress if approval of others occupies the role of false god in one's life. Congregations are often resistant to even the most obviously needed changes. I have heard all too often: "But we have always done it this way!"

Psychology tells us that the inordinate need for approval usually has its roots in childhood interaction with parents and other significant people. Childhood can be described as being a little person living in the land of giants. At knee-level to the giants, children tend not to question the judgment of parents. Critical parents or ones who believe that children will put forth more effort if approval and affirmation are withheld create an atmosphere in which children either strive constantly and unsuccessfully for approval or give up trying altogether. The elder sibling usually takes the former stance, while the younger typically sees that it does not work and abandons the effort. Statistically, most religion professionals are eldest children. Thus, the stage may be set in adult life for approval to become like a false god with which we define our self-worth. At times in my own ministry, it seemed as if I wore invisible vestments with "How am I doing?" emblazoned on the front and "Try harder!" on the back. When approval is a false god, it needs to be dealt with.

How does one repent in this situation? I have found three strategies in the form of reorientations to be helpful. The first is recognizing what is taking place within the mind and emotions and how that impacts on interactions with others, because an internal reorientation may be indicated. Secondly, the establishing of a support system to balance approval needs with healthy, honest, constructive feedback, support and encouragement can help free us from the tyranny of keeping the congregation happy at the expense of effective ministry and personal well-being. Finally, a circle of friends outside the congregation can orient our emotional needs and their fulfillment away from the vulnerability of the workplace.

First, if approval is a false god, we have probably carried into adulthood an inner belief system or philosophy of life which defines our self-worth in terms of the perceived attitudes and opinions of others. This originated in the childhood need for approval and acceptance from parents. Not adequately met in childhood, this need continues on into adult life as a never-ending quest.

David Burns, M.D., an expert in the field of cognitive therapy, coined the term "silent assumption" and has developed an effective way to identify the "silent assumptions" in our lives.[3] This can be done by choosing an event which was upsetting either because approval was not received or because disapproval was incurred. After discovering what I tell myself about me in relation to such an event, I can process this self-statement through a series of steps which lead to the underlying belief.

It might unfold like this. At a church council meeting, I propose that we allow our mission statement, our reason for existing, to determine the priority order in which we pay our bills. Like a leap of faith, it is a bit daring especially when funds are short. But it puts our money where our mouth is. I have carefully thought this out and believe it is a basically good idea. However the financial secretary, an influential and powerful member, takes strong issue with my idea, calling it financial suicide, and it is ultimately defeated. I feel angry, hurt and embarrassed. I tell myself, "I am unable to lead my congregation," almost as a reflex reaction which I may not even be aware of. If I can become aware of this self-statement, I can process it through its various levels of meaning to uncover my silent assumption:

> I am unable to lead my congregation. (self-statement)
> If this were true, what would it mean to me?
> —that I am an ineffective pastor.
> If this were true, what would it mean?

—that the church council will not listen to my ideas.
  If this were true, what would it mean?
—that my congregation will not move in the direction
  which I think it should.
  If this were true, what would it mean?
—that I am a worthless person. (silent assumption)

Notice the progression from having one idea defeated to being a worthless person. Of course this is distorted thinking. But it flows almost automatically, leaving me feeling hurt, embarrassed and, at a deeper level, angry.

In most cases, what we tell ourselves about approval is distorted. But since we have been giving ourselves the same messages for years, they feel natural and seem perfectly sound. Viewed with cold hard logic, however, the distortions will appear. Obviously, one defeated idea does not make me a worthless person or even an ineffective pastor. Identifying the distortions and correcting the logic in our reasoning can help lessen the impact of disapproval. This repenting or reorienting technique facilitates the shifting of the focus of evaluation for ideas and actions to the self rather than from others. The responses of others then become feedback which we can choose to use or not use as needed rather than an attack on our being. Due to its highly subjective nature, this issue may be difficult to address alone. A pastoral counselor or other therapist skilled in cognitive technique may prove to be a helpful asset.

In addition to an internal reorientation, some external supports may also be useful. A second strategy for repenting when approval is a false god is the development of a support group of a few persons not directly connected with the congregation. It is important to trust the judgment and the faith commitment of these persons and to be willing and able to be open, honest, and accepting of constructive feedback. Several pastors shared the cost of hiring a psychologist for two hours per month. The group of pastors, along with the psychologist, himself a minister, formed a peer support group with the added dimension of input from a mental health professional. The experience of sharing both personal and parish issues while receiving constructive feedback and emotional support was an excellent way to unhook sufficiently from the need for approval from members to maintain a healthy and balanced perspective. This was especially helpful when "counting the cost" of entering into a controversial area of ministry. The chapter on support systems in this volume explores the reasons for and possibilities of such groups in more detail.

A third reorienting strategy in breaking free from the false god of approval is to build a circle of friends and acquaintances outside the parish with whom you share common interests and who care about you and your family. They should have little vested interest in your congregation, synod, district, judicatory or denomination. Preferably, few should be clergy and/or clergy families. This is not to imply that a minister should not have friends within the congregation. However, if one takes seriously the call to be set apart for a ministry of word and sacraments, friendships within the congregation will have limits imposed by the nature of that call, without which either the prophetic or the priestly roles of ministry, or both, are likely to be adversely affected. Jesus said that a prophet is not without honor except in his own home town (Lk 4:24). As friendships with members grow in number and depth, the congregation can become more and more like our home town.

One minister enjoyed having a few drinks with certain members after committee meetings and on other occasions. Conversation flowed easily and the time spent was enjoyable and relaxing. One of the members, however, often drank to excess. The minister was unclear about the role boundaries as friend and pastor. But when he became aware that the drinking was causing family problems, he felt compelled to confront the situation. Becoming defensive, the member said that his drinking buddy had turned on him and pulled rank. Partly as a defense, he needed to see the minister as "one of the guys," thus weakening the minister's effectiveness in confronting his problem. When the dust settled, the minister had one less friend among that group of members. The others were more on guard and often "joked" about the minister suddenly switching roles on them. One might argue that the minister could have acted more as a concerned friend rather than "officially." In reality, he probably did. The role switching seemed more an automatic function of the member's perception than a conscious effort on the part of the minister. The fact is that it happened.

As a mediator between God and God's people, a minister brings words of hope, encouragement, strength, and forgiveness. The effectiveness of this priestly role of the religion professional can also suffer. In a sense, it is the reverse of the example just cited. Beverly belonged to a social group that got together for a monthly activity. Pastor Sam also attended the get-together and enjoyed "letting his hair down" once in a while. As Beverly got to know Pastor Sam better, she became less able to relate to him as a pastor. She had difficulty accepting Pastor Sam's less-than-perfect human nature. She needed to see her pastor as if on a pedestal. The more she got to know him, the more he seemed to fall off that pedestal. Pastor Sam was a competent and very effective minister. He was never inappropriate in the social group—just human. Beverly "knew" all ministers are human, but she could not seem to accept this in Sam and was sadly disillusioned when she sought counseling. It is probably safe to say that every congregation has some Beverlys. Some people cannot confess their sins to a buddy, but may be able to confess them and hear God's word of hope and forgiveness from one they know primarily as pastor. The dynamics between friends are different from those between pastor and parishioner. It seems to me that it is not likely for both sets of dynamics to exist at the same time. One or the other, the friendship or the pastoral relationship, is usually compromised at some point. When the primary circle of friends is outside the congregation one can go about the role of ministering without sacrificing needed and cherished friendship or lessening the effectiveness of the various roles of the ministry.

Achievement:
Healthy Productivity or the False God of Doing?

Pastor Jane, one of the first women to be ordained in her denomination, was well into middle age. Doing ministry had been a great sacrifice in her life. The commitment to four years of seminary and the demands of the parish influenced her decision not to have children and eventually contributed to the break-up of her marriage. Now in her second pastorate, Jane seemed to be thriving on the busyness of parish work. She rarely took time off and was typically on the go from early morning till late at night. Vacations usually took the form of an out-of-town conference or a continuing education event. Pastor Jane had an enormous amount of energy and a tremendous commitment to her work, factors which won her respect and appreciation both from the congregations she served and her denomination.

At age 48, Pastor Jane suffered a mild heart attack. Her doctor told her she had several risk factors for future cardiac problems and strongly recommended some changes in her lifestyle. Following recuperation for six weeks, he admonished her to limit her work week, taking part of each day for herself. The first six weeks back home were extremely difficult for Pastor Jane. Despite her wish to recover and remain healthy and the congregation's complete support of her reduced work load, Jane found it very hard not to be busy. Physically, she felt fine. Emotionally, she felt a sense of worthlessness and guilt. Pastor Jane began to recognize that these feelings were coming from within her. The congregation made almost no demands on her. She had "permission" from the church and her physician to take time to recover. Yet she was overwhelmed with feelings of lost identity and purposelessness. In counseling, Pastor Jane began to understand the extent to which she defined her being and her worth in terms of the work she did. She explored the roots of her drive to do and began to make some progress in changing her lifestyle in healthy ways.

Like approval, achievement is inherently a good thing. Healthy pride in our accomplishments makes us feel good, generates self-respect and motivates us to do more. Yet achievement can become the false god of doing. But when self-worth and security are defined by what we accomplish, achievement occupies a dangerous place in our life. Pastor Jane's situation is not uncommon. The religious and cultural work ethic has impacted upon most areas of life. As a child, I often heard "Don't waste time!" from a well-meaning teacher. My parents often praised my achievements. Far less often did they praise me for just being myself. So I learned early that achievement gets approval. In adult life, I pride myself on getting things done. Along the way, I encounter intense reinforcement from the media, such as advertisements for a host of products like car phones and personal computers to help me to do more, better and faster.

Achievement is also reinforced in ministry. First, the job of parish pastor itself is endless and complex. For one who tends toward workaholism, I found the ministry a veritable gold mine of things to do. A subtle, but sometimes fierce, sense of competition often exists among ministers who would do better to be in support of rather than in competition with each other. Yet I have often heard and been involved in the competitive spirit in meeting and talking with other ministers. "How many members do you have?" "What's your annual budget?" "Have you taken in many new families lately?" This is also precisely the information requested by the denomination each year. While it may be necessary for the running of the church, it tends to rekindle the old parental admonitions to shape up and get with it because bigger and more are better.

No congregation grows toward its potential as a people of God without a lot of dedication and effort on the part of its minister. But, when achievement reaches false god proportions in our life, when our work determines our worth, sooner or later it will let us down, as it did with Pastor Jane. When work determines our worth, much

needed leisure time to rest and replenish emotional and physical resources becomes difficult to justify. Often family is neglected and
many simple pleasures of life are overlooked. Retirement can be a
time of emptiness and despair.

Repentance from the false god achievement can reorient us to a
healthier balance of work and leisure. I believe the key word here is
balance. The absence of a desire for achievement in ministry can be as
disastrous as a preoccupation or compulsion to achieve. Somewhere
in between, in a place unique to each individual, is a healthy balance.
Repentance as reorientation need not always be a 180-degree turn-
around to be health enhancing. The drivenness of the obsessive-com-
pulsive personality, the behavior of the Type-A individual as defined
by Friedman and Rosenman,[4] creative time management techniques
and other such topics have been dealt with and can be reviewed from
other sources. I will focus here on the delicate balance between being
and doing in a culture and in a type of work which values doing as
all-important.

Perhaps a starting place is in remembering again that God calls
people to be faithful, not to be busy. Part of being faithful is keeping
in mind that the congregation or community we serve as minister
belongs to God, not to us. God comes to people and touches them as
God sees fit. We who are ministers are God's instruments in this
process.

In my own experience of fifteen years of parish ministry, I have
continually observed a phenomenon which I have come to accept and
trust as the working of the Holy Spirit in the midst of God's people.
After worship on many occasions, people have said things like: "Your
sermon was especially helpful today. It was as if you were talking just
to me. The scripture lessons really hit home this morning. I really
needed to be uplifted today and the choice of hymns couldn't have
been better!" I, on the other hand, may have thought the sermon was
dull, the gospel lesson confusing, the hymns dragged, and wondered
how anyone was nourished by the Lord's supper the way the acolyte
banged the glass trays around! It is as if something happens on another
level during worship to cause these responses from worshipers—
something outside my awareness and quite beyond my control. That
something for me is God doing what is promised: being present when
two or three are gathered in God's name and meeting people at the
point of their needs. While not a substitute for preparation and good
order, it has been tremendously freeing for me to come to realize that
God is the true presiding minister at worship. As a pastor, I am God's
instrument. God comes to people through the word: spoken and read,

sung and preached, through the sacrament, and through the interaction of those gathered together, touching them with healing love.

After a two-year leave for graduate study, I returned to active ministry as a pastoral counselor. In the course of seeing clients, I hear things like "This session was very helpful to me today" after a session I might have perceived as ineffective. A client may recall something I said in a previous session which helped shed light on an issue that I had long forgotten. Sometimes I gain some personal insight through what the client says to me. And then it dawned on me. The same phenomenon I had been observing in worship is happening in counseling. Outside of my awareness and beyond my control, God is present as we gather together. Using our words and the therapeutic relationship, God meets us at the point of our needs and works divine healing. Again, I experienced a freeing insight: God is the real healer. My perception of pastoral counseling began to shift from a task I do to "fix the client" to a way of being in communion with another person that enables the words and the relationship to accomplish God's healing. The subtle shift toward valuing being as well as doing has made me no less busy. It has, however, relieved much of the pressure and drivenness of the doing. The focus is more on being faithful to God's call rather than on doing as if I were God. The result seems to be a far more relaxed and healthy position for doing effective ministry.

The point is not that achievement is undesirable or unhealthy. Being productive can be tremendously satisfying. Success can be quite enjoyable. But the drive—the important word here is drive—for achievement gains us neither a place before God according to Judeo-Christian tradition, nor a healthy place before others and ourselves. A sense of inner peace and self-esteem is not dependent upon having the most, doing the best, or administering the largest. Yet the danger of this false god is that when it is operative, our feelings often tell us just the opposite.

Some Concluding Thoughts

We have looked at the tendency to base self-esteem on the approval of others and on our achievements. Framed as false gods, some ways of repenting or reorienting ourselves away from these ultimately disappointing sources of self-confidence have been discussed. The points made are probably not totally new information for anyone in ministry. Yet I can easily forget them, getting so caught up in my work that I spend much time as if dancing around a golden calf.

In the end, it seems to me that self-esteem cannot be earned by approval, by achievements, or by any other means. It comes first as a gift from God, who in both the Old and New Testaments declares people righteous apart from any efforts on their part. Secondly, our self-esteem is an assertion we make for ourselves as redeemed people of God in light of and in spite of any strengths and weaknesses we may have. I share these insights to help in the ongoing process of living effectively as people who have chosen to be God's instruments in the work of the kingdom.

Notes

1. Martin J. Heinecken, *Christian Teachings* (Philadelphia: Fortress, 1967), pp. 97–98.

2. Alan Richardson (ed.), *A Theological Work Book of the Bible* (New York: Macmillan, 1976), pp. 191–192.

3. David D. Burns, M.D., *Feeling Good: The New Mood Therapy* (New York: New America Library, 1980), p. 234.

4. Meyer Friedman, M.D., and Ray H. Rosenman, M.D., *Type A Behavior and Your Heart* (New York: Fawcett Crest, 1974).

Noreen Suriner Craley, M.Div.

Surviving Ministry from a Woman's Perspective: Celebrating the Joys and Avoiding the Pitfalls

Two roads diverged in a yellow wood,
And sorry I could not travel both
And be one traveler, long I stood
And looked down one as far as I could
To where it bent in the undergrowth;

Then took the other, as just as fair,
And having perhaps the better claim,
Because it was grassy and wanted wear. . . .

. . . Two roads diverged in a wood, and I—
I took the one less traveled by,
And that has made all the difference.
                                        Robert Frost

Surviving ministry from the point of view of an ordained woman compared with that of an ordained man is like comparing the towpath along Washington D.C.'s C&O canal with a climb up an unexplored mountain. For men, the road is worn, the ruts clearly visible, and the way well marked. For women, the risks of confusing role expectations, inconsistent deployment procedures, and unknown opportunities complicate the challenge of being a woman who ministers. However, with persistence, perseverance, and prayer one can overcome the obstacles, filling one's ministry with opportunities for great love, spiritual growth and personal enrichment.

Women are now doing what men have done for years: representing the holy to God's people, as a complementary mediator: allowing people to see God at work more fully in the world, interpreting the Holy to them, and enabling them to respond to God with commitment.

To start with, walking the less-traveled road necessitates that a woman follow *God's* lead down the path. A woman in ministry must be grounded deep within her call and possess a secure sense of empowerment from God. Her success depends solely upon this relationship; for it is only from her connection with Christ that she can effectively practice her ministry. Her call is not just a career, but a way of life that affects herself as well as her family.

The Reverend Phoebe Coe speaks about her call.

> What has become most important to me in my daily vocation is an on-going, still overpowering, sense of being in the right place and doing with my life the right thing. My experiences, successful and unsuccessful, all seem to be preparing me and making me ready for the days ahead. I am most at one when I am pursuing my studies, my Sunday preparations, the pastoral work and preaching. My heart beats faster just to think of it. Some people call this experience a verification of their "call." I simply know that my desire to serve the church and to grow into "the full stature of Christ" is a powerful drive that keeps urging me on and on.[1]

In order to withstand the difficulties of ordained leadership, a woman's identity must be well founded, worked through and secure. Both the institution and the specific people whom she is called to serve will challenge, yea, at times assault or victimize her. She must be clear on the theological issues, compassionate with those struggling with women's issues, and gentle with herself. With determination and commitment to God—along with support from some surprising corners—she can withstand assaults from within her profession and from the outside world.

For women currently ordained, there are few female role models and they are mostly submerged within their own congregations, hence unavailable for celebrity. They function somewhat like amoebae—taking an issue, surrounding it, taking it in, trying on solutions for fit, keeping the appropriate and discarding the rest—a slow trial and error process of living. Effectively, then, each ordained woman is, like it or not, her own role model. Each woman knows that she is clearing the way for others to follow.

Chotard Doll speaks about role models and how they affected her life and quest to serve Christ.

It's a question of role models. My most important understanding came when I realized that my father and the person
who served as my mentor were wonderful models, but that I
could not be like either one of them. Rather, I needed to
rejoice in that fact and not feel bad about it and to begin to
make my own decisions. I had to recognize that I had my
own gifts that I must use—my own intelligence, my own
instincts and my own faith. The sexual difference is positive
in that sense. Once I came to grips with it and accepted it as a
positive thing, I felt enormously freed.[2]

So, unlike the case with men, for women a process must evolve
where few guiding models exist. Fortunately, a partial result of this
ambiguity is to strip away old expectations of clergy and to furnish
new opportunities for changing social norms. In particular, women
can act on the feminine qualities society already accepts. Unlike men
who stereotypically are not allowed to display tender feelings, a woman is allowed to manifest her care for her congregation in important events affecting her people's lives. Societal norms allow her
to be cooperative and overtly nurturing, as well as singular and
independent.

So far as the author's observation discloses, the most successful
women in the church are those who present strong, coherent self-
images, comfortable and unashamed to be women, and conscious of
translating their male role models into female terms. They are
conscious of learning all they can from all available sources, while
fitting those learnings into theological contexts. Changes are occurring, but slowly.

Of course, there are—and will be—people who philosophically
cannot accept women clergy, or, for that matter, women in any position of real leadership. However, when confronted with the work of a
woman cleric, often they are "converted."

Pioneering offers the opportunity to incarnate an issue (i.e. women's ordination), and to watch the growth that emerges within people who allow themselves to receive her ministry. An issue once re-
mote and fearsome becomes familiar, comfortable and inspirational.
Frequently when a pastoral crisis occurs, the person in need does not
really care who arrives so long as he or she receives pastoral care.
Indeed, many opportunities for dialogue have emerged from a woman's simply going about her business.

In a larger context, women's ordination and how women clergy
are treated is symbolic for how all women are treated—as the hatred,

bitterness, and mean-spirited objection to the consecration of the first woman bishop, Barbara Harris, attests. That her consecration demonstrated the readiness of a majority of those in the Episcopal Church to accept women into the higher ranks of those who represent Christ's love does not mean that others in the church and the world are ready to accept it. Even though women have been ordained for decades, a deeper level of sex discrimination is detectable in places where resistance was thought to have diminished. The most guilty are people who speak in favor of women being ordained but show their ambivalence by not attending crucial events.

Sadly, ordained women share the fate of other career women. Betsy Freeman in *The Journal* observes:

> Almost every woman is familiar with these kinds of male behavior—stereotyping, exclusion and condescension. These and other forms of sexism are not as blatant as the outright sex discrimination and sexual harassment that have led to court cases. . . . But taken together, the gestures and remarks—sometimes unwitting, sometimes deliberate— form a pattern of subtle sexism that prevents women at all levels from achieving the success for which they're qualified. It's a kind of discrimination that often wears a cloak of sensitivity and deference to women.[3]

Women are most likely to experience this in the critical areas of entry into a congregation and deployment.

For men, the right to serve a congregation as minister is taken for granted. Only in extreme cases such as when there was moral or financial misconduct or too deep a love for the previous minister does a congregation withhold its spontaneous trust of the succeeding pastor. Trust is not as easily granted women. However, in the case of the above extremes, a woman can enter the congregation with fewer frustrations or projected expectations than can a man because of her visible difference from the offender or the previous minister. One vestry member of a congregation in which the previous two male clergy had had affairs with women of the congregation reported that his congregation's dismay and distrust was so great that they intentionally sought to hire a woman.

In another case, in which a young beloved rector had died suddenly, a woman was called and in time embarked upon a building program. When the hall was dedicated in the previous rector's name the congregation could allow his release. The building program facilitated the congregation's grief over the previous rector, thereby clearing the way for the new rector's acceptance.

Even in such cases, for women the authority to serve is never simply granted. They still must earn the privilege to minister and the relationship must be proven again and again. It takes the systematic building of relationships both by pastoral visitation and crisis intervention, as well as an adept hand at decision making.

Mary S. Donovan writes of an interview with the Reverend Phoebe Coe, whose congregation tripled in six months. Donovan reports Coe's reflection on what it is to build the church and to earn a congregation's trust.

> Pastoral needs must come first. She is faithful about calling on the sick and the shut-ins, about ministering to people in times of special crisis. In addition, the worship life must be strengthened. She takes particular care in arranging the worship services every Sunday and spends a good deal of time on her sermons, seeing them as a way to reach out to newcomers and old-timers alike. With an attentive ear to the unvoiced concerns of her flock, she has set up a schedule to visit every current member of the parish and every person who has been associated with the church in the past as well as those who appear in church for the first time.[4]

Unquestionably, the challenge of working with an unwelcoming congregation can be torture. For those who must search for their position, that road, too, is fraught with dangers. Statistics show that women are primarily accepting positions in smaller congregations with fewer financial resources and often outside of metropolitan areas. There persists a significant salary gap between ordained female and male clergy. Of the women ordained, just under half are serving as assistants, with an exceedingly large number serving as chaplains in institutions. Less that twenty percent of Episcopal women serve as heads of congregations.

Women earn less than their contemporaries for similar positions, are slower at moving to more lucrative pastorates, and have extreme difficulties in becoming (not being) rector or head minister of large corporate style congregations. Some of this is due to the unavailability of opportunities and some of it is due to women being in financial need and forced to take lower compensation for work accomplished. When women are hired, often employing congregations will look at her "financial need" and judge that since she has a working husband, her need is less than that of a man seeking the same job—even though *he* has a working wife.

An informal survey indicates that it takes a woman twice as long to find a position as it does a man. And when they are called to serve a specific church family, because of the time required to change, women must live a schizophrenic life as they work happily and intensely in a given congregation, only to be looking forward to a next position long before they are emotionally ready to move.

In interviewing, the call word is time. A woman must do her best to manage enough time with the search committee. The search committee will not understand the need, but with time each member will have the opportunity to see through some of their projections, thus seeing the strengths and weaknesses of a woman candidate.

Since many women serve as assistants, the bright side is that being an assistant offers a freedom of lifestyle that a pastor or rector doesn't have. More is demanded of a pastor in terms of personal behavior, role expectations, and relationships. If a woman is interested in a less traditional lifestyle, being an assistant offers freedom that is unavailable to a pastor or rector.

One woman who had served a congregation for nearly five years as an assistant found her experience happy and productive. However, once she was made interim pastor while the parish prepared to call another minister, her experience became quite difficult. All the authority and power issues from which assistant pastor status protected her emerged with a fury. Her peers, for example, treated her angrily, for they resented her being "in charge" and therefore in charge of them.

As in any business, there are standards for conduct—including dress—that are rarely spoken of and yet powerful socially. For an ordained woman it matters, perhaps more that it should, that she present a professional image. She must present confidence, strength, and poise. Good grooming and physical deportment are essential. Clothes with soft, feminine, but professional lines, attractive for the woman wearing them, are effective not only for the professional woman, but even more so for the ordained woman. A simple, classic, and attractive appearance facilitates acceptance for both the woman and her gifts and skills. A good guide: anything in excess detracts. By demonstrating her care for herself in her appearance, she conveys the importance she places on care and thus suggests her trustworthiness and interest in caring for others.

Any ordained woman wearing the symbols of her office, such as a clerical collar, will be the target for such questions as, "Well, what do we call you? Father?" "I've never seen a woman priest before. When did the Roman Catholic Church allow that?" "Can you get married?" As annoying as they are, how a woman cleric answers these questions, especially in first encounters with strangers, will provide an opportunity either for evangelism or for ill will. For many, their first encounter with the novelty of a woman minister will frame the context of any subsequent ordained woman they meet.

If a woman cleric's tradition allows clerical collars, she should wear one every day. The people become accustomed to seeing the symbol of office and eventually acknowledge the authority of the symbol. Full use of available symbols strengthens presence, makes grace concrete, and convinces congregants that, indeed, God's trustworthy representative is with them.

Romantic or sexual topics pose special challenges for women ministers. Here clear-cut distinctions about private and professional life become confused and each member of the congregation judges the minister by his or her own standards of morality. From a personal point of view, it is difficult to find the time or freedom for dating, much less privacy. The fishbowl aspects of clerical life direct serious judgment toward sexuality, its choices and its consequences.

However, while dating is extremely difficult, marriage can make being a pastor easier. Madge Brown, congregant of Peggy Bosmyer, a priest in Arkansas, observed the transformation marriage and two children made in Bosmyer. Brown says:

Marriage and then motherhood brought a new maturity and depth to Bosmyer's ministry. We feel that we've been able to share the excitement of their marriage.

For Bosmyer marriage meant a personal adjustment as well as an adjustment in her relationship with her congregation.

The congregation needed to learn that I had another, primary family; that they had become my secondary family; whereas before, as a single priest, they were my primary family.[6]

The Reverend Ann Struthers Coburn, co-rector, wife and mother in Danbury, Connecticut, expresses her frustration regarding the complexities of her many, at times conflicting, roles:

It is a hard lesson for me to learn that I can't have it all—career, family, personal life—all the time. I am always learning to sacrifice and compromise and balance.[7]

However, just as there are potential problems, there are potential advantages. Women clerics who deliver children while serving their congregations incarnate the experience of birth and rebirth. As she preaches, celebrates or reads while pregnant, a woman priest brings to life the action of God being made human in a way that only a woman can. When one incorporates the conscious and unconscious material of the holy, having a child becomes a holy event and the power for change is great. Preparing and working with that power helps to transform the options from potential liabilities into unusual opportunities.

An issue only recently acknowledged as a source of grief is the cost of sacrificing child-bearing years to the church. Women frequently put aside fully developing personal lives to fulfill the challenge of their calls. Just when they are in places to serve best, spiritually, physically, and professionally, they find themselves alone, and at times lonely. Looking back, some regret having put aside personal lives for service to God. Few regret the prospect of working for Christ's ministry, but a cleric, as with other professional women in our society, may wonder who, when she is eighty and in a nursing home, will really care about her work and life. A congregation she serves while she is forty may barely remember her years later. When these women are too old to have children, they must depend upon God alone to bear with them another cost of ministry.

A woman who finds her vocation later in life has the advantage of wisdom and experience on her side. Owing to her age, her congregation is less likely to see her as either seductress or victim, an all too frequent perspective. One woman related how, when she sensed that a man was beginning to express sexual interest, she pulled out the photos of her grandchildren. Suddenly the threat disappeared. She confessed that having the problem remained flattering. She had learned to take advantage of her age, creatively turning a threatening situation into a humorous one.

No doubt the conditions of social compromise for women clerics will make some readers angry. Indeed, the pain of continued discrimination and the thorny paths it makes of forming personal and professional relationships discourage many. Those who remain endure it because, even with the struggle, they are called by God to serve.

They are in ministry not in their own name, but in the name of Jesus Christ. And, called and prepared, most will survive. Most, though angry and hurt that their call is slow in acceptance and still at times feared, manage not to let their justifiable anger subvert their mission. Women ministers who are angry are clearly less effective within their congregation, for most people cannot cope with the intensity of avoiding the minister, as well as the issue. Hence, women clergy serve everyone's interest well by learning to manage anger and conflict without negative face-to-face confrontation. Members of a congregation are less forgiving of anger—justified or not—than of almost any other negative behavior.

Humor with its capacity to enhance well-being and perspective on life offers both an antidote to anger and a vehicle for esteem. While humorless men are perceived as serious or thoughtful, humorless women are seen as angry or grim. Preaching, living, and working with humor captivates the congregation and facilitates the proclamation of the gospel. The use of humor is generally a survival tactic for women in ministry. It may be the tool of choice for dealing with anger.

While colleague groups are helpful for men and women, for women they are essential for the help they provide in keeping perspective and in facilitating theological reflection on various issues confronting all ministers today. Along with a women's group, necessary for translating traditional male roles into roles in which women fit, women also need a trusted group of both men and women to help clarify common issues. Peers' views help to distinguish between issues common among all ministers, those more relevant for women, and those which are strictly personal. In any case, the personal support is critical. Few people work well in isolated or hostile environments. Having a source for reaffirming one's call and mission and one's value and direction can help realign priorities and reconfirm purpose. In supplying these important resources, a trusted support group can supply the difference between effective and ineffective ministry.

As a whole, although women are increasingly seeking ordination, the road to successful pastoral life remains less traveled and unworn. No long tradition exists upon which they can plan or base experience. Few guideposts mark the way just yet. Gradually, however, they are emerging through accumulated data and shared experience. Together, all of today's women clergy are writing and will be rewriting this chapter.

Notes

1. Mary S. Donovan, *Women Priests in the Episcopal Church: The Experience of the First Decade* (Forward Movement Publications, 1988).

2. Ibid., p. 75.

3. Betsy Freeman, "Breaking the Code," The Journal (November 1, 1988).

4. Donovan, pp. 59–60.

5. Constant H. Jacquet, Jr., *Women Ministers In 1986 and 1977: A Ten Year View* (Office of Research and Evaluation, National Council on Churches, New York, September 1988).

6. Donovan, p. 43.

7. Ibid., p. 52.

Roy M. Oswald, M.Div.

Building Support

Support has been a key issue for me throughout my ministry. Unhappily, I see in retrospect the large chunks of ministry when I did not feel support. I recall the loneliness and despair I often experienced when I believed that there was no fire escape from the turmoil I was in. How different those times would have been had I had people around me to give me perspective and encouragement. A few times a good swift "kick-in-the-pants" would also have been a caring, supportive gesture, because I was feeling sorry for myself and was afraid to do something about my malaise.

The times in my ministry when support was available were growing, exciting times. I recall moving out with perspective and confidence when setbacks occurred. I did not feel abandoned. As I reflect on these times of support and non-support, it becomes clear to me that the effectiveness of my ministry is directly proportional to the quality of support I am feeling at any given moment.

I am taking this opportunity to share what I have learned about support while in and out of the garbage pail.

Occasions of Need

Role Confusion

Carrying the role of resident religious authority is possibly the most confusing and unsettling assignment in North America today. The "holy man"/"holy woman" designation is a projection phenomenon. Everyone has a different idea of what a parish pastor ought to do, and how she or he should execute that role. Clergy themselves have been given complex and sometimes contradictory role models—some coming from early childhood experiences with clergy, some from seminary, others from "successful" clergy in their judicatories. In the midst of this confusion clergy often find themselves lacking helpful feedback from their denominations and clear messages from their parishes.

Stress technology proposes that the more confusing your role the higher your stress level. I meet many clergy who are experiencing high stress in the midst of role confusion.

A solid peer support system works to alleviate stress by offering distance, perspective, and experience. This makes for role clarity. A good peer group can help the individual priest pull away from the parish scene and see his/her role through other eyes.

The case study method (i.e. Jim Glasse in *Putting It Together in the Parish*[1]) is one of the most potent tools I know. In the hands of fellow professionals it can help regain clarity at critical points when other routes lead to confusion and self-doubt.

Role Conflict

Role confusion may come from confusing or competing models of ministry. Role conflict occurs when there are competing external expectations for a pastor, placing him/her in an untenable position. It can be a "shootout" when two individuals or two groups insist that the pastor do it their way. These situations can be highly threatening and they jeopardize one's future in that parish.

In such a situation a group of caring professionals can weigh the pros and cons of various options and again provide invaluable experience and perspective.

Isolation/Loneliness

Regardless of how much laity may talk about clergy needing to learn to share the ministry, the majority of the laity do not understand and do not wish to understand what it is like to be the religious authority in their midst. This phenomenon causes a kind of isolation and loneliness in ministry that is generally only understood by other clergy. Ninety percent of parish ministry is invisible to ninety percent of the people involved in a parish. If a pastor must put in an eighty hour week during a time of crisis, most lay people will have little idea of how those eighty hours are spent. At such times we often need support in caring for ourselves and our loved ones.

Lack of Pastoral Care

Who is the pastor to pastors? The majority of clergy function with little or no pastoral care for themselves or their families. When their prayer life runs dry and they become disillusioned and cynical, there is rarely anyone to intervene and set them on a more constructive spiritual course.

Effective support systems can offer this kind of constructive care. When trust level is high and individuals share their pain and vulnerability, a group can offer a theological or scriptural perspective on the malaise. Some time can be spent in prayer. Members of the group often then proceed to follow up individually as one of their members moves through a crisis of faith.

Burnout

Even the most energetic parish pastor can become depleted. After years of continual giving out without much coming back in return, an individual can feel burned out. Most social scientists agree on the four primary characteristics of burnout:

(a) physical/emotional exhaustion
(b) cynicism
(c) disillusionment
(d) self-deprecation

Alban Institute Research[2] has shown that one in five parish clergy exhibit these four characteristics. Burnout is lethal for parish ministry, as it is nearly impossible for "good news" to come through a person who is exhausted, cynical, disillusioned, and self-deprecating.

Burnout literature often points out the need for support in counteracting the destructive lifestyle that has led to burnout. Burnout does not necessarily occur because people are putting in long hours. Those hours may contain work that is enjoyable and fulfilling. Burnout occurs when clergy feel that they have lost control of their lives and that other people are continually writing their agendas for them. They feel drained dry and helpless in getting their lives back within their own control. In such situations a solid support network can be invaluable. When it is frightening to say "no" to powerful parish people, support networks can affirm an individual's right and need to do so. Without such support it is easy to crumble in the face of parish demands.

Clergy Transitions

Clergy not only need occasionally to execute a geographical relocation but they also need to traverse some key transitions within their ministries and personal journeys.

Pulling up stakes is often painful and stress-producing. Support persons can minister effectively by helping the transiting clergyperson to identify the sources of the confusion, grief, and anger felt during times of change. While traversing the shoals, support can make the difference between an effective transition and start-up and a transition that is destructive both to the exited parish and to the pastor-parish relationships in the new situation.

Personal and career transitions can include: mid-life crises, career changes, long pastorates, divorce/marital crises, a new multiple-staff situation, or the change from staff support to working alone. Each of these transitions can disturb our equilibrium, landing us in confusion and uncertainty. At such times support persons lend stability and perspective. Most helpful are those who have been through similar situations and whose stories can significantly ease anxiety.

Alban's work on clergy transition identifies stress as a key factor in both geographical and personal transitions. In fact, stress is defined by Holmes and Rahe[3] as exceeding one's threshold level in social readjustments. While in stress, a support community can be of great assistance in helping us see the options open to us. While under stress we tend to become myopic. Self-pity causes us to arbitrarily limit our options. We should never make crucial decisions at such times without first consulting with the "encouragers and supporters" in our lives.

Marital/Family Crises

Often the crises in our ministries are not professional but personal. Marital difficulties are particularly stressful, as clergy and laity collaborate in the delusion that clergy have ideal marriages. Clergy will need to feel a good deal of safety in a group before revealing that everything is not perfect at home. When the trust-level is high, however, and someone does risk his/her personal pain on the home-front, others will usually take this opportunity to share their frustrations/anger/anxieties on this issue.

A front-page article in *Us Today* (January 1986) cited a study that correlated longevity in marriage with the availability of one close friend in whom one could confide. Both clergy and spouse can improve a marriage by increasing the quality of support in their lives. Without such a place to expose the deeper side, we tend to load our marriages with too many expectations. Marriages break up not so much for the lack of intimacy but for the focus of too much intimacy.

A study done years ago of the survivors of the Cocoanut Grove

fire in which 491 people were killed supported the conclusion that
the availability of support can improve the management of crisis. In
that situation those who had a lot of supportive human contact recov-
ered much more quickly than those who had little help of this kind.

Barriers to Support

The Myth of Accident

There is a common myth that support happens by accident. You
either get it or you don't. The truth is that a quality support network
takes hard intentional work. It also requires skills that are rarely
taught by either families or school systems. Professional community
organizers know that the first thing one should do in a new community is to build a support network. Clergy appear to rarely follow that
strategy. Too often they move into new congregational settings and
dive into their work, hoping that support will happen by accident or
as a natural byproduct of the situation. Only when they are in a jam do
they then belatedly realize that no support is there for their lives and
their ministry.

Rugged Individualism

Rugged individualism is another barrier to support. According to
Robert Bellah and his co-authors in their book *Habits of the Heart*,[4]
independence, self-sufficiency and individualism are particularly
strong values in North America. Bellah claims that our unique American heroes are the cowboy and the hard-boiled detective:

> Both the cowboy and the hard-boiled detective tell us some-
> thing important about American individualism. The cowboy,
> like the detective, can be valuable to society only because he
> is a completely autonomous individual who stands outside it.
> To serve society, one must be able to stand alone, not need-
> ing others, not depending on their judgment, and not sub-
> mitting to their wishes. Yet this individualism is not selfish-
> ness. Indeed, it is a kind of heroic selflessness. One accepts
> the necessity of remaining alone in order to serve the values
> of the group. Yet it is part of the profound ambiguity of the
> mythology of American individualism that its moral heroism
> is always just a step away from despair.

There is much in the clergy role which supports this kind of rugged individualism. The heroes in church systems are generally Lone Rangers who get a few Indians, both male and female, to support "their ministry." The model is hierarchical rather than collegial. Many clergy, like the cowboy or the hard-boiled detective, feel that their characteristics are so unique that they can never fully belong to society. For them their marginality is their strength. Yet their heroism is just a step away from despair.

Gender

According to Carol Gilligan in her book titled *In a Different Voice*,[5] gender can be a factor in the support issue. She cites studies of early care patterns which reveal that:

> . . . masculinity is defined through separation while femininity is defined through attachment. Male gender identity is threatened by intimacy while female gender identity is threatened by separation. Thus males have difficulty with relationships, while females tend to have problems with individuation.

Daniel Levinson, in his book *Seasons of a Man's Life*,[6] concluded:

> In our interviews, friendship was largely noticeable by its absence. As a tentative generalization we would say that close friendship with a man or woman is rarely experienced by American men.

Herb Goldberg, in *The Hazards of Being Male*,[7] says that American men must learn once again to be buddies with one another. Men will rarely call up a friend just to talk. There always has to be a reason for the call. Yet isolation and loneliness contribute to more alcoholism and suicides than females experience.

Failure To Commit to Work Involved

In spite of such evidence the biggest barrier to support is, I believe, the hard work required to build a quality support group. We can speak nostalgically about really supportive groups we have known in the past, yet we are unwilling to pay the price required in the formation of such groups.

Scott Peck in his book *A Different Drum*[8] writes descriptively of the painful stages a group must go through if it is to reach genuine community. For him the four stages of community development are:

Pseudo-community
Chaos
Emptiness
Community

In pseudo-community we are pleasant and nice to one another, covering our real feelings about one another and the process. A group moves to chaos when people do start to level with one another, where their main goal is either to "fix" another person in the group or to change another person to their point of view. The result is anger, frustration, and chaos. Unless there is a covenant to stay together, some group members will say "Who needs this?" and bail out. In order for the group to move forward, it needs to go to emptiness, where people give up their notions of what the group should be about and allow it to become what it will.

Such giving-up does not come easily. It threatens our self-perception and our worldview. Yet emptiness is the necessary prelude to genuine community where people can share who they are and how they feel, and others listen attentively without trying to change or fix them. It is in this kind of community that support is going to be felt most profoundly.

Given the price for quality support, many clergy look at the risk and back off. They hold tightly to the myth that in-depth relationships with peers will happen magically. If they do not, it is because of other kinds of screw-ups.

With all these barriers to peer support groups, it is no wonder that so few helpful ones are functioning today. Denominational executives know that their clergy need more support, yet they feel powerless to help facilitate such groups. It is ludicrous to believe that by simply herding clergy together in some corner of the judicatory there will then be beneficial in-depth sharing groups. If anything, this kind of process will result in more and more clergy becoming disillusioned about the possibility of quality support ever coming from their peers.

A Dependency Model

If a peer support group is to work, it will require leadership. Someone is going to have to take some initiatives and get people together. This first step is sometimes the key barrier. Clergy are weary of always having to take responsibility for others. They would relish the idea of someone else being in charge.

Leadership is going to be needed if a group is to move through the painful stages of group development. Someone is going to have to hold people's feet to the fire or the group will disintegrate with people turning away disillusioned and cynical.

The Grubb Institute in London, England has a theory of oscillation which speaks to this issue. The director, Bruce Reed,[9] claims that healthy people oscillate between states of intra-dependence (dependence upon one's own internal resources) and extra-dependence (dependence upon an external resource), and they do this so as to gain some distance and perspective for healing in their lives.

For a support group to work, members need at some point to be able to move to a state of extra-dependence, trusting that someone competent and caring will look after them while they are in this state. Without that kind of confidence in the leadership of the group, people will rarely trust enough to make the commitment to the healing dimensions of extra-dependence.

To be sure, shared leadership is a distinct possibility in quality support groups. Members learn to trust each other when they move to share their pain and vulnerability and thus some leadership can emerge so that the group can function productively.

Another model I have seen work is for a group to hire a leader. The choice of leader is of crucial importance, as one might guess. It is my sense that this leader needs to have three characteristics: she/he needs to be *competent, sensitive, and safe:*

—*Competent* enough in human dynamics and group process to help the group manage the worst that it may cough up.
—*Sensitive* to the complexities of the clergy role, suggesting that the leader must have some first-hand experience of being a religious authority for others.
—*Safe,* meaning that in no way can he/she affect the life and career of group members, thus probably disqualifying people influential in the judicatory or anyone who can influence a career-path.

Generally, for this model to work, the leader needs to have a clear contract and should be paid. Since a quality support system is unavailable in terms of professional competence, it is worth the investment of some funds on the part of the group members. Some clergy build such a commitment into the church budget.

In addition to leadership, the group must have stability. The same people need to be meeting over a period of several months if trust is to develop. Generally, this means that members should contract for four to six months at a time and commit themselves to being at every meeting, barring emergencies. If someone new wants to join the group, he or she should wait until the next contracting period.

How often the group meets, where it meets, how long meetings last, and what the focus of the group is are all items up for grabs. Members need to reach mutuality on all these issues.

Most groups that work well start out with some sort of getting-on-board exercise. As it becomes clear that certain members are hurting, time and attention needs to go to them. Beyond those immediate concerns, the group needs to decide how it can best be supportive of each member. This may mean addressing professional issues, reviewing case studies or peer evaluations or theological/biblical issues. At other times personal/family/spiritual issues can be shared and addressed.

For the past two years I have been part of an all-male group of four which meets for four hours each month. We have focused mainly on gender/psychological/spiritual issues. We share leadership in this group, and the agenda flows from our personal sharing time.

I am also part of a professional group called "Phrogs" which meets for an overnight twice a year. We designate certain people to be in charge of parts of our twenty-four hours together. Friday evening we share a meal and get on board with one another. All day Saturday is given to one or two members who lead us in some subject-area which they have found useful—a theory, a design, a book. This group has been functioning for eight years. When someone misses two meetings without notice, we assume they have left us and we discuss invitations to colleagues we respect to replace them. There are generally eight to ten of us present at each meeting. The value of this support group to me has varied over the years, but I remember clearly the times this group has come to my aid in a time of need.

In the final analysis a good support group offers us protection against pain, affirmation of values, and challenge to move away from dead-center. Such a return makes all the effort of starting and sustaining a support group worthwhile.

Notes

1. James A. Glasse, *Putting It Together in the Parish* (Nashville: Abingdon Press, 1972).

2. Roy M. Oswald, *Clergy Burnout: A Survival Manual for Church Professionals* (Minneapolis: Ministers Life Resources, 1982).

3. T.H. Holmes and R.H. Rahe, "The Social Readjustment Rating Scale," *Journal of Psychomatic Research,* 11 (1967), 213–218.

4. Robert N. Bellah, Richard Madsen, William Sullivan, Ann Swidler and Steven Tipton, *Habits of the Heart* (Berkeley: University of California Press, 1985).

5. Carol Gilligan, *In a Different Voice* (Cambridge: Harvard University Press, 1982).

6. Daniel Levinson, *Seasons of a Man's Life* (New York: Knopf, 1978).

7. Herb Goldberg, *The Hazards of Being Male* (New York: Nash Publishing, 1976).

8. M. Scott Peck, *A Different Drum* (New York: Simon and Schuster, 1976).

9. Bruce Reed, *Dynamics of Religion* (London: Grubb Institute, 1984).

W. Benjamin Pratt, D.Min.

Burnout: A Spiritual Pilgrimage

In June 1966, following graduation from Wesley Theological Seminary, I was assigned to found a new congregation in a planned residential community twenty-five miles south of Washington, D.C., in Virginia. In the following four years, my wife and I had two daughters. One of the fastest growing congregations in the Virginia Conference was also born. In eight years I received more than one thousand members, provided oversight for a major sanctuary and educational project, spawned twenty small groups, founded an orchestra and performing arts society, was an officer in the Civic Association, and acted as an active member of the fire and rescue squad. At the end of my pastorate, I was preaching to nearly six hundred people each Sunday, working a part-time job in order to survive financially, and averaging seventy to eighty hours of work weekly.

On the surface, life was exciting and accomplishments were viewed as many. Behind the scenes there was a different reality. In 1971 I went to the Institute for Pastoral Psychotherapy, ostensibly for the purpose of enhancing my pastoral skills. Before long it was clear that I was there to work out some deep personal conflicts that manifested themselves in my body, my marriage, my emotional and spiritual life. My wife and I sought marriage counseling. I went into therapy for myself to begin dealing with my depression. I was exhausted, depressed, withdrawn, irritable, physically, emotionally and spiritually depleted. I grew doubtful about my work. I felt frustrated and unappreciated. My depression often led to feelings of despair and sometimes suicide. My thinking became clouded. Sometimes I would sit in my office and be unable to make phone calls or accomplish any reading or writing. My prayer life diminished. I functioned, but I was dying inside. I did not know it then, but I know it now. I was burned out.

It is clear that my M. Div. seminary experience gave me a good education in Bible, theology, ethics, preaching, education, and classical literature. It is also clear that it gave me little assistance in how to be a parish pastor and survive. Above all, I was given no guidance in my spiritual formation. Only in recent years have I taken this dimension of my life seriously enough to have witnessed its vital place in my pilgrimage. While in the parish, the majority of my sermons were on the subject of grace. They reflected my deep need to hear the word of God's love for me as I sought constantly to work out my salvation through endless hours of labor.

Only recently have I been able to proclaim honestly that I cannot save myself. My salvation is only in the gift of God's grace through Christ.

"Io non mori, 'e non rimasi vivo." (I did not die, yet nothing of life remained.) These words of Dante reflect the state of burnout, near death, in me and many other ministers.

Where does the fire go? Again and again, persons in the helping professions burn out. They lose their enthusiasm and energy and they become exhausted with their profession or major life activity. Literature on burnout has focused primarily on its being an issue for persons in the service professions, but the phenomenon is not restricted to these people.

What is burnout? Definitions include that of psychiatrist Herbert Freudenberger, who describes burnout as "a state of fatigue or frustration brought about by devotion to a cause, way of life, or relationship that failed to produce the expected reward."[1] Freudenberger's work, an anecdotal study, stresses the intrapsychic variables of over-dedication, over-commitment, insecurity, power and control needs, and an unfilled personal life as key contributors to burnout. Jerry Edelwich and Archie Brodsky define burnout as "a progressive loss of idealism, energy, and purpose experienced by people in the helping professions as a result of the conditions of their work."[2]

Burnout results in exhaustion physically, emotionally, intellectually, socially and spiritually. Physically, the symptoms usually begin with fatigue or general malaise in all areas of life, difficulty in sleeping, lack of interest in good nutrition, weight loss or gain, headaches, and gastrointestinal disturbances.

Emotionally, burnout is indicated by a decline in sharpness, empathy, sensitivity, and compassion. The person often begins treating colleagues and family carelessly and callously. The most common emotional symptom of burnout is the over-investment of energy in the job with little interest in anything beyond work. When the job, which has provided identity fulfillment, begins to go poorly, the result is a feeling of anger, helplessness, and depression. This alone hints at the need for varied interests and activities in a person's life, to provide various avenues of satisfaction.

Intellectually, burnout is indicated when a person loses his sharpness to think and solve problems. Creativity will generally diminish and will often be coupled with cynicism toward the innovative and creative approached of others.

Socially, the burnout victim suffers from a greater sense of isolation and feels less involved personally with colleagues, friends, and family. Often the individual becomes more distant from his or her own feelings and less able to give and receive in intimate relationships.

Spiritually, the burnout victim often experiences a loss of meaning and direction in life. That which was once valued is questioned or treated with cynicism. The purpose for which one worked and the world view which gave meaning to the person's life is often significantly altered or at least viewed with suspicion or cynicism. The feeling of despair often leads to a loss of belief in the goodness of life and God.

Welch, Medirios and Tate in *Beyond Burnout* list two broad causes which seem invariably to be present in burnout: expectation and distribution.[3] A major cause of burnout is the expectation of accomplishment rather than an expectation of striving. When dreams of accomplishment are not fulfilled, frustration ensues. The failure to handle this frustration adds to the possibility of burnout. "Burnout is generally limited to the dynamic, goal-oriented, high-aspiring idealist."[4] Freudenberger has noted that "to anyone who enters this world with a vision, as the individual with a burnout temperament does, the actuality is shocking."[5] The second problem leading to burnout, according to Welch and his colleagues, is broadly described as distribution. Using the metaphors of Death Valley and the Dead Sea, they point to two common characteristics of persons who burn out. Death Valley, though now a desert, was once an ocean teeming with life. Water flowed into and out of this ocean. This changed. Whatever fed the ocean stopped, but the outflow continued. "It gave so much that it dried up and became not an ocean but a desert. Death Valley is a phenomenon of nature in which there is an outlet but no inlet. It simply gave up what it had and, since nothing new was coming in, it died."[6] This points metaphorically to the distribution problem which characterizes the work of many clergy who burn themselves out by giving and caring and not receiving or even taking. They fail to let themselves be fed.

> The Dead Sea is a body of water that is stagnant. The Jordan
> River flows into the Dead Sea. It was once a body of water
> that supported life, but it no longer does so. It has an inlet

but no outlet. It collects the waters of the Jordan River, accepts life, and then doesn't let it out again, with the result that it is smothered and dies. Nothing escapes from the Dead Sea. It has nowhere to go. It takes in but lets nothing out.[7]

This metaphor characterizes the burnout victim who is unable to distribute the richness within himself or herself. Such people take but do not give. Such an inability leads to isolation and a failure of intimacy.

Many of the warning signs of stress and burnout are seen by others before they are seen by the victim. The most insidious and devastating aspect of stress and burnout is the way it gradually consumes a person over an extended period of time. Stress is the non-specific psychological and physiological response to events which are believed and perceived to be a threat to one's well-being. Burnout is the exhaustion of our resources due to excessive striving based on unrealistic expectations. The key element is that stress relates to beliefs and perceptions, while burnout relates to expectations. The biblical figure Elijah illustrates many of the burnout symptoms and the contributing factors, as well as the healing potential. The story of Elijah appears in 1 Kings 18 and 19. Elijah had a great triumph over the priests of Baal when his sacrifice to Yahweh was consumed by fire from heaven, even though it had been drenched with water. The terrible drought ended as a result of his sacrifice and prayers. But within a short time the prophet also was consumed, burned out. After his initial experience of high enthusiasm and expectation, Elijah retreated into defeat, pursued by Queen Jezebel's headhunters, as a disheartened and bewildered man. Elijah did what many burnout victims do. He retreated in frustration, leaving his servant behind (19:3). He not only wanted to flee the wicked queen, but he wanted to detach himself from people who could support him, a common symptom of burnout.

As Elijah sits under the broom tree, he manifests symptoms of the advanced stages of burnout: apathy, depression, despair, and loss of faith. He no longer believes in God's goodness and mercy, and he believes himself a failure. He says, "It is enough: Now, O Lord, take away my life; for I am no better than my fathers" (19:4—Revised Standard Version). Elijah suffers from the despondency that often follows prolonged intensity.

It's the let-down that comes in between crises or directly after "mission accomplished." Frequently, following a triumph, high achievers suffer periods of deep melancholia somewhat akin to the post-partum depression some women experience after giving birth. The feelings are remarkably similar: sadness, separation, sluggishness, and above all, emptiness.[8]

Yahweh is not as impressed with Elijah's sense of failure as Elijah is impressed with his own zealousness and omnipotent indispensability. He proclaims to Yahweh, "I, even I only, am left" (19:14). So Elijah's sense of indispensability, coupled with a deep feeling of being unappreciated for how much he had done, leaves him with the common burnout feelings of being frustrated, angry, out-of-control, self-pitying, mistreated and even paranoid and persecuted. Elijah is able to continue in the service of Yahweh only after he has a "personality re-orienting dialogue with God."[9]

Elijah illustrates how the burned out person can be drained of energy and purpose. His sense of failure, coupled with his anger over not being appreciated and not being in control of the world as he wanted it, illustrates his sinful pride and narcissism. God did not think he had failed, and God was not unappreciative. Elijah had failed to grieve properly the loss of *his* dream. His despair was a result of inappropriate sorrow about not changing the world to be the way he wanted it. He was angry and self-pitying, so he lashed out in a passive-aggressive, self-emulating way, denying the goodness and mercy of God.

Elijah denied his mortality, his limited human nature. Denial is often one of the first responses in the grief process. It is the stage in which a person refuses to accept what is. One refuses to accept the death of a loved one. One refuses to believe that something precious has been denied or taken away. One refuses to accept his human limitations and inability to have the world be as he insists it should be. Brooks Faulkner suggests:

> Perhaps that is what burnout is to some ministers. It's part of
> the grief process. We have not become all that we think we
> should have become and therefore we deny the hurt. We
> face one of the same stages as in grief. If we deny it, we bury
> it. We keep it in the closet and pretend it does not exist.[10]

Fundamentally, it is a refusal to grieve, to let go of omnipotent narcissism, and to accept human limitations. Clinging to high expectations is refusing to mourn omnipotent, prideful illusions of playing God. Sin is whatever we do that violates our life in God. Burnout has in it an element of the sinful posture of pride which refuses to let God be God and man be man. This refusal to mourn omnipotent illusions and accept limitations is found at the heart of *acedia* in which one's "soul ceases to be refreshed by the fountains of sanctifying grace."[11]

The literature is exhaustive with detailed analysis of the physical, emotional, intellectual, and social consequences and causes of burnout. Little attention has been given to the spiritual dimension of burnout. I want to let this brief summary suffice and move to amplify the spiritual depletion and malady that prevails, or, as I am suggesting, that underlies the phenomenon of burnout. I will further explore the little known ancient sin of *acedia* which is richly informative of the spiritual condition in the modern day burnout victim.

When Dante descends to the Fifth Circle of the Inferno, he finds there a black and loathsome marsh made by the dark waters of the Stygian stream pouring into it. There, in the putrid swamp, he sees the souls of those whom anger has ruined. They are hitting, tearing and maiming one another in ceaseless, senseless rage. But there are others there, the Master tells him, whom he cannot see, whose sobs make bubbles that rise to the surface. What sin has thrust them down into this uttermost wretchedness?

> Fixed in the slime, they say: "Sullen were we in the sweet air, that is gladdened by the sun, carrying lazy smoke within our hearts; now lie we sullen here in the black mire." This hymn they gurgle in their throats, for they cannot speak it in full words.[12]

This is a penetrating and terrifying picture of unbroken sullenness, of willful gloom that has shut out light and love forever. It is the worldly grief and sorrow that produced death (2 Cor 7:10). It is not grief that produces *metanoia* (a turning around) and leads to the joy of salvation. It is not grief that disciplines the soul and turns it toward God searching for God's presence in the mystery of pain. It is the sorrow that is fueled by anger and envy, for it is the sorrow of the world. It stands in contrast to the sorrow and suffering of Christ which heals and restores and leads to salvation.

Dante may well be describing persons who are committing the sin of *acedia*. This sin, which ranked among the seven deadly sins of pride, envy, anger, avarice, gluttony and lust, is not commonly known in the twentieth century. Its original meaning has been lost to many because it became translated as sloth, torpor, or laziness. A recovery of the original meaning and history of the word enables one to understand its designation as a deadly sin, as well as its place in the modern phenomenon called burnout. In addition to the similarity of symptoms, it contains specific spiritual elements which suggest that it is especially applicable to spiritual burnout.

Acedia is a subtle and complex evil which has resulted in many definitions. As one compares these various understandings of the sin, a few key elements common to its nature become apparent. *Acedia* is spiritual apathy. *Acedia* is a form of spiritual suicide, characterized by a refusal to experience joy. Symptomatically, it is characterized by an oppressive grief or gloom, sloth, and bitterness or irritation. Thomas Aquinas, commenting on the sloth, observed that it "implies a certain weariness of work," but focusing on the gloom, he called it a "sorrow in the divine good."[13]

Acedia is a certain sadness which weighs down the spirit in such ways that the person seeks that which is not good for the soul. It is characterized by sluggishness, boredom, melancholy, moral lassitude, distaste of the good, a sadness or grief which weighs upon the spirit so that a person has no energy for joy, but rather is bitter in the heart. Francis Paget offers an excellent summary of *acedia*.

> There settles down upon the soul a dire form of accidie; the dull refusal of the highest aspiration in the moral life; the acceptance of a view of one's self and one's powers which once would have appeared intolerably poor, unworthy, and faint-hearted; an acquiescence in discouragement, which reaches the utmost depth of sadness when it ceases to be regretful; a despondency concerning that goodness to which the love of God has called men, and for which His grace can make them strong.[14]

David Read describes *acedia* in a manner that suggests its similarity to burnout.

> Don't we all know, in varying degrees, that gray mood that settles on the soul, when nothing seems really worth doing, when meaning drains out of life, when we find it hard to respond with real interest to things we care about, when we tend to despair of ever being better or stronger characters than we are now, and to take a cynical view of people around, of mankind in general? *Acedia* strikes at the most unexpected people at unexpected times. The sin is not that it comes, but in our glum and unresisting acceptance of the mood.[15]

The word *acedia* is a linguistic foreigner to many. The word was most clearly attached to Christian asceticism from the Greek by Evagrius Ponticus, a fourth century desert monk in Egypt, southeast of Alexandria. His amplification of the word and that of his student Cassian are important, but of greatest interest and value is the treatment of *acedia* by Thomas Aquinas. The place it holds in the scheme of his writings reveals its true character, the nature of its harmfulness and its antagonism to the Christian life. Aquinas speaks of *caritas* as the form, root and mother of all the virtues. *Caritas*, the true friendship of man with God, is the basis for receiving the fruits of the spirit of which Paul spoke in Galatians. Love, joy, and peace are the result of *caritas*, which is the energy of the Spirit of God in man's heart. For Aquinas, *caritas* is the greatest Christian virtue and *acedia* is the negation of that joy that is strength, springing from the presence of the Holy Spirit. *Acedia*, being the negative of that joy, is Aquinas' basis for his strong declaration that *acedia* is a sin. Aquinas says:

> Accidie is a shrinking of mind, not from any spiritual good, but from that to which it should cleave as in duty bound, namely the goodness of God. (Disputations, xi *de Malo*, 3, ad 4)

> The repulsions are about good things, wrongfully regarded threatening our own proper good, and which, therefore, are grieved alone or actively combated. Spiritual values menace our physical pleasure, hence *acedia* or boredom, a sadness about spiritual good. *Envy* is similar; it asserts another's good qualities because they lower our own self-esteem. To flare out at them is *anger*. (Disputations, viii *de Malo*, I)

It is opposed to the joy of love because all the upward longing falls out of the heart and will. It is the fruitless gloom of sullenness, the sour sorrow of the world, an inappetence, a lack of desire for God and cheerlessness in activities that relate to God directly. It is a willful self-distressing that numbs all love and zeal for the good.

Aquinas marks a deep affinity between *acedia*, envy, and anger. All are forms of sinful gloom, standing opposed to the fruits of *caritas*. The joy that comes from *caritas* is twofold. First, there is the joy that is found in God and God's goodness and love. Second, there is the joy which concerns one's neighbor's good and delights on seeing another's welfare and happiness. In contrast stands *acedia*, the sorrowful despondency or listlessness concerning the good things of God.

Acedia precedes envy which negates the joy that should result from contemplating the good of one's neighbor. Envy can lead to constant bitterness and anger about what others have and one does not have. For Aquinas, these are moral acts in which the vices lie at the roots of man's appetitive faculty. *Acedia* is a chief vice because it is responsible for other morally wrong actions that a person commits while trying to avoid what seems to one to be an evil.

Symptoms such as dejection and sorrow, absence of elation in spiritual exercises, impatience in work and devotions, anger against brethren, and despair of ever reaching one's spiritual goals were common to both. The two concepts were fused in the works of Thomas Aquinas. St. Paul had already distinguished between a positive and negative form of sorrow, with one leading to penance and salvation and the other leading to death (2 Cor 7:10).

I am not suggesting that burnout and *acedia* are interchangeable terms or concepts, but rather that one serves to illuminate the other. The two concepts were developed within the context of different worldviews and different anthropologies. *Acedia* originated as a technical term of Christian asceticism among the fourth century monks. In this setting, the Orthodox Christian worldview prevailed, as the early church believed that the ascetic life was a war against demons. Phenomenologically, demons were a fact of life during this period, and the "noonday devil" was responsible for *acedia*. The fundamental psychological power that was active in this struggle continued to be devotion in faith to the person of Jesus, who, as the sum total of divine revelation, formed the center of Christian life. On the other hand, the concept of burnout is developed in the context of a humanistic worldview that seeks to scientifically consider the interface between the intrapsychic and interpersonal observations of psychology and sociology. This is a worldview informed by systems theory and intrapsychic models that takes seriously the unconscious, intrinsic psychology of the human soul.

I am suggesting that at the heart of burnout is a spiritual dilemma. An understanding of the sin of *acedia* informs us of the spiritual issues and struggles of the burnout phenomenon. This understanding is helpful to the healing process.

If a person is to prevent or cure burnout he or she must first acknowledge his or her limitations and thereby begin to understand the consequences of ignoring those limitations. To live without a full awareness of one's limitations is to play God and pridefully insist on omnipotence. It is to pretend that one can secure his own existence and control things—indeed, all things. The acknowledgment of humanity, finitude, and limits is to confess vulnerability in this world.

> We don't want to admit that we are fundamentally dishonest about reality, that we do not really control our own lives. We don't want to admit that we always rely on something that transcends us, some system of ideas and powers in which we are embedded and which supports us.[16]

Ministers strain at limits and search for transcendence in their political, religious and cultural ideologies, in their identification with leaders and popular stars, and in their occupations. Ernest Becker says that when, by denying limits, one engages in the *causa sui* project, the endeavor is to see oneself as self-caused, self-controlled, self-determined, and therefore unlimited.[17] When a minister seeks to establish the grounds of his self-esteem, prove his value and worth as a person, and secure his life by his zealous, unrelenting work, he is omnipotently, pridefully, denying the grace of God in Christ and living to work out his own salvation. Such an effort will be plagued by constant stress and anxiety about the success of the effort or project. Often the cause of burnout is false motivation. The correction for this is service motivated by grace and the love of Christ. The minister who is working to secure his or her own existence, to work out his or her own salvation, uses the congregation as an extension of his or her own narcissistic ego. At this point the minister and the congregation that colludes in this project are grounding their identity in illusion and sin. At this level, the roots of stress, burnout, and *acedia* become problematic, theologically.

In this sense, burnout is the symptom of sin—the attempt to justify one's own existence. Burnout may be the vehicle by which clergy are brought to their knees before God to confess that they have been whoring after false gods. Burnout witnesses to the failure to succeed at one's own project. It witnesses that there is nothing one can *do* to save oneself; it shows one that being obsessed with one's own foolish projects can bring one to his or her knees with the possibility for forgiveness and the reception of God's grace. Burnout brings one to the possibility of receiving God's grace.

> Burnout can be a very special time of giftedness. While on the one hand it may be experienced as a dismembering of one's ego, it also offers an opportunity to reassemble one's

self as a more functional and loving human being. While it is a time of losing one's life, it can also be a time for finding it again in a new way. It can be a time spiritually for giving up one's desire to be omnipotent, and psychologically for giving up one's desire to be completely in control of one's life. Above all, burnout can be an opportunity for growth in holiness and wholeness.[18]

If burnout becomes the refiner's fire, and the person is born in grace with new hope and vision, then he or she is able to realize that success and failure are determined by God. The person is able to let go of the need to exert God-like control over all his works. It is living in the gospel security of sinner and saints struggling to trust in grace and live in forgiveness and freedom, rather than trusting in oneself and living in self-justification and bondage.

Once this grace-note has been sounded in a person's life there are some basic ways a person can care responsibly for himself. This is accomplished through some crucial elements in the fostering of a well-balanced life: pacing, balance, and continued renewal of one's physical, emotional, mental, spiritual, and social life.

Notes

1. Herbert J. Freudenberger, *Burnout—The High Cost of High Achievement* (Garden City: Anchor Press and Doubleday Co., 1980), p. 13.

2. Jerry Edelwich and Archie Brodsky, *Burn-Out: Stages of Disillusionment in the Helping Professions* (New York: Human Sciences Press, 1980), p. 14.

3. David Welch, Donald Medirios, and George Tate, *Beyond Burnout* (Englewood Cliffs: Prentice-Hall, 1982), p. 12.

4. D.G. Kehl, *"Burnout: The Risk of Reaching Too High"* Christianity Today 20 (1981) 26.

5. Freudenberger, p. 172.

6. Welch, Medirios, and Tate, p. 13.

7. Ibid., p. 14.

8. Freudenberger, p. 110.

9. John Sanford, *Ministry Burnout* (Ramsey: Paulist Press, 1982), p. 86.

10. Brooks Faulkner, *Burnout in Ministry* (Nashville: Signet Books, 1949), p. 11.

11. James Joyce, *A Portrait of the Artist as a Young Man* (New York: Signet Books, 1949), p. 70.

12. Dante Alighieri, *The Divine Comedy*, The Carlyle-Wicksted Translation (New York: The Modern Library, 1932), p. 50.

13. Robert Maynard Hutchins, ed., *Great Books of the Western World*, 54 vols. (Chicago: Encyclopaedia Britannica Inc., 1952), Vol. 20: *The Summa Theologica* by Thomas Aquinas, pp. 563–564.

14. Francis Paget, *The Spirit of Discipline* (New York: Longmans, Green, 1928), p. 46.

15. David H.C. Read, *Virginia Woolf Meets Charlie Brown* (Grand Rapids: Eerdmans, 1968), p. 142.

16. Ernest Becker, *The Denial of Death* (New York: The Free Press, 1973), p. 55.

17. Ibid., pp. 115–123.

18. Louis Savary and Patricia Berne, *Prayerways* (San Francisco: Harper and Row, 1980), p. ix.

Daniel C. Henderson, M.Div., M.S.

When the Bridge Comes Tumbling Down: Bearing the Weight and Tension of the Task of Ministry

There are times in the life of a minister when he or she bumps up against personal and professional crises. It is as if the bridge between service to God and service to a congregation is crumbling. The stress of ministry seems too much to support. The footings are giving way. The minister starts to question his or her own integrity. Emotions surface in different ways than ever before. Spiritual life is in chaos. It is difficult to trust the very ones who care the most. Resources are depleted. It feels as if the bridge is tumbling down.

When a bridge is built, solid footings are laid out to support the columns. Decisions are made on the best way to span the chasm. Trusses made up of geometric triangles form a lacework for strength. The physics of compression and tension are calculated to hold up enormous weight. The bridge is built to bear the weight and to endure the storms that pummel it. Tension is an intrinsic part of its strength. Yet there are those times when hurricanes batter it. Periodically the bridge is inspected, surveyed for alignment and continued strength, inventoried for the presence and condition of all its parts. The inspection determines its ability to endure the future stress it will undergo.

It is for times of stress that the minister takes personal inventory of those components which bridge between God and the congregation. The minister must be continually cultivating resources in order to bear the weight and tension that comes with ministry. The tension inherent in relating God to the congregation in a significant way will always be there. Strength comes from emotional and spiritual foundations.

Eric, the pastor of his present congregation for five years, had no big plans for the congregation when he first arrived. He had been in the ministry fourteen years and he knew he had been at many significant junctures of individuals' lives. Making it a point to be available to parishioners, he was with them in their pains of illnesses and death and in their joys of births and weddings. Yet, with this congregation, something felt empty.

Eric knew that he was an average pastor. There was nothing in which he considered himself an expert. Yet he was unique in a special, pastoral way. Often he would sit in a waiting room with a family to find out if their loved one made it through surgery. He was fairly effective in focusing in on a teenager who had family conflicts. He would make a point of trying to understand cantankerous parishioners. Most of the time he was effective in relating to them. Yet, with this parish, he was disheartened in his attempts to interact. Though Eric could not understand it, something was conflicting the relationship.

In late November his mother had died. She had lived in a nursing home for her last few years and Eric could see steady deterioration of her health. A few weeks after her death, his seventeen year old daughter was in a car accident. Thankfully, she was only shaken up with a few cuts and bruises, yet he was disturbed about her.

In February he discovered that the chairperson of the building committee had not fulfilled proper legal requirements which resulted in the county not issuing building permits. The contractor began complaining about working with churches. A few of the parishioners told him that he should have managed the building committee more effectively.

Eric's relationship with his wife had had its ups and downs throughout their marriage. Now they were at one of many dry periods. She was busy with other things, limiting her time for him. He was aching for her attention, but could not bring himself to share his loneliness. Eric was the type of man who held his feelings inside, not knowing how his wife would react if he were to talk about his fears and loneliness. This created a distance between them, but someday, he thought, things would improve.

In early spring Eric met with the pastor and parish relations committee, and he decided to share his feelings with them. After all, this committee was to be used for his support. The more he talked, the more his feelings bubbled to the surface. Then one of the members spoke up: "Well, Reverend, you are a minister. You of all people ought to be able to handle anything that comes your way. Besides that, we need to let you know that we are hearing complaints of you being distracted with family problems. The folks are saying you are not doing your job."

It was as if they had not heard him. He was sharing deep feelings, but they were unable to understand the enormous stress he was experiencing. When someone came to his defense by pointing out that additional members had joined the church, another suggested that they would have joined anyway. Eric was depressed and hurt, emotionally beaten up. He began to question his faith and to doubt God. Being caught up with sorrow and pity, he had lost hope. His spiritual and emotional supports were giving way.

Times like these can leave a minister feeling drained of energy. The stress of ministry can seem to have unbearable weight. It is for these stressful times that the minister needs to take a personal inventory of the spiritual and emotional components that hold him/her together. One of those components is the call to ministry.

The Call to Ministry

When God calls a person to ministry, it becomes the foundation for support during the stressful times. God calls the minister to serve people in different ways and at different times. The Old Testament's prophets were pulled out of history to guide the Hebrew people for specific ministries. Jeremiah was called to challenge King Jehoiakim. He taught that serving God is a personal matter and that each of us must take personal responsibility for serving him. Hosea was called to denounce the sins and unfaithfulness of the people, but he also said that God was wonderfully loving and forgiving.

In the New Testament, Jesus called the disciples to follow him. Who would have considered Simon the fisherman to be Peter, the rock from which Christ would build his church? Here was the boss of the waterfront, a bit of a loudmouth, with calloused hands and the smell of fish. Yet Jesus worked with Simon, at times confronting him. Simon had the spirit of being open to his confusion and lack of understanding. One can almost see Jesus praying for different ways to reach this man.

God calls men and women to serve in particular ways and God presents special opportunities. Several years ago I participated in a study of the dynamics of migrant workers and agribusiness in Florida. The community we studied had a year-round population of 3,500. Then from November until April the population increased to 17,000. This annual influx of people changed the community. We interviewed migrant workers, fruit and vegetable farmers, warehouse shippers, health officials, law enforcement officials, and ministers. It became clear that the migrant workers, though cheap labor, were not wanted in the community. Their influx brought serious social problems such as housing, education and health. The migrant workers were poor. Hunger was common. Often their only place to sleep was in a cardboard carton. The social pangs taking place in this community were enormous.

I interviewed a minister in this community, who was depressed, angry, empty. He saw the ministry to his congregation as the worst place in the world to be. He could not understand that his ministry could take many different forms, such as an evangelical bent or a social activist approach, or a congregational caring and support emphasis. Instead, this pastor felt defeated, had little hope. Wanting a better church, it seemed as if he wound up with nothing. He was missing the opportunity for a challenging ministry which could have significantly changed the lives of that community. As a result he was distressed and broken.

When God calls men and women into ministry, he never leaves them abandoned. Moses was called by God from the burning bush to go to Pharaoh to demand Egypt's labor force be let go. Moses, convinced that Pharaoh was not going to cooperate, tried three times to get out of God's calling. "Moses said to God, 'Who am I that I should go to Pharaoh, and bring the sons of Israel out of Egypt?' God said, 'But I will be with you' " (Ex 3:11–12).

Here is the foundation for ministry. If a minister is sincerely called by God, God is with him or her. God calls men and women for specific tasks at specific junctures of history. It is the wise pastor who ponders the task for which God has called him or her in the particular congregation he or she is serving.

The first and basic task, then, of being called is to understand the calling. On this basic level the pastor is called to be fully aware and to experience being alive. Most people develop a routine or rhythm in the day to day pulse of living with positive and negative effects. On the positive side, life can be fairly predictable. The negative side to routine living is that life always has interruptions. Some are small and insignificant like the broken window from a neighbor's child playing baseball. Some are large and life-changing like the tragedies of accidents and death or like receiving results of medical tests indicating that an unborn child has Down's syndrome. The minister is called to be where people are in the midst of struggling. To be a pastor is to be fully present with those parishioners.

Emile Durkheim, one of the early founders of sociology, became interested in the way society impacts on an individual's religious and ethical life. He studied the native cultures of the South Sea islands for years. In his book *Elementary Forms of the Religious Life* Durkheim concluded that religion helps people to get in touch with each other as a community. People share birth experiences as well as deaths. Communities come together to celebrate marriages, but also to share the worries of catastrophes. The individual is important, but the individual is always incorporated into the community.

When we compare native cultures with those of the modern world, we get a sense of the excluding of the individual. Life is fragmented in more ways than it has ever been before. No longer are children growing up and returning to their home communities. The population trend for young adults in the United States is to strike out on their own and to settle in different communities. The young adult's new home setting and support groups have to be restructured, redefined.

Ministering in the modern world means that the pastor is called upon by the congregation to make sense out of birth and death issues in this terribly complex and broken world. The pastor can view the calling to ministry as a resource for building a sense of community with individual believers. The pastor more than any other professional has opportunity to interface with individuals in the midst of their struggles.

In Pastor Eric's situation mentioned earlier, the congregation was caught up with the reality of their pastor's struggle, denying their own frightening impulses. If Eric could become overwhelmed with life's circumstances, what could happen to them? Eric was, in fact, not abandoned by God. Rather God was in Eric's life. When a person is pressed against life's catastrophes, as Eric was, the faith community can lend support. Members of Eric's congregation had not experienced caring about each other as a community of faith. This was their growing edge, a focus of ministry for Eric. By relying on God's presence in the call to help his congregation to develop a sense of caring and community, Eric can be strengthened and empowered in his own life struggles. His life can be an example of God's presence in the lives of members in their own individual struggles. In this way the calling to this specific aspect of ministry can be a source for renewed strength and commitment. The parishioners can realize that the pastor is taking their faith struggles seriously.

A second task for the calling to ministry is to claim the talents and gifts a pastor brings to a congregation. Most clergy are trained to be scholars in biblical studies, religious history, pastoral counseling, preaching, and parish administration. Beyond training, every pastor has certain gifts which are brought with him to the congregation. The pastor who ignores or denies these gifts is doing a disservice to God and self. Biblical and church tradition cry out for the ministers of the faith to acknowledge and use these gifts. Experiencing life, understanding what one has been called for, and utilizing God-given gifts and talents are crucial to understanding the task of ministry as a call.

Knowledge and Use of Transference

Another element in the support structure for ministry is the knowledge of and use of the phenomenon called transference. Frequently members will transfer on to the pastor their view of what they believe God should be like. Psychotherapists help us to understand how a person uses transference. Transference takes place when a people project their feelings, desires, and, at times, fantasies about someone from their past on to someone else. In psychotherapy, the someone else is the therapist who will usually allow the transference to happen. The therapist will use the transference to aid in healing the patient.

With a pastor, transference can take several forms. First, the pastor can represent God. Often parishioners transfer onto the pastor their feelings toward God. The pastor, in an incarnational way, becomes to the parishioners the representation of what they would like God to be.

Every pastor has experienced walking into a room and seeing people nudge each other until a hush comes over the group. Someone once said, "All a pastor has to do is walk into a room and people will feel guilty." Everyone feels some guilt for things they are ashamed of doing. Everyone has experienced some shame and embarrassment. Sometimes people have hurt or abused others with their anger. They may have asked for forgiveness, yet not forgiven themselves. The shame, guilt and embarrassment hangs on. On an unconscious level, the pastor is a bridge to God. Incarnationally, the pastor is God. Thus the pastor's presence stirs up guilt and embarrassment.

In every congregation there are those who have been affected by a major life crisis. Their hurt and anger comes out in subtle ways. People are often angry at God, yet they cannot bring themselves to express their anger. Instead, their hostility is aimed at their pastor.

Pastor Eric's life was being crushed by several personal crises. But the members on the church's committee expected him to be unaffected. He was mustering all the energy he could to keep going. Yet he could not satisfy this committee. Their anger at God was being transferred toward Eric like vindictive rage. The transference of Eric's committee was deep and unconscious.

The second type of transference often projected on the pastor is a form of manipulation, the unconscious need to work out desires and wants from mother, father or God with the pastor. If a person can manipulate the pastor to do what his unconscious desires are dictating, then he is in control. Like the Israelites at the foot of Mount Sinai, he is creating a golden calf, a god that can be controlled.

Eric's pastor and parish committee yearned to create another golden calf. The unconscious reasoning of the committee might be described as follows. God is above pain and hurt. The pastor, they think, should likewise be above pain and hurt. If the pastor hurts and has pain, then where is God? It is easier to believe in a god who is stoic. In reality, however, a God who is alive and real is one who will care for the hurts of people. The greatest gift Eric was giving to this committee was an opportunity to experience the way God aches when people hurt. Just as Jesus cried at the tomb of his dead friend Lazarus, God aches with his children. The people at Eric's church needed this different experience of God's care.

In the third form of transference, the pastor represents authority. When "all you have to do is walk into a room and people will feel guilty," you represent authority. Members' experience with those who had authority over them can be subtly projected onto the pastor. The pastor may represent the third grade teacher who punished them for homework not done, the coach who demanded they run until exhaustion, the sergeant who criticized them into conformity, the boss who intimidates them. The pastor represents the authoritarian God who makes demands from on high and who gives little care and concern, the angry God who can wipe out a life with a blink of an eye. One cannot satisfy a god like that. This can result in harboring a rage toward God. The parishioners may transfer their infuriated feelings onto the pastor, since he or she can represent this wrathful authoritarian view of a god who will constrict their desires.

A subtle way to express hostility toward a wrathful god is to criticize the characteristics of the person who represents God. This is what happened to Pastor Eric. Eric opened himself up. He was vulnerable not only to the committee but to the whole congregation by sharing who he was and what he thought every time he preached. Rather than seeing the remarks of the committee as misplaced anger that needed to be processed, Erick took the remarks personally.

The fourth form of transference is that the pastor represents the parent to the unconsciousness of an individual. The ideal mother and father are caring and nurturing. They provide unconditional love to their child. They are excited when the infant takes that first step away from them. They celebrate the curious investigations the toddler makes. They seek to understand the ambivalence of a teenager. When there are temper tantrums, they patiently encourage the settling down and the thinking through.

However, most people do not have ideal parents like this. All parents make some mistakes. Often child-raising takes the form of criticism and punishment. The ten year old boy gets hollered at by dad for not cutting the grass the "right way," or the nine year old girl is scolded for not acting like a "lady" when taken to a restaurant and is treated harshly. If this is the child's experience, nurturance and care are not likely to be trusted. Criticism will seem more familiar. The tendency may be to rebel against the critical parent. The same dynamics can be transferred to the pastor-parent. Pastor Eric had been there when someone needed pastoral care. This is often unfamiliar, perhaps mistrusted. The parishioners can act out their unconscious hostility to the pastor-parent. They who once were the victims now become the persecutors.

However, transference can be used as a strength. The pastor can use transference as a resource for ministering effectively. Jesus gave the people an understanding of what God was like. It is easy to view God as the harsh rule-maker. Yet when the woman who was caught in the act of adultery was thrown down in front of him, Jesus said, "He who is without sin cast the first stone." The law was clear. If you commit adultery, you are to be put to death. Jesus came with a higher law of God's compassion and unconditional love. God loved not only this woman, but also those who lusted for her death.

It is the pastor's responsibility to ask those spiritual and soul-searching questions. What were the real issues with Eric's congregation. What was their neglect or insensitivity to Pastor Eric all about? What was God like for them? How were they to represent God to the community?

The late Jewish theologian Abraham Heschel, in his book *The Insecurity of Freedom*, has said, "You will not enter the gates of religion through the door of speech. The way to God is through the depths of the self. The soul is a key; the depth is the door. In the depth of the soul there is prayer, and invocation, a cry for meaning, a craving for justification."[1] Transference, too, springs from this place. The psyche and the soul are the same thing. The only difference is which discipline is talking. The pastor is the one who deals with brokenness of the soul. Yet, the pastor can use the tools of the psychologist. When a person experiences God in depth, then that person will be affected. It is spiritual encounters that bring about healing change.

The bridge between the pastor and the congregation does not have to come tumbling down. The pastor can use the stress to energize himself or herself. God's call carries with it the conviction of doing first what God wants and second being the vessel through which God moves. The strength for being a pastor comes from the spiritual trusses found in doing the work of pastoring.

Notes

1. Abraham Joshua Heschel, *The Insecurity of Freedom* (New York: Schocken Books, 1959), p. 124.

B. John Hagedorn, Jr., Ph.D.

Clergy Families:
The Struggle To Be Free

This book is on surviving in parish ministry. For most people surviving any occupation, or for that matter simply surviving the trials and tribulations of life, their family is a haven. Their family is a place to escape to from the stress of the job, from the interpersonal relationships of the job, and from the constant pressures of the expectations placed upon them by the job. It is my premise that the real crisis for most clergy today is that this family haven is often not available to them in the way it is available to many other people. The clergy family is too related to the job, too intertwined with the job, and too synonymous with the job to be a haven. The clergy family needs to free itself from the job in order to be a place of refuge for the clergy and therefore an aid to surviving in ministry.

What has made the clergy family so intertwined with parish ministry that it is often unavailable as a health-giving refuge for the minister?

Family System Theory

Family system theory states that identity formation is the major task of family functioning. The family helps in defining the unique individuality of each of its members. The family helps in defining the communal nature of human identity. The family is the arena in which separation and differentiation of the self occur. The family is also the community in which togetherness and belongingness are experienced.

It is my premise that when a clergy family enters a new parish setting the movement toward entry often takes on the characteristics of a new person joining an already established family system rather than the characteristics of a new employee joining an already established occupational institution. Issues of identity formation, of individual separation, of communal belonging, and of appropriate boundaries all become primary during the movement into a new parish setting. The identity of the minister, of his/her family, and of all the clergy family members is tested and re-defined in the process of entry.

Lyndon E. Whybrew in *Minister, Wife and Church: Unlocking the Triangle* describes a threefold process of entry. In the first step of the process the clergy is tested by the parish as to his/her personal strength. How will the new pastor handle criticism as the parish begins to subtly evaluate his/her performance? Can issues become open and be confronted? It is important during this phase that the pastor have a clear understanding of his/her own identity and interpersonal strengths, and that he/she have the support and backing of his/her family.[1]

The second step in the process of entry is that of testing the pastor's professional authenticity. Once it is known that issues can be made open and be honestly confronted, the pastor is sought out by many to share their concerns and problems. The pastor must be able to set appropriate boundaries on his ability to care for all. John Fletcher refers to the "madness of God," the concept held by the pastor that he/she ought to be able to meet all the needs of the flock.[2] If appropriate boundaries are not established between the pastor and the parish, the personal identity of the pastor can become diffused and the line between his/her personal authenticity and professional authenticity disappears. Here again the clergy family is vital in helping to keep the occupation clearly defined and limited by giving the pastor a space to step back and reflect. If this boundary setting does not happen the family may become lost or absorbed into the job. The parish must learn to transfer its dependence on the professional competence of the pastor to their mutual dependence upon God.

The third step of entry is called the crisis of particular authenticity and refers to the pastor and the congregation exploring the pastor's unique capacities and skills and the congregation's unique needs and opportunities. Here, too, the pastor must struggle with his/her identity as a pastor and with the limits and goals that must be established. As the pastor is perceived more appropriately as the human person he/she happens to be, with certain skills and certain limitations, a healthier relationship will be established between pastor and parish. This clearer definition can be supported by the clergy family and can help in freeing the clergy family from the work of the parish.

Clergy Family Identity and the Parish

A number of factors affect clergy family identity and the process of joining a parish.

(1) The Pastor's Self-Concept

It is vital for the pastor to examine his/her reasons for entering ministry if the issues of identity, separation, togetherness, and boundaries are to be handled in a health-giving manner.

What unresolved family-of-origin issues have led to the choice of ministry? Are there issues of seeking attention, of needing to please others, of securing love, of earning affection, or of living out unfulfilled dreams of a father or mother? All of these issues, if unresolved, will help to blur the line between parish ministry as an occupation and parish ministry as a chance to join a new family. The more the pastor needs the parish to resolve these family-of-origin issues, the more clergy family identity will be affected and harmed.

There is a subtle but powerful difference between caring for a parish and its members out of Christian love and caring for a parish and its members out of personal identity needs. Personal therapy and an in-depth study of the pastor's family of origin system will greatly enhance the process of cleanly defining the reasons for entering ministry. I have found in my own practice as a pastoral counselor working with pastors that unresolved issues with one's father affects one's definition of God and relationship to God, and that unresolved issues with one's mother affects one's definition of the parish and relationship to the parish. Sometimes a demanding father pushes a pastor into excessive work to please a demanding God, and sometimes a needy mother pushes a pastor into excessive work to meet the expectations of a needy parish.

(2) Ministry Seen as an Identity

Another issue affecting clergy family identity is the distinction between ministry as an identity in and of itself, and ministry as an occupation. I am the first to admit that the line is almost by definition fuzzy, but a clear boundary is needed to survive in the ministry. Ministry is a vocation; it is a calling; and as such it is a personal commitment to the sense of personal selection by the Spirit to do the will of God. Ministry is service to God; it is an act of praise; it is a response to personal forgiveness and personally experienced grace; and it is a witness to faith.

It is therefore difficult at times to place boundaries around the time and energy expended in ministry. Ministry is not an occupation that exists between 9 and 5 and that can be left at the office at the end of the day, especially at the end of a Friday. Ministry can be all-consuming. Fifty-five to ninety hour weeks are not uncommon for pastors, nor is the sense of being on call twenty-four hours a day, seven days a week. The "madness of ministry" confuses the line between what one does and who one is.

A major issue for many pastors is the extension of these first two concerns from themselves to their families. Often it is assumed that the clergy family identity includes a sense of being part of the ministry of the pastor. The family is defined as entering the work of ministry, of having its own sense of call, and of having its own acceptance of the excessive demand, time consumption, and needs of the parish. The pastor must clarify his/her own identity from his/her own family. I find it interesting that the term "clergy family" blends together the role of the pastor and the identity and role of the family and its members. Other occupations do not define as precisely as does ministry the name or role of the "teacher's family," "the doctor's family," or the "plumber's family."

(3) The Pastor and the Clergy Family as Living Role Models

Another major issue in clergy family identity is the assumption that the pastor and the pastor's family are to be living role models of Christian life. The pastor is thought of as the resident "holy person" and his/her family as the resident "holy family." When David and Vera Mace interviewed clergy couples in 1980, they found that over eighty-five percent felt the pressure to be models of perfection and Christian living. The pastor and his/her family are expected to be better, to be more wholesome, and to be happy examples of blessed lives.[3]

As examples, the pastor and the clergy family members are watched and evaluated and emulated. It is true that in most ordination services the candidate is charged with living a "holy life" and engaging in "holy conversation." This charge is accepted by the pastor, received with the response, "Yes, by the help of God," and struggled with throughout the life in ministry. As such the pastor does have a responsibility to be an example of sorts. The problem most often lies in who defines "holy life." The definition given by the parish is far more restrictive than that given by the pastor or by the pastor's denomination. And in most cases the clergy family is not included in the service or the charge of ordination, but is expected to take on the role of godly example simply by the act of marrying the pastor and/or being born into the pastor's family.

Survival in the parish needs clear expectations of what is important in public and private behavior and what is needed for realistic growth and development. The pastor and his/her family can be models, but they must be allowed to be models of healthy interaction and not stereotyped examples of restricted behavior. Issues of dress, personal hygiene, style, morals, habits, and general behavior need to be given freedom of expression if the pastor and clergy family is to model individuality, differentiation, and uniqueness as well as community, belonging, and relatedness. It is true that there has been a great deal of easing on some of these issues during the past decade, but much more freedom is still needed.

The concept of role models extends to all areas of life. Not only are the pastor and his/her family to be models of Christian life, they are often used as models for more general life issues. What does it mean to be a man or a woman, what does it mean to be a husband or a wife, what does it mean to be a son or a daughter, and what does it mean to be a brother or sister? All of these questions are sometimes referred to the pastor and his/her family for answers. The answers are sought not only by asking questions but through observation.

Currently one of the most stress-producing areas in the concept of modeling is in the area of marriage. Clergy marriages are supposed to be models of success and happiness in a world filled with marriages that are not succeeding. My major concern as a pastoral counselor is not that clergy marriages are sought after as an example, but that clergy marriages are often not given the freedom to be healthy examples. Marriages need to be worked out through constant struggling to clarify roles, expectations, and identities. The tension of "separate togetherness" must be allowed to exist and to be worked through again and again and again. Clergy marriages need both connectedness—the ability to stay within the emotional field of the spouse and the family—and boundaries—the ability to define one's individuality without being absorbed by the spouse and the family. In order to be such a model the clergy marriage will have to go through times of togetherness and times of separatedness, times of joy and times of anger, and times of love and times of struggle. Clergy marriages that can express all these aspects, that can feel free to keep private what needs to be private and to share openly what can be shared, will in fact be a healthy example of Christian life.

The same "freedom" concept applies to the clergy couple's parenting and to the clergy family's life together. Struggling, failing, succeeding, growing, hurting, forgiving—all need to be part of Christian life together.

In conclusion, the clergy families who choose not to be role models, who don't want that expectation, ought to be allowed to so choose. Congregations need to struggle with letting the family of the pastor be a "normal" family. A number of years ago it was important to make the distinction between the pastor's wife and the wife of the pastor. Today it is still important and must be applied to the family as well—it is the family of the clergy and not the clergy's family. All too often the positive actions and behaviors of the clergy or the clergy family go unnoticed or unrewarded as if they were simply assumed, but negative actions and behaviors of the clergy or the clergy family can have devastating effects. A clergy divorce can hurt the pastor's ability to be accepted and in some denominations can remove him/her from the active role of the ordained ministry. A problem with a teenage member of a clergy family can affect future appointments and positions within the denomination. The whole church needs to work on granting the freedom to be human to its pastors. All too often the church is harder on its clergy families than it teaches and trains its clergy to be with their congregations' families. A useful book on this subject is *The Clergy Family: A System in Need of Support* by Margaret M. Sawin and Lyndon E. Whybrew.[4]

(4) Parish Life and the Clergy Family

A number of issues arise within parish life that add to the problem of clergy family identity. Who ministers to the clergy family? If the pastor himself/herself attempts to fill this role he/she is often doomed to failure. The pastor needs his/her own pastor, outside the parish and sometimes outside the denominational structure. Pastors often feel trapped with no place to turn when it comes to their own emotional needs and spiritual growth issues. Luckily, many pastors are choosing to find spiritual directors, pastoral counselors, and pastoral mentors for themselves. Clergy spouses and clergy family members need to do the same.

Pastors also need to struggle with the expectation or temptation to be the family chaplain, not only for their immediate family but for their extended family of origin. To be asked to perform marriages, baptisms, and funerals within the family system is meaningful. But such requests can lead to an inability to grieve, celebrate, confront, or struggle in an appropriate way with the person or event involved. To preach at the funeral of one's parent can lessen the natural flow of grief work and can present a model of strength and grieving that is not necessarily healthy.

Spouses and children of pastors find it hard to choose their own spiritual community. It is assumed that a spouse and family members will be members of the pastor's congregation. What if that hinders the individual spiritual growth and development of the spouse and/or child? It is sometimes hard to receive spiritual guidance and inspiration from the person who is your spouse or parent, especially when interpersonal tensions are high. It might be awkward for the pastor's spouse to be a member of the church down the street, but it might be more spiritually freeing.

It is also difficult to define how some members of the clergy family can participate within the parish if they choose to join. Many clergy spouses feel disenfranchised within their spouses' parishes. It is sometimes expected that the spouse will be a member of the woman's or men's group and that the children will be members of the appropriate youth groups. But can that membership be free and can participation really meet the needs of that person? Stereotyped expectations can be a problem. A clergy wife should have the right to run for president of the woman's association just like other women, but she should not be expected either to always be the president or to never be the president. The same can be said for the right of the clergy spouse or child to take a stand on an issue. That stand should be given the respect due the stand and the person making the stand and not agreed with or disallowed because of the clergy family role that person fills. Conflict of interest charges restrict the individuality and freedom of the spouse and child.

The clergy spouse also needs to be sensitive to the role of go-between within the parish. The clergy spouse can take messages just like any other spouse, but should not have to defend or present issues raised by members of the parish. Clear lines of communication and availability need to be established between the parish and the pastor. The clergy spouse also needs to guard against becoming the sole listener and counselor of the pastor. All of these concerns blur the line between the life of the clergy family and the expectations of being fellow employees and workers of the parish.

And of course the "fishbowl" concept must also be addressed when it comes to clergy family identity. Clergy families are more increasingly living in their own homes, but the parsonage concept is still the norm in many parishes. Issues of privacy and feeling watched need to be addressed and appropriate steps taken to insure the separateness required for healthy family life. Being too public can lead to playing "let's pretend" for the sake of the audience. Any action that can be taken to protect the clergy family from inappropriate observation and invasion of privacy will help to insure survival within ministry.

(5) Triangularization Within the Parish

Family systems theory helps in understanding clergy family identity and some of the issues of parish survival. The concept of triangularization states that any two persons or groups, when faced with a tension or disagreement which they are unwilling to face directly with the other person or group, will pull in, or triangulate, a third person or group to stabilize the tension. The resulting arrangement teams the newly recruited person or group against the remaining person or group. The issue for parish and clergy family survival is that often the three components of the triangle are the parish, the pastor, and the pastor's spouse, family, child, or children.

In *Minister, Wife and Children: Unlocking the Triangle,* Lyndon E. Whybrew[5] clearly describes the problem and some of its potential results. If the pastor is having a problem with the parish, he/she often enlists the listening ear and support of his/her spouse against the position of the parish. This entwinement complicates even further the boundary between the spouse and the parish. The parish will also wish to gain the ear of the spouse to either let him/her know what is being said about the pastor, or to attempt to use him/her to confront and change the pastor. Boundaries must be kept clear. The parish needs to confront the pastor directly, just as the pastor needs to confront the parish directly, leaving the spouse and family out of the tension.

The same pattern can be constructed when the spouse has an issue with the parish, or, vice versa, when the parish has an issue with the spouse. Again the pastor will be brought in by each side to gain added support. And again the pastor must keep very clear boundaries and not get in the middle. The spouse needs to go to the appropriate leaders of the congregation, and the parish leaders need to go directly to the spouse, to resolve issues.

Marital discord between the minister and his/her spouse is also subject to the triangularization of the parish. Pastor and/or spouse can enlist the aid of the parish to put pressure on the other in an attempt to resolve a tension. Here the parish needs to get out of the way and give the pastor and his/her spouse the freedom and the support to work out their own issues through the use of appropriate community resources.

Help for the Clergy

How can the clergy family survive in the parish? Understanding the need for individuation, differentiation, separateness, togetherness, belonging, and boundaries is a needed first step. Education of the pastor, the clergy family, and the parish are needed to produce the desired results. A pastor wishing to keep clear boundaries can be sabotaged by a spouse who feels a need to be the "pastor's wife" and who blurs the limits. A clergy spouse can fight hard for clarity around his/her separateness from the parish only to be nominated or volunteered for a position by the pastor. And the parish, uneducated in the concept of boundaries, can constantly push and pull the pastor and clergy family into unclear situations. The first step is a complete education program within the parish on the issue of clergy family survival. It is probably best done by an outside consultant who understands family systems theory and pastoral ministry.

A second help can be therapy and growth work for the pastor and his/her spouse. An in-depth study by the pastor of his/her family of origin can clarify unresolved family issues that might be the source of unclear boundaries between the pastor and the parish and the clergy family and the parish. The same can be true for the clergy spouse and his/her family-of-origin and its effect upon expectations and boundaries within the parish. Ongoing therapy and/or support group involvement for the clergy and his/her spouse are excellent practices for surviving parish ministry. As a pastoral counselor I am in and out of my own personal therapy continually. Therapeutic support is a part of continuing education and survival for all professionals who work daily with the deep emotions and daily conflicts of others.

Marriage encounter and family enrichment seminars are also helpful for the clergy and his/her family. Consultation from outside experts often helps to give a situation reality and to open up other alternatives of action for examination. Since the clergy and his/her family are going to be viewed as models even if they don't want to be, it is good for them to work constantly on their own lives and on their life together.

Sometimes it is useful for clergy families to meet together with other clergy families in a retreat setting just to share successes and failures. Clergy family clusters have been established in some denominations to give such support on an ongoing basis.

The most important process for clergy family survival in the parish is constant work on negotiating clear boundaries: boundaries between the family and the congregation, between the clergy and his/her spouse, and between the individual members of the clergy family. Contracts are very useful in defining boundaries. Time together and time apart should be scheduled and contracted. Expectations and priorities should be clearly stated and reworked often to allow for flexibility as well as continuity. Contracts need to be shared with the entire family through family meetings. And the clergy should share family decisions with the leaders of the congregation. Clarity, sharing, and education are the by-words for success in this process.

Time availability is a special problem within the work of ministry for the clergy and for the clergy family. The boundary around the parsonage needs to be honored so that privacy can be secured. Clergy offices should be in the parish buildings and the home reserved for private usage. The phone needs to be controlled so that access is limited. A system of on-call, trained pastoral care providers should be organized to help handle pastoral care needs that do not necessarily require the clergy. Clergy cannot be responsible for everything and need to model acceptance of their own human limitations and their need for support and help.

It is also valuable for clergy and their families to consider alternative ways of meeting their own spiritual needs. Attending another church during the week as a couple or a family can be useful as well as having private services just for the family. And the clergy and his/her family should secure their own pastor from another congregation or even another denomination to attend to their pastoral care needs.

The clergy needs a family separated from the job by clear boundaries if the family is to serve as a refuge and a place of freedom. Survival in the parish can sometimes depend upon it!

Notes

1. Lyndon E. Whybrew, *Minister, Wife, and Church: Unlocking the Triangle* (Washington, D.C.: The Alban Institute, Inc., 1984).

2. John Fletcher, *Religious Authenticity in the Clergy.* (Washington, D.C.: The Alban Institute, Inc., 1979).

3. David and Vera Mace, *What's Happening to Clergy Marriages?* (Nashville: Abingdon, 1980).

4. Margaret M. Sawin and Lyndon E. Whybrew, *The Clergy Family: A System in Need of Support* (Washington, D.C.: The Alban Institute, Inc., 1985).

5. Lyndon E. Whybrew, op. cit.

Suggested Readings

John C. Harris, *Stress, Power and Ministry*, The Alban Institute, Inc., Washington, D.C., 1977.

Barbara G. Gilbert, *Who Ministers to Ministers?* The Alban Institute, Inc., Washington, D.C., 1987.

Keith J. Reeve and Priscilla Shows, *The Goal: Strong Clergy Families*, The Episcopalian/Professional Pages, September 1983.

John P. and Nancy Jo von Lackum, *Clergy Couples*, Professional Church Leadership, National Council of Churches, 1979.

Donna Payne, Ph.D.
R. Alex Lutz
Sarah Carol Adams

The Millstone Around Their Necks:
Children of Religion Professionals

The Bible contains many examples of professionally religious families. David, son of Jesse, was the spectacularly successful spiritual and
political leader of a kingdom in its golden age, "a man after God's own
heart," whose failure as a father was echoed in those saddest of sad
words, "Oh my son Absalom!" (2 Sam 18:3). Then there was Eli,
mentor of the great prophet Samuel and an important religious leader
in his own right. Eli could be understanding and spiritually wise with
his parishioners as evidenced by his compassionate treatment of
Samuel's barren mother and of Samuel himself. Yet in spite of these
qualities, Eli raised sons who were sexually and religiously profane
and whose evil deeds were a byword in the land. Add to these examples those of most of the kings of ancient Israel, who were supposed to
serve as religious as well as political leaders, whose offspring were
seldom righteous, and the perception exists that being a religious
leader definitely does not guarantee success in child-rearing. These
biblical models have their spiritual heirs today: those whose name in
the community is good, but whose children grow up to reject their
parents' heritage and sometimes the parents as well. Against these
examples are the many religious leaders, who like Zachariah the
priest and father of John the Baptist, are able by God's grace to successfully guide their children to maturity.

In the families of most religion professionals, I would guess, there
is neither complete failure nor complete success, but rather a tension
between these two extremes. For, as Mr. Lutz points out later in this
chapter, these families are subject to the same human tensions as are
lay families, tensions created by a fallen nature stamped with the
image of God. The question then becomes not whether there are
problems, but what are the problems peculiar to being raised as a

140

child in a professionally religious family? The related questions are: to what extent do the parents and congregation contribute to these problems and what behaviors can minimize detrimental influences?

Before we consider these questions, we draw attention to the fact that they are questions of "nurture," not "nature." The nature of the child undoubtedly enters into the equation. One can easily think of examples of apparently righteous families which raise both righteous and unrighteous children and of disfunctional families whose children do not follow the examples of their parents. We do not consider the "nature" aspect here.

What then are the unique problems faced by children of religion professionals? Perhaps they are summarized by the tension created between perception and reality: the perception of perfection (or near perfection) and the reality of trouble in Eden. The editor of this book had a difficult time finding people who would write candidly about their experiences growing up in such families. One prospective author wrote a chapter and then was unable to expose it to public scrutiny. Like physicians unwilling to discuss malpractice in their profession, perhaps the children of religion professionals find it difficult and sad to expose or discuss, even among themselves, the tensions inherent in their upbringing.

In our democratic country, there is no institutional royalty. Our de facto royalty are the unreachable movie, rock and sport stars, and, perhaps on a local level, the reachable priests, rabbis and preachers. These latter minor celebrities are subject to both the benefits and the pitfalls of being placed on a pedestal. Their children know that their parents are on a pedestal (the perception of perfection) and indeed they are unwillingly often on it themselves. When the children face the reality of their own and their parents' failings, conflict results. In the following essays, two young people eloquently express their feelings of growing up "on a pedestal." Pay careful attention to the common themes of blessing and curse in this experience.

"Not Ordained"
by R. Alex Lutz

I'm seventeen now. My dad was the pastor of our church for as long as I can remember. My mom tells me I used to stand up and wave to him during the sermon. But what I remember most are the stories he would tell about me during the sermons. This embarrassed me. Sometimes it was funny and sometimes it wasn't. The congregation got to know more about me than I ever wanted them to know. We have a deal now—he won't tell any stories without my approval first. I like it that way.

One of the nicest things about being a pastor's son is that you are always around people—people of different nationalities, life-styles, wealth, and even attitudes. Being a pastor's son enabled me to meet many strangers. I loved being with my dad when I was younger, going to people's houses and hearing something like, "Yes, this is Pastor Lutz's son." It made me feel important. And why not? At that age, he was my role model and a big influence in my life. I was with him a lot before I went to school and later just in the summers. I would go to church and work with him. I'd also go with him to visit parishioners. I suppose that influence has stayed with me later on in my life.

This influence always put me on my best behavior. But, as a kid, I would do things wrong. Then I'd get that horrible look which said, "How could you do that in front of these people?" I wasn't all that different from other kids. But I guess to the people of the church I was because of who my father was.

When I was a little older I felt I had to work harder to fit in with a group. When I was with new people in a conversation and we were having a good time, someone usually asked, "So, what does your dad do?" I'd say, "He's the pastor of a church." Immediately the conversation changed to a more suitable note for my "ears." One time someone walked in and said something "wrong." I heard, "Don't say that! His father is a pastor." It was as if I couldn't fit in with the group. When something like this happened I wanted to say, "All right, let's just talk normally and we'll all be fine." I usually had to prove to them that I was not the one ordained.

I knew someone who always asked, "So, what's it like being a pastor's kid? Is it different?" I usually replied jokingly, "Yeah, hell fire and brimstone every night!" I didn't mind the question, but not every time we talked!

It's sort of funny now, but I remember that in third grade I went to a Catholic school and had sisters for teachers. I forgot what I did but Sister scolded me with, "How could you! And you are the son of a pastor!"

I think that because my father teaches the word of God to a congregation, people tend to think we don't live normal lives. The truth is, we do. We say things we shouldn't say, do things without thinking, and fail to do things we should do. This all adds up to being human. I think people tend to forget that. I tend to dramatize things I see on television, how superheroes do no wrong. Maybe it's the same when it comes to religion.

Now you're probably saying, "Wait a minute. You were a little kid. How could you know what's just part of being a kid and what's unique to being a pastor's kid?" The truth is I didn't know until about two years ago when my father changed professions. Instead of being the pastor, he now is a pastoral counselor at a psychiatric hospital. I am no longer looking out toward a congregation; I am looking in through the eyes of a congregation. Life seems to be more fun this way. I can get away from the "eye" of the congregation and be myself more easily. Not having to worry so much about what other people might say or think takes a big burden off me. I can make friends on my own with people who don't know my father as their pastor. I'm older now and on my own most of the time. I like who I am in my own right. And it seems that people tend to like me for who I am, rather than for who my dad is. There are ways of surviving when your dad is a pastor. I think they involve talking with your parents. Letting a kid be a regular kid without having to be a superkid is the most important thing.

"Whose Child I Am"
by Sarah C. Adams

Being the child of a pastor has been a difficult task for me. In the early course of this experience I strove hard to overcome the many hills and pitfalls that came my way. At an early age I was forced to realize that my father was not just another ordinary dad with a normal career. This startling realization frightened me.

School for me was a time of great learning, not only about the world, but about the people around me. Soon I came to learn that people didn't see me as an average kid; they saw me as a pastor's child. When asked what job my dad had, I became reluctant to answer. If I replied, just as I expected, I received looks of horror and surprise. As I now know, it is the young children of this world who know the true beauty of accepting people. Unfortunately, as they begin to grow older they lose that precious gift. It was my teacher's attitudes that changed after they discovered who my dad was. Although I cannot recall in which specific ways, I know that my teachers treated me differently. Perhaps it was their reserved behavior when I was around. It was as if they had to watch what they said for fear of offending my beliefs. I didn't resent this too much in my early life, but the situation became progressively worse.

During my pre-teen years, I found that I was making more enemies than friends. This simply amazed me because these people didn't know me; they only knew that my father was a pastor. My peers laughed at me, talked behind my back, and called me names to my face. Many tearful nights passed with my wondering why God had cursed me with this awful life.

During this time I was going through real emotional trauma. I often prayed to the Lord, asking him to help. Sometimes the next day seemed worse. Inside I was crumbling from the tremendous strain to my sense of worth. In addition I was also under the pressures of getting good grades and being the best role model for others. This was a difficult time for me. I was expected to be the perfect child and excel in everything. Many times it was not only my parents who pushed me but it was also the members of the church. It was impossible for me to fulfill the role the world had created for me. People demanded that I be knowledgeable in every aspect of the Bible. In Sunday school the difficult questions were always directed toward me. Even though I could answer most of them, I came to resent that I was expected to know so much.

Even now, in my teen years, people sometimes look at me very differently. My supervisor at work is very cautious about what happens around me. My schoolmates angrily call me names on occasion. The parents of friends and boyfriends are afraid to curse or drink around me. I wish that they could see that I am not a saint and that I am a normal human being.

Until now I've only written about the negative side of being the child of a pastor. As I look back on my years growing up, I see now that a curse wasn't placed on me. Instead I was blessed with a gift.

Since my father's job required it, we moved around a lot. I've lived in three different states, and I've attended about ten schools. At times I feel very lost and lonely because of this. I've never really had a friend for more than five years. And just when I'm getting comfortable with my surroundings, it seems as if I have to move again. But as I know now, this was an excellent experience for me. I've had the rare chance to meet people of many walks of life and see so many sights that others will never see.

I was always forced to go to church when I was younger, and I hated it. But I realize now that it was at that time I was first introduced to God. I grew in God's love and peace and my faith grew very deep and strong. Due to the nature of my father's job we lived in a very family oriented environment. Unlike many of today's American families, we spent a tremendous amount of time together. I quickly developed a close relationship with my family that I value even today.

In my teen years I've had the opportunity to attend several retreats and special church functions. There I received strength and courage to face my daily struggles. God has also given me special friends whom I have met through the church. I've shared the abundance of love and friendship that God first gave me.

There are not many ways to avoid the painful situations that I often suffered through. But I offer some advice to the parents of the children and to the congregations.

- Accept your children as God made them.
- Realize that children are only children; treat them as normal, growing humans.
- Don't expect them to be perfect.
- Support them as their minds and spirits grow in God's love.
- Teach them to love as they would like to be loved.

I honestly do not believe that there are any true solutions to the problems that I faced. In my times of greatest need, I turned to my God and he offered me strength and love. That in itself is the best solution that I can offer.

In closing, I would like to share with you something I have written that may remind you of who you are and whose you are.

As I walk into this world
of shattered dreams
and lost hopes
I hold my head up high.

My Father is by my side,
holding my heart
in his big hands.

Not fearing what the
future will yet unfold,
I raise my chin
and smile.

My eyes are those of
my Father's—

full of love and
faith and help.

And I realize that
I am proud of who I was
and who I am.

And all that I hope to be
is
what my Father is.

In the preceding two essays, the young authors suggest many of
the blessings of being "set apart." These include pride and self-worth
by association ("I am Pastor Lutz's son") and exposure (in successful
environments) to faithful teaching about God and to a family oriented
environment. Even the heavy burden of personally representing God
as the child of an ordained parent can have a special blessing. As
suggested by Miss Adams' poem, learning that one may hold her head
high as a pastor's child can teach the vital lesson that one is principally
the child of a king and represents a Father who *does* have high expectations and will grant help to realize them. It *is* important to know
whose child you are.

As mentioned above, children of religion professionals often
profit from a melting-pot environment. They often move from place
to place, meet, hear about, and entertain in their homes people from
varied places and of varied personality. A child who has heard his or
her parent counsel a suicidal person in the middle of the night may
learn compassion. A child whose parents have lived in several states
and met people from other countries or cultures or economic classes
may learn flexibility, adaptability and appreciation for people different from himself or herself. I recall a close-knit ministerial family of
my acquaintance whose daughters left their small southern town to
attend college six hours away. The congregation believed that this
indicated a parent/child rift. The children were secure in the knowledge that love and independence can co-exist. They were not wedded
to one community's world outlook.

If the benefits of being raised in a professionally religious family
can be great, the flip side is the potential for great conflict. In the
preceding essays, the fallout from being set apart and placed on a
pedestal is discussed. These include, to varying degrees, a loss of
identity (the child's importance in society being absorbed in that of
the parent's); a sense of isolation, of being considered different from,

or better than, mere layfolk; and a sense of failure in being unable to live up to expectations of sainthood. The extent to which society, in the form of the congregation or the child's peers, promotes unrealistic expectations is variable and largely unavoidable. Parents cannot protect their children from incidents such as occurred to a friend of mine. She was deeply hurt and confused by a teacher who told her that although she deserved the lead in a play, it was going to an emotionally needier child since the preacher's kid would surely be much better able to handle the loss of the part. Religious parents can only assume that such circumstances exist, and try to exert damage control. This can be done by clearly differentiating for their children God's reasonable standards and the false standards of society. They can consistently call attention to their (the parents)' own failures and need for forgiveness and renewal. I compare two clergy families of my knowledge in the same field of service. In one family, the father, unwittingly and with good intentions, fostered unreasonable demands on his children to their sorrow and hurt by requiring pristine Sunday behavior and by constantly demanding that they be spiritual models to the community. The other father explained to his children that, under certain circumstances, certain behavior was appropriate, not because God specifically mandated it, but in deference to a local community's standards. This same father modeled what I believe is crucial behavior in a clerical parent. This father was acutely aware of his own considerable personal liabilities. Throughout his life he prayed for the spiritual, physical, and emotional well-being of his children. The children certainly suffered from his inadequacies but the father's prayers, to a large measure, were answered. "If any of you lacks wisdom, let him ask of God, who gives to all men generously and without reproach, and it will be given him" (Jas 1:5).

In the discussion thus far we have assumed that the parent is both willing and able to promote the benefits and defuse the liabilities of growing up in a religious home. However, these conditions, at least to a certain extent, may not exist. From the child's point of view conflict is directly related to the discrepancy between the perception of righteousness and the reality thereof. Isaiah (29:13) speaks of "these people who come near me with their mouth and honor me with their lips, but their hearts are far from me. Their worship of me is made up only of rules taught by men." Hypocrisy is a trait vilified by our society. When children see it in their parents they are confused and angry. It is especially damaging if the parent is God's official envoy. Where children see "a form of godliness, but power thereof denied" (2 Tim 3:5) they are often inoculated against religion as the polio vaccine protects them against polio. They receive the deadened germ of religion by repeated participation in and observation of devitalized religious ritual, and so are forever protected against the real thing, should it ever come along. The religion professional who does not deal with his or her personal sins or who sits with colleagues to discuss his or her calling as a business, in terms of numbers of church members or amount of money collected, is hurting his or her children. The hurt is perhaps only different in degree from that produced by the few who totally ignore their vows and are "like a coating of glaze over earthenware: fervent eyes with an evil heart" (Prov 26:2).

The most common biblical pictures of God are family ones. One is as the husband and lover of our souls. Another is as a parent, primarily as Father, but also with motherly characteristics, as the hen who gathers her chicks under a protective wing. The religious parent has a double obligation to represent faithfully the parenthood of God to his or her children. The failures hidden from the congregation are clearly seen by the children. They are failures not only of parental leadership but of spiritual leadership, and a child's upbringing may become a millstone around his or her neck. Those in religious authority can profit well from the warning of Jesus who indicated where the millstone should be placed. "But whoever causes one of these little ones who believe in me to stumble, it is better that a heavy millstone be hung around his neck" (Mt 18:6).

Evelyn R. Chesnutt, M.A.Ed.

Surviving in Ministry: Stresses, Strategies and Successes from the Clergy Wife's Perspective

In the ministry, as in many occupations, there are satisfying aspects as well as problems. In some ways it is like other professions, yet the ministry may have more chances for renewals. I happen to think that the joys outweigh the stresses. From my own experience and that of other ministers' wives with whom I have been in touch, I would like to share some of the pitfalls encountered, the sources of renewal available, and the blessings that can be present.

I conducted a short survey of sixty-two other United Methodist Church ministers' wives in the Maryland and District of Columbia area. These were persons I had known through church activities over the years. They have a broad base, including active and retired persons, and also a few whose husbands were second career ministers. I was pleased to receive more than a fifty percent return! The comments from this sample showed amazingly similar, yet unique ways of responding to the topic. They represent a total of over one thousand years spent as ministers' wives, with the average being about twenty-eight years.

According to my survey, a few of the older wives recall very little stress, or else the term was not consciously so named. However, it was clear that they certainly had emotional reactions to their daily lives and specific decisions that had to be made through the years regarding their commitment. Many others were not shy about responding bluntly and were grateful for the opportunity to express their ideas.

I will discuss my findings under the following headings: Expectations; Self-Identity and Interests; Couple/Family Support and Communication; Isolation, Loneliness, and Vulnerability; Congregational Life and Politics; Finances, Moving and Parsonage Living; Dealing with Grief; Personal Faith and Spiritual Nurture.

Expectations

A great deal of stress results from trying to fulfill what one might feel are the myriad expectations of the congregation. These are often unrealistic, because no minister and wife are infallible and superhuman. Expectations can also be conflicting. A clergy spouse soon learns that she cannot be all things to all people or please everyone, so she might as well be herself. A husband's expectations, as well as those of the rest of the family, enter in here also. When you become comfortable with who you are, it will be easier to deal with the expectations of others.

Responses indicated that some church members expect the wife to step into certain jobs as soon as she arrives in a new church. These jobs include teaching Sunday school and vacation Bible school, leading devotions, becoming active in the women's group, playing the piano and singing in the choir. In addition, wives are asked to be the "go-fer" and message conveyer, be intelligent, cheerful, attractive and well dressed, bring up model kids, cook and bake beautifully, and keep a neat house.

Unfortunately, some congregations expect "two for the price of one." A wife might also think that she should emulate the wife she followed, even in areas where she may not feel comfortable or skilled. However, it is really up to each person to decide the areas in which she, as an individual, is capable and interested. At other times she can graciously say "no" and not allow herself to be taken for granted. I suggest letting people know where you can and are willing to help, explaining other commitments, if that seems to be appropriate.

In some churches it is not appreciated, and even resented, if the wife is too visible or appears to "take over" things. Personally, I have stayed away from becoming an officer in church groups, preferring to help out in many smaller ways and staying somewhat free to be available when needed on a short term basis. Each person can develop her own style and comfortable methodology. Since the pastoral family generally is more transient than the church members, it may be more appropriate to encourage, train and support other laypersons in leadership positions.

It is important to be very clear that *you* may have hidden expectations yourself about the church members, so it is not just a one-way street! Try to develop mutual acceptance of each other. Some people will assume that the wife's expressed point of view is the same as her mate's. Therefore, exercising discretion and cautious reserve in expressing opinions regarding church political issues is in order. Although the minister's wife may be afforded a certain status, she should contribute her ideas as a fellow layperson, not as a theological expert.

Some people in the secular business world may treat the clergy wife differently, being a little stand-offish. This is a sort of "reverse status" procedure in terms of being accepted as another human being. It is best not to try to be someone you're not. Learning and growth can take place, but not as a substitute for self-acceptance of skills and limitations. This brings us to the second area, that of self-identity.

Self-Identity and Interests

Maintaining identity as a unique person in your own right can be a difficult aspect of any life. Being a strong supporter of the clergy spouse and his role in the church is important, but the wife's own personal commitment is crucial also. Developing your own abilities and interests within and outside the congregation is important and helps give needed perspective. Opportunities for continuing education abound in the larger church and also in the community.

A great many ministers' wives have followed the current trend of having their own careers outside the home. This is partly for financial reasons, but also it is because of a need for self-identity and individualization. The involvement of the wife and children in community activities is often helpful for all concerned. The danger here, of course, is trying to be "Super mom/wife/career person/church member" all in one, and, if time and effort are not carefully prioritized, being exhausted most of the time. Striving always to be a model family may bring on even more trouble and stress. A key need here is developing good support and communication as a couple and also within the total family.

Couple-Family Support and Communication

It is important that a clergy couple grow together with new experiences. This can be a great gift and wonderful challenge, provided ideas and feelings are shared along the way. Mutual trust, understanding and support are needed. The marriage takes work to keep it new and exciting. Hopefully the clergy couple can be best friends and lovers as well as colleagues in the ministry. Some say they are first: wife of the man; second: mother to the children; third: spouse of the minister. Others say they share a career and act as co-worker. Nevertheless, heavy demands on the husband's time and an excessive amount of overtime duties can keep the clergy husband and father from adequate family time.

A clergy wife should become a productive person in her own right. It may also be the wife's role to *insist* on the sacredness of the "day off" each week, and on vacation times which are so important to the re-creation of the family. There seems to be a large proportion of "workaholics" in this profession. Although weekends off are very rare, an overnight or evening out for a movie, play or dinner is important, as is making time regularly for just the two of you, without the children. A wife can put herself on her husband's calendar; it may not seem as romantic or spontaneous, but waiting for "free time" may be a long wait!

Families can arrange for a cottage out of town for the family to use, thus having a focal point for family life far from the ever-ringing phone and doorbell of the parsonage. One friend said this made it possible for them to know quality family life through the children's growing years and even when they became "empty nesters." Finding family time is not easy; it is necessary to accept the fact that this often might have to be worked in according to the schedule of the pastor. Opportunities such as travel, camping trips, and sharing activities with those in the community can also help.

It is so easy to get in such a time bind that the only activities of a clergy couple are church related and the only people they have as friends are those within the congregation. Getting together regularly with friends from outside the congregation, either clergy or from another occupation, will pay dividends. Sharing and receiving support from such friends and taking advantage of personal and family counseling is sometimes needed to get over the rough spots.

Despite mutual commitment to the church, expecting perfection, either in self or spouse, is usually unrealistic. Praying together, going on retreats together, laughing and playing together are good ways to relieve stress. I have found that the support and understanding of a minister spouse is indeed a blessing. In return, being a good listener when he agonizes and mulls over the cares and responsibilities of the church, while maintaining a healthy detachment from the many problems that are constantly a part of life in the church, can be invaluable to him. A wife can be a sounding board and help her husband cope with a personal problem within the congregation without his needing to disclose the confidentiality of the situation.

A favorite book of mine, perhaps because I love being by the ocean, is Anne Morrow Lindberg's *Gift from the Sea* (Pantheon Books, 1955). It emphasizes quiet times for reflection and renewal. This is needed by anyone in a high stress society, but perhaps it is even more crucial for those associated with the helping professions. A clergy wife can feel that everyone else in the congregation, or another meeting, or another appointment, comes before her! The goal of service and serving others is important, but not to the neglect of self and family.

Isolation, Loneliness and Vulnerability

Many of my friends at times have expressed feelings of isolation, loneliness and vulnerability. A minister's wife is often in the background or on the sidelines, and she is sometimes overlooked in social situations in the church. She may be seen only as an appendage to her husband. The pastor husband has a unique closeness to many of the church members because of his role, and it is easy to be a little resentful when he gets so much attention. Also, he often gives so much of himself to others that the family feels neglected. He may need to be reminded that his family is also God's gift. Therefore the wife needs to develop interests and friends of her own for added support. She may also enjoy recognition as a valued individual in either paid or volunteer work in the community.

Sometimes when a minister's family experiences trouble, accidents, serious illness or death, they do not receive enough support from church members, who may feel that they, of all people, should be able to cope well with their own stress and grief. At other times churches will pitch right in without being asked and have been very helpful in times of emergency. Since the clergy family has often been in the "helping" role, it may take some effort to be the recipients of caring ministry from the congregation.

To whom can a clergy wife go? Since we move so often, friends and relatives may live far away, making it difficult to keep in touch. It is important to cultivate meaningful friendships with colleagues. We have learned that in the ministry it is easy to fall into a "lonely" trap. Sometimes we are fearful to show our vulnerability, especially to those who may have appointive power over us. Sharing can take place with other ministers' wives, not in gripe sessions, but in a positive manner. Sometimes even an occasional short phone call is helpful. I believe clergy wives need to intentionally be more supportive of each other in both joyful and sorrowful times. I have received overwhelming numbers of comments that wives who are retired and widows of clergy have often been the most helpful friends. They seem to have the time, interest, experience, and freedom to speak honestly and openly. They have so much to offer. There can be a mutual friendship need fulfilled here.

Another source for friendships are women from the community, perhaps of another faith, and not necessarily the wives of ministers. If they are not judgmental or in a position of authority over you, they can also help to put things in perspective. On the other hand, many clergy wives feel that the fellowship they have had over the years with other clergy families within their own denomination has been one of their greatest blessings. We have been talking about a type of outside networking, but what about congregational life and politics?

Congregational Life and Politics

It is important not to play favorites in the church, even though the wife may feel she has more in common with some persons than with others. Sometimes women in the church, with whom the clergy wife may have felt close, became cool when they or their family disagreed with programs or policy changes in either the local congregation or on the general church level. Also, members who are unhappy with the pastor may target their unhappiness toward the wife.

Stress may also come by having to watch women whose mid-life crises turn into a crush on the designated "care giver"—in other words, the clergy husband. It is hard learning to share your husband constantly with everyone. But if a minister's wife allows herself to be jealous or selfish, she is doomed to a miserable life! Occasionally there are persons who delight in spreading rumors about others, including the minister. This is awkward, but the wife can learn to cut off gossip or exaggerations with a few choice but tactful statements.

Unfortunately, criticism comes with the territory and can really hurt. Taking out of it what can be used and discarding the rest can be challenging. It is very painful when a person you love and respect is attacked unfairly. Nevertheless, trying to have a positive rather than a negative attitude, praying for him or her daily, and finding that forgiveness is healing for you as well as for the critic are some ways of coping. When people come to the clergy wife, she can listen sensitively but perhaps should consider referring the problems to the pastor or to the proper church official rather than trying to handle them herself.

Most ministers' wives I surveyed avoid taking on chairmanship of church committees, feeling that it is better to be an "enabler." They avoid being the "switchboard operator" and the "middle woman" between the church and the pastor. A better stance is to be helpful, friendly, and interested but somewhat detached. People can be encouraged to speak directly to the person involved instead of expecting the clergy wife to run interference. It is also not a good idea to volunteer spouse or children for things. My motto: "Be your own self"—and allow others to be the same and speak for themselves! Although you will meet and know some wonderful people in the churches, there will be some pettiness within congregations. It is important to let people know, in a kind way, when their words are offensive. Covering up and being meek and mild is not a helpful response. Brutal honesty, of course, is seldom good either.

One important blessing is the probability of your having an "instant community" in most places the clergy couple serve. This is not always true of persons in other occupations. However, much damage is done by clergy and their families who encourage continuing close ties with special church members after they have moved on to another parish. This undermines the new pastor and divides a congregation.

Finances, Moving and Parsonage Living

Although salaries have much improved in recent years, finances are always tight on a minister's salary. Especially in the early years, the couple may be on a shoestring budget and unable to live on a level near that of parishioners. Double careers are often necessary, especially with regard to the expense of children's college educations. However, this may cause scheduling problems. In the United Methodist Church, job security is a plus; nevertheless the need for retirement planning is crucial. The minister may end up having no equity built up over the years and be left without a viable retirement home. Where one lives can be an ambiguous matter. It may be convenient to live next door to the church, but the lack of privacy can be an infringement on family life.

It is good (and often expected) that clergy wives entertain church groups in the parsonage so that they can see their house, but it is also important to set limits on the time and types of visits. Sometimes the couple feels that their house should be ready for a "walk through" check-up at any time. Children can learn to keep the living room neat and ready for unexpected visitors, but they need to have privacy in their own bedrooms and not be unduly subject to the fishbowl mentality. Being under constant scrutiny and observation can cause strain and anxiety for the parsonage family.

There is great deviation in the type and condition of parsonages. The clergy family should be good stewards of the church's property, but it is often difficult and sometimes embarrassing to get the trustees to take care of certain needed repairs or replacements to the house. Getting the sympathetic ear of an influential woman member may help to speed up the process. Parsonage problems may stem from the fact that the church budget may be tight and care of all buildings, not only the parsonage, may be put off and may suffer from neglect over the years.

Living in the church parsonage often means being restricted from making decisions about the location, furnishings and decor of your home. However, the clergy couple should establish it as a personal residence, not an extension of the church building. Having a vacation cottage can be the one permanent home in a long line of changing parsonages experienced by the clergy family. Moving is a fact of life, and is more probable in some Protestant denominations than others. There is the blessing of "built-in" friends when one moves to a new congregation, and moving creates the opportunity for making wonderful friendships all over the state area—something that others may not have. However, it is still not easy uprooting the family and experiencing the uncertainty of where the family will be assigned from year to year.

There is a special stress of a mid-year move with school age children. It requires adjusting to a new area, new surroundings, and new schools, as well as the necessary and difficult task of a job change for the wife. It is good to involve the children in the whole process. Children are really quite adaptable, and will usually pick up your favorable "can do" attitude.

I find that unpacking bags entirely (hanging pictures, etc.) is an important way to "bloom where you are planted." A friend of mine notes that she tries not to have a part of her standing outside evaluating and deciding whether the new church is worth the move. She says that it is making a commitment, almost like marriage, to accept the frustrations and disappointments that are an inevitable part of moving to a new church.

Nevertheless, moving every three to six years is harder as time goes on; we hate to say goodbye to people we have come to love and serve. This takes a lot of flexibility, and some people can develop this ability more easily than others. At this point, I want to be sure to say a few things about dealing with grief.

Dealing with Grief

Do not underestimate the *grief process* that accompanies a clergy family's move. This may take two years or more after the move, depending on many factors. Not only may the pastor and his wife deeply miss the members of the former church and the comfortable ways of doing things, but the new church members may *also* be going through a period of grief. This is true especially if the preceding pastor and family were dearly beloved, and if they have not broken their ties after moving on. Acceptance of a new pastor may be a long time in coming, because most people crave stability and dislike extra changes in today's already transient society.

One of my favorite resources for individuals and groups is a book by Ann Kaiser Stearns, entitled *Living Through Personal Crisis* (Thomas More Press, 1984). It discusses coping skills and describes the difficult processes of moving and relationship changes, which involves a type of grief different from that related to physical illness and death, but which is real nevertheless.

Another friend finds that by getting involved with the new congregation, by getting to know them and by working with them, it doesn't take as long to feel a part of them and to be accepted by them. Although she still missed the people from the former church, the friendliness of the new church soon made her feel at home. Sometimes a clergy wife may feel closest to churches where her own children were teenagers. However, different phases of life can have their own satisfactions.

A minister's wife has to be careful not to let exhaustion take over. One of the dangers is that there is always more to do than can ever be done in any church—large or small. That is when burnout is a real problem. We have to draw back at times and relax. An option may be to get away and focus upon our personal spiritual life.

Personal Faith and Spiritual Nurture

We have talked about the low discouraging moments, as well as the high exciting ones in being a minister's wife, and whether we consider them problems or challenges. The Chinese language has one character for "crisis" which is made up of two parts: danger and opportunity. A clergy wife can learn to be open to growing personally and spiritually, realizing that God speaks to us often in the midst of storm clouds. How do you learn from failures and setbacks, welcome an ambiguous future, and dare new things? One gets such strength by having faith and by trusting in God's love and constant presence in our lives.

Being strong comes by developing a personal devotional life, through reading religious and secular materials, through prayer and Bible reading. It comes through sharing with special prayer partners or groups, and participating in retreats. Walking in the fresh air is a great time for praying; car pooling or commuting can also be time for "quickie" prayers. Enjoying art, music, creative hobbies, and keeping a journal can add to personal devotional life.

A favorite meditation in our family is the passage from Isaiah 40:31 (Revised Standard Version): "They who wait on the Lord shall renew their strength; they shall mount up with wings like eagles. They shall run and not be weary; they shall walk and not faint." (To which we add, "Help us, Lord; help us, Lord, in thy way!") It is important for every person to assume responsibility for one's own spiritual growth and development, and to take advantage of self renewal opportunities.

Conclusion

Is there a way to summarize the stresses, strategies and successes that we've discussed? The role of a minister's wife allows a way to share with her clergy husband on many levels and serve as a team, if that is what they both want. Growing together as a couple in new places with rich new experiences can be a real blessing. The clergy wife needs to keep open communication lines with her husband about her feelings as they learn to trust, support and laugh with each other.

Having a good self-image and a secure personality can insure a tolerant attitude toward the demands placed upon a clergy husband. The wife also needs to be committed to his vocation, and it certainly helps to like people! Although it is a joint commitment, the wife has to make a life for herself also. She can utilize her unique personality and God-given talents, intentionally broadening her horizons and interests for a clearer perspective on daily stresses, and not accepting unhealthy and unrealistic expectations from other sources. She should not allow herself to be imposed on, but be her own person and give her time, talent and gifts in her own way.

It is important to preserve an individual identity consistent with one's own sense of self, and not assume the burden of trying to fit into someone else's "mold." Try to see the humorous side to situations and laugh instead of becoming hurt or resentful.

In the potential loneliness of the pastoral role it is so crucial to cultivate meaningful friendships with colleagues and others in the community. The fellowship and support of the larger extended "church family" is beyond measure.

One key to survival is to focus on the many positive aspects, benefits and opportunities in the ministry, rather than on the negative experiences that happen from time to time to all of us. I agree with many of my colleagues and friends who are ministers' wives in saying: "I couldn't have chosen a shared career that was more fulfilling, challenging, and rewarding!"

James S. Rosen, M.A., M.S.W.

The Spouses of Religion Professionals

The nineteenth chapter of the book of Numbers records a ritual that described well the dilemma that we face in ministry. A red heifer is slaughtered in order to offer purification for the person who has contact with a dead body. But what a paradox! The very ritual which purifies the impure also defiles the person who offers the sacrifice. The Bible makes no attempt to answer the dilemma. That task is left to later traditions. Yet I suggest that the dilemma is one that many of us feel keenly. We who purify, that is to say, who teach and serve and help our communities, find ourselves and our characters threatened with a certain kind of defilement. There are elements in the work we perform that threaten our self-perceptions, our own ego strengths, perhaps even our visions of who and what we are and what we might do. Understand that these are elements that have a clear impact on spouses as well.

Indeed, to a large extent the religious leader is seen as God's representative on earth. He or she stands apart. Some don robes which help inspire awe and authority. Many of us act in ways that maintain an aura of mystery about us. Sometimes all of this is in stark contrast to very real human weaknesses that we may or may not be aware of.

It is tempting to feel a sense of power at times. But as it is lonely at the corporate top, it is especially so in the "high heavens." We often become unapproachable for informal and simple human contact, and if we become too human, too revelatory, we risk undermining the power that lets us serve in the first instance.

If you serve God you are ripe for manipulation in every kind of dispute. After all, who does not want God on his or her side? Though some see you as representing God, it is the board of trustees that represents your security. A thirty-second vote decides if and where you will do your representing. The temptations are so strong to follow not what conscience dictates but rather what politics demand.

As a result, religious leaders often act in ways that invade their roles as husband and father, or mother and wife. As Rabbi Harold Kushner describes: You schedule an appointment for an hour that is convenient for the caller but not for family. You rush through a Sabbath meal so that you may go to preach about the Sabbath as uninterrupted family time. You leave a sick child or spouse at home and go to teach religious values to a synagogue or church youth group. There are days when you have to cancel family plans because you must officiate at a funeral. Then you praise the deceased as a man who never let his business interfere with obligations to family.[1]

Carl Jung once wrote, "We overlook the essential fact that the achievements that society rewards are won at the diminution of personality."[2] We often don't realize what price we pay by serving the way we do. Must it be so? There is such tremendous pressure to serve and to help. I sense that pressure is largely due to the decline of the traditional family and of religious commitment. Most of the people we serve feel a strong sense of the disintegration of stable, predictable family life with its permanent relationships. The family is in flux and this fluidity causes ambivalence, guilt, and ever-changing expectations that demand an anchor.

As Christopher Lasch has so clearly demonstrated, the family has in the past been a "haven in a heartless world." The haven has disintegrated so much that today it seems powerless to protect its members from all manner of external dangers. And so the school, the helping professions, and peer groups have taken over many family functions over time.[3] The family itself provides companionship, but is seen by many as the stepping-stone to individual growth. Not surprising then is the tendency to see marriage as a non-binding commitment. Who amongst us has not seen a couple which rejects any mention of permanence in a marriage ceremony? "Till death do us part" is simply not realistic, they say. Embodied in all of this is the tremendous distrust of the future.

The nuclear family simply has ceased to exist as a comfortable and predictable embodiment of the family organization. In fact, if, as predicted forty-nine percent of all American children will live in a single parent family for at least part of their lives by the year 1990, we must sense what a loose and shifting foundation there exists for the establishment of any family life.[4]

I think as well of expectations for women these days. Fifty-nine percent of married women work outside the home, earning, incidentally, only sixty-five cents to the average man's dollar.[5] Half of all women with pre-schoolers and two-thirds of women with children under eighteen are now working.[6] Such women are saddled with tremendous ambivalence: how to be supermom at the same time as a success in the marketplace. It's not that women cannot have careers, It is not even that a woman cannot become pregnant while at work. It is really all right as long as she agrees to wear a designer maternity business suit and return to her job within six weeks after birth, fending for child care on her own.

There is undeniable nostalgia in our communities. Nostalgia, we know, is so often a form of depression, a mourning over a past that never quite was, in reality, as it is envisioned, and never can be realized in the future. So people everywhere look for role models of stability. The clergy represent, together with spouses, an authoritative tradition that hearkens back to a hoary antiquity in which families were stable, people seemed happier, and problems that seem so rampant today were not around at all. That this picture is simply untrue is not the issue. It is the perception. And so we discover that we religious figures with our spouses counsel not so much by what we say but by what we are. We are perceived to be husband and wife in love, committed to ethical and transcendent religious values, who minister to others in need. We are open and caring people who want to help. Such role modeling is a heavy burden indeed. It is not that changes in the family have not touched clergy and care-giving families. We have our own share of ambivalences and traumas. But here is a clear hope amongst others that the changes will not touch our families too much.

The decline of religious commitment is a second factor that complicates the care-giving role of the clergy and its extension onto his or her spouse. So many of the people we serve have abandoned the religious and ethical values of our faiths, but do see us as practicing them *in toto*. Such commitment inspires others and makes us worthy of being approached for help. It is what we stand for, after all. Yet our traditions call for entire networks of support for families and individuals in need. Often those networks are lacking due to insufficient support in the rank and file in our communities. When that happens, clergy remain the professional Jews and Christians of our communities, caring beyond our means and resources.

It is too much for one, so ideally you have two. The spouse becomes the partner of a single unified team. It is he or she who cheerfully answers the telephone when a person calls during dinner time with the statement, "Pastor, Minister, Rabbi, I didn't want to disturb you at the office, so I'm calling you at home." He allows an extra fifteen minutes or so for grocery shopping, never knowing whom he will meet. It is necessary to catch up on news of the congregant's family. Clergy long ago discovered that some of the most significant counseling we do is outside of formal settings. Often our spouses discover it too, right there in the frozen food section. Moreover, she will always yield the right of way on a highway to a driver who cuts her off. It is the only appropriate thing to do.

Often the work is wonderful. We help people. A human touch makes a major difference, especially in unanticipated settings. But let us realize the price we must pay. The fishbowl existence that extends to our spouses, the denial of his or her humanity, the tendency to limit the spouse's identity and individuality and to see her or him as an extension of the religious leader is inescapable. I think of a friend, married to a clergyman, who works for a major technological corporation. When she met members of the congregation and discussed her occupation, she was met with the comment, "I didn't know that there was a religious services committee at your firm."

There's another role that the spouse plays as well, one that is double-edged. It is that of direct supporter to the care-giving husband or wife: the voice of encouragement, of sensitivity, of shared fate. There is another aspect to that role which is perhaps more important, however. I am reminded that the Hebrew term used in the description of the creation of Eve in the garden of Eden is *ezer k'negdo*. It is translated as "helpmate," but very literally, it could be translated as "the helper who is in opposition to." That is, of course, the way in which a spouse plays a terribly important role. We need an objective voice in our work. At times we need a critical one as well.

You have perhaps heard that story about the rabbi seized with bouts of indecision. He is presented with rival claims by two litigants. He tells litigant A, "You are right," after hearing his presentation, and tells litigant B, "You are right," after hearing his presentation. When his wife points out that they cannot both be right, he says to her: "You are right as well." I must admit to knowing that rabbi. I am especially grateful that I know his wife.

It is something we have all encountered. There has been a terribly difficult week with five emergencies. We are confronted with the need for a sermon and we write something that we feel is simply awful. At best, we hope that congregants will think that we were simply a guest speaker who will disappear in due course. And then someone comes up to you and says, "What you said today has changed my life. You are talking exactly about my situation and now I know how to handle my affairs." Or you spend hours crafting a masterpiece. It is fresh, it is free of clichés, it contains such a novel interpretation of scripture that you are considering having it published. You get up to deliver your masterpiece and discover the Pavlovian reaction that greets so many speakers and especially preachers. You barely open your mouth and the yawns start, then the coughing, and then someone in the fourth row starts nodding off. So, the clergyperson desperately needs a voice that will help him or her to keep a firm sense of reality. A voice that will be critical and constructive. A voice that will prevent him or her from being led solely by consideration of popularity.

But what a price there is here, too! Dr. Leslie Freedman in a study of role-related stress in the rabbinate had this to say: "The more his wife is involved in a rabbi's actual work, the weaker may be the psychological boundary between work and marriage. Therefore, the harder it may be for husband and wife to be intimate with each other as persons, without the trappings of work getting in the way."[7]

It is a message I believe we need to take to heart. There is always a price. Our humanity is not less precious than that of anyone else. What Dr. Freedman found true of Conservative and Reform rabbis, I would suggest is true of all religious leaders and of other helping professionals, too. Dr. Freedman concluded that the average rabbi has a level of distress statistically greater than sixty-three percent of the general population of the United States. In his statistical scheme, the experience of chronic psychological distress experienced by these religious figures was at a level higher than the brief period of peak distress felt by males in reaction to the Three Mile Island accident. Perhaps it is not surprising then that thirty percent of his sample reported feeling "fairly often" or "very often" that their wives would prefer that they were not rabbis.[8]

So we are left with a dilemma: We do vitally important work in helping other human beings. Most of the time, most of us enjoy it. Yet the demands of that work invade our marital and family lives, often induce marital stress, and cast spouses in roles they would never have to play if their husbands or wives had chosen a different profession.

We will not meet this dilemma through simply reducing physical symptoms of stress. We must recognize for ourselves that we are individuals, complex people who are separate from the roles that we play, who need to relate to our spouses, children, and friends on a plane wholly different from the all-consuming care-giving and religious roles that we assume. It takes balancing and skill if we are to preserve the authority we need to function, but we dare not evade the issue.

We preach constantly that any loving relationship involves constant work, that human beings must play very different roles in their lives to feel a sense of competence and happiness. It is, I believe, a lesson we must learn and embrace ourselves, for our sake as well as for those we serve.

Notes

1. Harold Kushner, *When All You've Ever Wanted Isn't Enough* (New York: Summit Books, 1986), p. 24.

2. Ibid., p. 23.

3. Christopher Lasch, *Haven in a Heartless World* (New York: Basic Books, 1977), pp. 97ff.

4. Paul C. Glick, "Marriage, Divorce, and Living Arrangements—Prospective Changes," *Journal of Family Issues*, Volume 5, No. 1 (1984), p. 24.

5. Anne Taylor Fleming, "The American Wife," *New York Times Magazine*, October 26, 1986, p. 32.

6. Cited in *Baltimore Jewish Times*, October 31, 1986, p. 73.

7. Leslie R. Freedman, "Role-Related Stress in the Rabbinate" *Proceedings of the Rabbinical Assembly*, Volume 66 (1984), p. 47.

8. Ibid., p. 45.

Kay Stanford, L.C.S.W., A.C.S.W.

When the "Mrs." Is a Reverend

"We are not the typical family" was a frequent response of men married to women clergy. To explore the special issues faced by clergy husbands, twenty phone interviews were conducted with husbands whose wives represented many different faiths, among which were Episcopal, Lutheran, Unitarian, Jewish, Methodist and Presbyterian. In interviewing the clergy husbands, it became clear that they do indeed represent very different backgrounds, differing in their histories, personalities, religions, and careers. A recent demographic study by the Methodist Church concludes, "Clergy husbands represent a highly diverse group and few general statements can be made about them."[1] This chapter will affirm that finding. Clergy husbands is the phrase used in this chapter to describe non-clergy men married to women ministers or rabbis. By numbers there are more men married to ministers than rabbis, but the issues are so similar that the terms church and synagogue could be interchanged.

Despite their individual identities and struggles, there are some common issues that are perceived by clergy husbands. Hopefully this chapter will help clergy husbands identify some of their experiences and struggles and feel reassured that they are not alone. At the same time, spouses, friends, family and religion administrators reading this may begin to appreciate the hurdles clergy husbands face. Besides identifying some of the challenges confronting husbands, it might be helpful to shed some light on how these couples cope and deal with the dilemmas presented to them.

A search of the literature reveals that research on the roles of clergy husbands is sparse. In 1986, the Alban Institute published "Men Married to Ministers." Laura Deming and Jack Stubbs presented the results of 258 questionnaires that they had gathered from clergy husbands describing their lives. They stress that the spiritual "call" brings a different dimension to ministry and marriage than to other two-career marriages. They stress the pioneer status of these men along with their wives as the ministers face discrimination, career dilemmas, unclear expectations and sacrifices.[2] Their work presented a springboard for these interviews.

Expectations: Unclear/Uncrystallized

Lee and Kathy Stanyun were married while Kathy was in seminary and Lee was in engineering school. He described himself as quiet and shy and was apprehensive when Kathy took a position with two small rural churches. They lived in the parsonage and Lee commuted thirty miles to his job with a construction company. Lee expected to be involved with church but was unclear as to how. He felt that the congregation expected him to be at the weekly coffee hour and to keep the manse in good repair. The congregation's discomfort with his role was made clear early when they received a letter addressed to "Rev. and Mr. Stanyun." Lee wanted to be supportive, but he did not want to go to two church services each week. He decided to offer to publish a newsletter using his computer skills. Kathy made a lot of hospital calls as her parish had many elderly members, and once or twice a month a middle-of-the-night emergency arose. Lee felt positive about his wife's helping others in crisis, but really resented her attendance at denominational meetings, which caused her to return home at midnight. "Reasonable and realistic" expectations was their hope as they discussed their relationship, dreams and goals. Lee thinks that he will have a better career opportunity if he takes a job offer in a large urban area, but there are no denominational openings for clergy in that area.

Inquiring about the expectations of the new role of clergy husband brought forth a number of comments. "There are no expectations." "There is no precedent." "They don't know what to expect of her, let alone of me." "I probably have not fulfilled them." "I don't know what they are." "No baking cookies or washing windows." "They don't know how to deal with me." Clergy husbands in general guess that there are some expectations, but claim they have the freedom to develop their role as they wish. They are quick to share that there are no role models available, that they frequently do not know other clergy husbands, and that there are no clear concepts of what their behavior, participation, or investment would be.

Most agree quickly that their wives had "no firm idea" of what their role should be. Some husbands felt that their spouses expected them to participate, but the arena or the level of involvement was completely up to them. A frequent response included, "I became active because I wanted to, not because I was pressured into it." Clergy women made it clear in the hiring process that the clergy husband was not part of the hiring package. The levels of participation, which will be discussed under spirituality, varied greatly among the clergy husbands.

Some husbands had negative expectations starting with their initial reaction to their wives' consideration of a career in the ministry. One midwestern clergy husband charged, "My sense of expectation was a feeling of loss—loss of attention, loss of a helpmate; she was having an emotional affair with the congregation." Conflict arose for some husbands who felt that they wanted to support their wives as individuals but not their choice of becoming a clergy person. Some marriages have survived this conflict and turned it into a workable though tense solution, while other marriages have not been able to survive.

Unlike traditional clergy wives, no stereotypes seemed to face the husbands. It was clear that all congregations expected the husband to work outside the family. Respondents felt they could focus on interests of their own, such as involvement in the music program or the outreach program, but they were not expected to do any traditional support services as a clergy wife might be. In the congregation's struggle with expectations for them, they also felt that the people grappled with the expectations for the clergy women at the same time. One husband whose wife serves a small rural church shared that "they expect her to do what a pastor's wife would do as well as what a pastor does." Some clergy husbands struggle with their expectations being so unclear that they wonder if they meet them adequately. Other husbands felt they could support their wives by becoming involved, but they let her define what events they would attend.

Marriage: Choices and Hurdles

Bob and Sue Adams were married twelve years ago while he was in college and she was in seminary. After ordination nine years ago, Sue accepted an assignment in a parish in another state. Bob decided to go to graduate school and selected one in the same urban area where she accepted the position. While she served as the associate pastor in a large congregation, they had several children. After Bob completed his graduate studies, he took a position in the academic world where he had developed a unique specialty. He did not feel any clear expectations from her congregation toward his involvement, but instead actively participated in the congregation out of his own desire. He felt that he had always been active in prior church activities and would keep up the same investment. Bob felt that at times he remained silent out of respect when he might have otherwise spoken out on certain issues. Early in the marriage, Bob and Sue decided to assume a cooperative arrangement, dividing all the household chores and child-care responsibilities, and have continued to work that out. He emphasized the need to communicate frequently because little assumptions and differences in priorities seem to cause the conflicts. The time demands on Sue from her pastorate are a stress on the family that requires both to be constantly aware of their needs and their children's demands. Some times are much more hectic than others, but they have chosen to structure "planned getaways" times for just the two of them, made possible with a large church staff. Sue is currently considering a move toward her second pastorate, in which she would like to be a solo pastor. Trying to anticipate both their careers developing, they are looking for geographic areas where he might be able to teach in his specialty and she might have the opportunity to be the only minister of a congregation.

Communication patterns, attitudes of the partner, and flexibility seem to be the keys for successful marriages of women clergy and non-clergy spouses. Most respondents agreed that it takes work by both partners to surmount the hurdles created by a dual career couple complicated by congregational expectations and religious policy.

Communication is essential to promote an atmosphere of compromise and cooperation as well as love and respect. Discussion of the pressures of both their jobs is vital for good mental health. Couples need to be a release valve for each other. With whom does the clergy person talk? The spouse is the natural person, but then next week he must participate alongside the congregational member who has created conflict with his wife. This inter-relationship does not happen in most two career families. There is generally little contact between the co-workers of each partner except at the annual holiday party or an occasional social event.

It appears vital for clergy and spouses to take time to learn about each other's style of communication since they will often be in stressful circumstances. Couples reading the same books on communication styles can be helpful. Jointly taking a communication or marriage workshop can help highlight conflictual needs. Becoming familiar with a personality profile such as the Myers-Briggs Type Indicator is beneficial because it enhances awareness of communication styles.

Attitudes of partners are affected by many features including when the minister was ordained, personal self-esteem, child-care issues, and marital security. It would appear from the respondents that those husbands who were married close to the wife's ordination adjusted more easily to the new role than those whose wives were "called" to ministry as a second career.

Husbands of more mature women, who entered ministry later, had to deal with the loss of her attention, publicly sharing her with other people, changes in child-care responsibilities, redistribution of household tasks, and internal upheavals created by her choices. Many husbands replied with awe at the intensity of their wife's "call," often finding the wife more assertive and goal-directed than ever before. This was frequently not comfortable for the spouse. One husband remarked that while in Vietnam he made a strong commitment to place his family first and felt that his decision was "devalued by her choice of ministry."

Husbands reflected that their own personal sense of security seemed to be an important factor. An Idaho husband said that he was very supportive of his wife's second career, but wondered aloud if he could have been so encouraging if he had not been a successful businessman already. It seemed essential for husbands to have their own interests besides their work. Some of these activities included reserve duty, scouting, hobbies, and sports interests.

Most respondents felt that they had more child-care responsibilities after their wives entered ministry. Some felt that was a rewarding and unique opportunity they might not have taken advantage of in a traditional pattern of child care. Resentment about the additional child care was verbalized by others. Several spoke specifically about the pressure of Sunday morning—being on time, having children dress properly to be a "public family."

Those husbands, who married knowing that the ministry would be her career, seemed to make a smoother adjustment because they expected some of the clergy marital pressures and because they were a member of a society at a time when shared responsibility was more accepted within the marriage. Many of the spouses related sharing household tasks ("We try a fifty fifty split"), shared child care issues ("My wife arranges child-care during the day and I do evenings and weekends") and pooled income ("All the money goes in one pot"). Acceptance of the issues created by dual careers seemed much more agreeable and less personalized for them.

In general, husbands had greater incomes than the ministers regardless of their educational backgrounds, most agreeing that their wives did not get fair compensation for the hours worked. Several felt that the church was "proud of its low salary as part of social responsibility." Many felt that there was a clear expectation of all clergy families to live modestly as an example. Some were quite angry when they encountered the attitude, "She does not need as much money because she has a working spouse." One wondered if church boards might negotiate salary differently between men and women. It is usually thought that money reflects power issues as well as affirmation of value, both of which these couples must consider.

Time demands were a stress regardless of when the wife was ordained. Having time together was a high priority of most couples. "We have to make extra efforts to touch base." Most couples agreed that their work week was out of sync. Ministers traditionally have their peak of energy Friday through Sunday and slow down on Sunday afternoon, while the husband is starting to get energized for Monday—the beginning of his work week. Some husbands said that their wives experience "every day as a work day."

Flexibility seems to be essential in helping to achieve a balance. Some couples planned which nights they scheduled meetings and which nights they kept for the family. One respondent explained, "She decided that she did not have to go to everything." Several families made a strong commitment to have dinner every night, some letting the answering machine handle any interruptions. With conviction, one respondent clearly stated a helpful attitude, "We are both amenable to being interrupted." One physician shared their solution, "Each of us decided to do a little less professionally."

Accommodating schedules takes work, but seems to have rewards. Those personalities who can "go with the flow" seem to be less frustrated than those spouses who like to adhere to a tight schedule. True emergencies for the minister seem universally to bring genuine understanding and support as well as admiration from husbands. On the plus side, couples with children find some advantages with her flexible workday schedule in responding to their child-care needs.

Career choices also demand a lot of flexibility. Ingenious adaptations to difficult employment situations were discovered through the interviews. When both careers dovetail, all are grateful, but that did not happen for each couple or each career move.

Commuting became a major part of some couples' lives. Living in an apartment midway between their jobs still caused a couple each to commute forty miles one way. A New York couple had a house on Long Island near her church and an apartment in the city near his job. They divided the week between the two residences. One minister commutes sixty miles each way so her husband can keep his job which is tied to a local business. There were no closer employment opportunities for her.

Working out career choices seems to require much give and take. A twosome moved to a large western urban area where he had a job. The chances for her employment looked good. But, despite many speaking engagements, no job developed, probably because she was one of so few women. After two years she found a job in the eastern area where he also found a suitable position. A Chicago based company offered one husband a transfer and a promotion to a rural southern town. Since there appeared to be no position for her, he eventually turned down the offer with some regrets. Several husbands felt that the family move should be based solely on their opportunities, because they made more money. Considering college tuition for children and retirement needs, one couple felt that they had to accept a move when the corporate headquarters relocated. He had been with the company twenty-five years, while she had been an associate pastor for three years. None of these decisions were clear-cut, nor without struggle.

Sometimes complicating these decisions even more is the discrimination felt by the wife and the unsteadiness of the job market for clergy in general. Women had the experience of being considered for interim pastorates, substitute preachers, or conference speakers, but these did not translate into permanent positions. They were seen as a novelty or as a "token woman" on a program, but rarely taken seriously as a potential pastor. One spouse reflected that it was difficult for a woman "to get beyond the paper stage of the hiring process."

In a recent study focusing on outlooks for women in ministry, the following conclusion was reached.

> Since this is a male-dominated profession, it is unlikely that
> women will become equal participants until men are willing
> for them to do so, and, indeed, until the women overcome

any reluctance of their own to assert themselves equally. Until this prejudice is openly recognized by the profession and its leaders, it cannot be addressed and equal participation will remain limited.[3]

Men married to ministers do not deal with this in the abstract, but experience the frustrations of discrimination whenever career choices need to be made.

Spirituality: Form and Substance

Chuck and Mary Hoffman have been married five years, having met at an ecumenical gathering four years after she was ordained an Episcopal priest. Since they were from different faith backgrounds, they discussed their religious beliefs and traditions extensively before marriage. After several years, Chuck joined the congregation where Mary was the priest. He felt Mary appreciated that his spiritual journey and expression of faith were different from hers. Chuck did a lot of "soul searching" before deciding how he would participate in her congregation. He wanted his participation to be genuine, not in response to some unclear expectations of others. Singing in the choir was consistent with his love for music. Chuck had always felt a strong pull to local hunger projects, so he volunteered for the mission committee. Remaining uncomfortable with his role as the minister's husband, he thought that he was not meeting the congregational expectations, though he did not know what they were. Chuck felt awkward when members asked, "Are you proud of her?" or "What is it really like to be married to a priest?" When criticism was directed toward how the church was run, he felt distressed, wanting to defend his wife. Chuck and Mary talked about his dilemma, but they did not know any other clergy husbands with whom to talk. Chuck's family was not supportive of him, since he had changed his faith tradition.

How does a clergy husband focus on his own spiritual development with so many factors involved? For most interviewees, spiritual development is entwined with their marriage and church affiliation. There was only a hint in several answers of a personal spiritual process of reading, reflection, retreats, or private prayer life. One can only wonder why these are unreported behaviors.

Many respondents felt that their religious faith was less formalized than their spouse's. The biggest fear for one husband was the expectation of the congregation that his spiritual life was completely developed. After converting to his wife's religion, a spouse expressed appreciation that "she respected my faith struggles." Wondering aloud, one husband stated with some bewilderment, "Maybe hers is a more valid expression of faith than mine, but I really don't know." Another shared that he felt his attitude, as a teacher, reflected his spiritual and religious convictions. All expected their spouses to be more articulate about faith development and felt no expectations that they should be able to articulate their faith as clearly. Several speculated that it must be quite different for a couple where both were clergy.

Most clergy husbands who were interviewed attended the churches where their wives served. Their involvement included singing in the choir, attendance in worship weekly, being a member of a mission committee, working on landscaping around the religious facility, being a member of the board of trustees or serving at regional levels within formal religious structures. Most were involved to the degree that they wanted to be. Some said that their current involvement was not related to her pastorate, but a natural progression from their prior church-related activities. Others stated that they felt it was important to share her ministry by involvement. One husband of a newly hired pastor expressed his need to "go slowly," having been a church leader before and now cautiously finding a new role. In their participation, many sensed a need to be "guarded," "think things over carefully before I speak," or "hold my tongue." Being sensitive to his wife's position, one active young husband said that he would politely excuse himself from any discussion of her salary. Affirming worship participation, a husband stated, "Her involvement in services enhances my experience." Another felt that his wife as a clergy woman had a big impact on his own spiritual life. It is of interest that a number of clergy husbands were members of administrative boards and regional bodies. This would be highly unusual for a wife of a clergyman.

Going to a church other than the wife's was not uncommon for a number of reasons. A father of teenagers in New Jersey continued to attend the church the whole family had joined together before the wife entered seminary. She was eventually assigned to a church thirty-four miles away. Another spouse, who had many organization abilities, decided to go to an urban mission church where he felt his skills were needed and he could express his faith commitment. One spouse of a rabbi continued to attend his temple in a metropolitan area while his wife's assignment was sixty miles away. Some husbands of different faith backgrounds worked out alternating attendance at her church and at his denomination. One associate pastor from a mixed religious marriage tried to go with her husband and child to his church when she was free of worship responsibilities at hers.

Serious conflict was present for other husbands in finding a comfortable expression for their spirituality. A young father in a rural midwestern area had been very active until he was asked by a regional administrator not to be so outspoken. "Gravely disillusioned with the conventional system," this husband withdrew from all church activities, experiencing a mixture of sadness and anger that his commitment was rebuffed. The impact on his marriage and his wife's career is yet to be determined, but it is clear that the conflict in resolving this dilemma is painful for both of them. Another spouse was so angry at his wife's choice of a second career that he quit any formal expression of religious faith. Still another quipped, "It's her problem that I am not involved." Yet another husband acknowledged with sadness that his lack of involvement probably caused her distress.

Support: Scarce and Resisted

Since they were married twenty years ago, Dick and Pat Carpenter had lived in an urban area in the midwest. Over Dick's objections and after much soul-searching, Pat decided to enter seminary, feeling "called" when their three sons were teenagers. Dick's responses to her decision were feelings of loss, abandonment, and anger. Dick felt he had to assume most of the supervision of the teenagers, as well as making other adjustments. It was not what he expected out of life. He finds it hard to bend, making it difficult for her to make the choices that arise between work and home. Dick does not wish to participate with her in her career or her church. Bouts of anger have been expressed and much negotiation is needed for the marriage to survive. The congregation sees him as unsupportive; he sees himself as trying to be supportive of his wife as a person, not as a pastor. As a couple, they struggle alone. There are no support groups or church administrators sensitive to their pain.

Our hope would be that support reduces the stress we are under. However, for women who are ministers and rabbis, and for their non-clergy husbands, there seems to be little support outside of immediate friends, family and each other.

The lack of formal support for clergy husbands from religious authorities is one area of concern. Husbands answered that they were always invited to spouses' meetings adjacent to the clergy affair, but felt awkward, like "a third foot." Often the only man attending, they did not feel deeply welcomed. Several spouses suggested that a general introductory workshop would be helpful for all spouses, male and female, to have a clearer understanding of what to anticipate, how to handle parish issues, and how to balance living in a "fishbowl." One diocese in a mid-Atlantic state did have a two-day retreat addressing these issues, which was praised by one husband.

Generally, there is a lack of interest or perceived need for any type of support for husbands. Husbands, except those few who were dissatisfied with their wife's career choices, did not feel that they needed outside attention. One husband insisted that it would not be "macho" to need support. Most respondents only knew one or two other clergy husbands and had no substantive contact with them. "I only know three or four men whose marriages have survived." That kind of comment belies the apparent minimizing of the stressfulness of their situation and the stress level of their wives' occupations. Rayburn, Richmond and Rogers concluded.

> Somehow, clergy women as a group have not adequately communicated their pain and stress or its harmful nature to the men in their lives: to their husbands and to their male colleagues in the clergy. Perhaps these men have not listened well either.[4]

Disillusionment about congregations was expressed by one respondent. He expected the congregation to be a source of nurture for him and his wife. But when his family was preoccupied with a seriously ill child, he felt as if they suffered alone. He speculated that their trauma somehow minimized the crisis of congregational members and that the members were disturbed by that. He concluded bitterly, "You should never expect emotional, spiritual, or psychological nurture. You won't get it!" Perhaps more husbands have found this to be true, but since they never expected caring, they may not be as aware of its absence.

Friends are often a source of strength for individuals and couples, yet developing friends as a couple has been a hurdle for many. Some were friendly with other clergy families, especially where the congregation had a multiple staff. Very few couples had close friends in the churches where their wives served. Couples also stated that there was little time or opportunity to develop friendships outside the church. Those in small rural areas had even more difficulty finding compatible friends since the local people did not always have the same interests. Some tried to keep up with seminary friends, but that was not possible to maintain for long. A Friday night event with friends was a commitment for one couple, but few others did this. In general, developing joint friends got very low priority.

Ministers' wives are quick to talk about the stresses created by overly dependent or demanding parishioners. It is not uncommon for some congregational members to see the clergy as an authority figure or parental replacement and to have unrealistic expectations. These individuals unconsciously try to complete unresolved developmental issues by their attachment to parental substitutes. When such situations arise, they often intrude into the clergy family. In this survey, this intrusive behavior was never mentioned as a stressor. It is a curious omission for which there could be many theoretical explanations. Denial of this behavior may be one way this emotional threat is handled by husbands. Congregational members may be less intrusive, sensing a husband's presence rather than a minister's wife. Perhaps authority figure issues may be slower to develop in a congregation with a female clergy, but one might expect the parental substitution issues to arise quickly. Whatever the reasons, this concern needs further study.

Conclusion

Men married to women clergy are diverse in their attitudes and approaches to life but face many common challenges. These couples are to be admired as they handle the stresses of clergy life with unfolding expectations. By virtue of the inherent pressures, their marriages need constant attention and nurture to flourish. Perhaps more support could be offered. Women clergy have formed support groups both denominationally and geographically. Creative thinking by clergy and religious administrators could generate support to clergy husbands in new ways. With the higher percentage of women in seminary, these issues need to be addressed with new ideas. Religion professionals with administrative responsibility need to develop a roster of therapists and counselors who are skilled and sensitive to these unique circumstances to be a referral source. Providing orientation to all spouses or potential spouses could enable more open discussions regarding expectations and roles.

Some respondents had the experience of their wife being the first woman clergy in the area. These husbands saw themselves and their wives as pioneers. In a broader sense, all these couples are pioneers. They are participating in changing a societal role as they venture into ministry. It is well stated by Charles L. Baker in the Foreword of *Men Married to Ministers:*

> They are a microcosm of our society and its response to the new and developing role of gender in western civilization. They demonstrate that the events which free women from oppressive gender-based constraints also can free men, but only if men choose to accept their newly available empowerment and responsibility.[5]

As traditional roles change, we all are presented with new opportunities for growth. We owe a tribute to these couples as they open new doors for themselves and us.

Notes

1. Harlan London and Katherine Allen, "Family Versus Career Responsibilities," *Marriage and Family Review* 9 (3–4) 203.

2. Laura Deming and Jack Stubbs, *Men Married to Ministers* (Washington, D.C.: Alban Institute, 1986), Foreword.

3. C. Rayburn, L. J. Richmond, and L. Rogers, "Outlooks of Seminarians and Ministers on Women in Clergy," *Journal of Pastoral Counseling* 23 (1) 43.

4. Ibid., 30.

5. Laura Deming and Jack Stubbs, op. cit.

6. One final thought: SPICE is a newsletter that addresses clergy spouse issues of all kinds and can be a source of shared experiences. SPICE is published by Clergy Family Publications, Inc., P. O. Box 127, Alpha, Michigan 49902. Laura Deming, who co-authored *Men Married to Ministers,* is founder and editor.

Matthew Schenning, M.Div.
Norma Schenning, M.Div.

=============================

Clergy Couples

Clergy Couples in Historical Perspective

James and Thelma Mowrey, United Methodists, argue convincingly that the apparent new emphasis on husband-wife teamwork is in reality simply a return to old ways of doing things. In a pamphlet accompanying their 1982 Doctor of Ministry project, "A Team Ministry Model for a Clergy Couple Serving in One Context," is the following historical overview used with the authors' encouragement.

Clergy couples are "new" on the religious scene only in their numbers, the publicity surrounding them, and their increasing availability to serve as denominations open ordination to women and opportunities to couples in ministry. The earliest recorded Christian couple in ministry is Prisca and Aquilla as found in Acts, Romans, and 1 Corinthians.

An overview of clergy couples requires first a consideration of women as church leaders. Authors such as Joan Morris, Rosemary Ruether, and others bring to us little-known facts of history which show that women have had important leadership functions in the church in administrative and hierarchical matters, as well as spiritual ones. History tends to show that women have had fewer leadership roles in the church in the nineteenth century and twentieth centuries than in earlier periods.

During the formative monastic period in the church, many prominent male leaders labored in partnership with female companions as, for example, St. Francis of Assisi and Clare, and Benedict of Nursia and his sister. The influence of Susannah Wesley and the Countess of Huntingdon upon the Wesleys cannot be overemphasized.

Prior to the industrial revolution, husband and wife team labor was common. Very likely the tailor used material made by the spouse

179

and the family. The farm family toiled side by side. Shopkeepers and craftpersons frequently were couples working together.

The industrial revolution which took manufacturing from the home and shop to centralize it in large factories tended to break down the couple labors. Men began going away to work. Women tended to stay at home, managing things there. A fairly rigid division of labors became the new norm for the family.

World War II saw a dramatic rise of women in the labor force and armed services, but the end of the war saw this temporary situation ended. America entered a low period in the number of women gainfully employed in industry and the professions.

In the 1970s, with the phenomena of labor saving devices, predictable family planning methods, and increased numbers of women going off to work, men and women began more to share incomes, household duties, and child care. Women expanded their vision of call into areas formerly reserved for men or single women. As this spirit affected the church, it led to women as well as men recognizing calls to ordained ministry. Today, most main-line Protestant denominations ordain women, and pressure is great within the Roman Catholic tradition to move in this direction.

In historical perspective, clergy couples have gone full circle: recapturing the pre-industrial revolution norm of husband and wife working together in their common calling, and recapturing the earlier truth that God indeed does call women as well as men to be ministers and leaders in the church. Clergy couples are a significant minority here to stay and to be understood and seen in their full potential.[1]

Although clergy couples are on the increase, as yet there are no accurate figures on how many couples are working in ministry in the different denominations. However, the Evangelical Lutheran Church in America reportedly has two hundred and forty clergy couples (twenty of which are married to a non-Lutheran partner).[2]

Clergy couples, to us, are a team in the most complete sense of the word. It is a team that is able to experience great joy and freedom in working with a partner not only respected, but loved, and who loves in return. It is a team that is able to share thoughts, visions, problems, fears, joys and tears with one another with honesty, much more so than might be attempted with someone not a partner in marriage as well as ministry.

Naturally, there are pitfalls to be aware of, but speaking for ourselves we consider being a clergy couple to be basically a blessing because the blessings far outweigh any pitfalls or problems that can occur from being a couple in ministry. Matt and I have always enjoyed working together, whether in the home, on a hobby, in the church, or whatever. Married for twelve years, our relationship has always been a true partnership, even before we were both ordained, so it follows that we would also view ministry as a partnership, a partnership that is a blessing.

Currently, we pastor two separate congregations, but our goal for the not too distant future is to co-pastor one congregation. We believe we will be an even better team when we are serving in the same church. On the other hand, there are some clergy couples who feel they simply could not work in the same church together, because their differences in personality are too extreme.

Either way, the same church or two churches, it is a blessing for us to be in the same vocation and to be able to understand the joys, frustrations, and challenges that are part of being a pastor. To be able to understand completely what the other is going through enables us to be good listeners and to offer support and perhaps even some advice if we have already been through a similar ordeal.

Another blessing is being able to relieve one another of a work overload. We have, on occasion, made hospital visits for each other, and we have enjoyed traveling together if we both have parishioners in the same hospital or nearby hospitals. We have also co-taught confirmation classes, preached for one another in the case of illness, and fielded telephone calls when the other needed some uninterrupted time.

Sharing sermon ideas and reading our sermons to each other is also a great help. Sermons ideas can be shared in any group of pastors who meet on a weekly basis, of course. But we are able to bounce ideas off each other at any time during the week as fresh new thoughts and insights come to us. Plus, we can divide up the research work that goes into sermon preparation.

A big advantage of working together in ministry is flexible hours. While we are not always able to spend our evenings together because of meetings, we can arrange to go to lunch together during the week, or share other time together whenever we both have a morning or afternoon free.

However, as any clergy couple knows from experience, there are pitfalls to be aware of and, hopefully, navigated around. Conflation is one of those pitfalls. Conflation is when a clergy couple's professional and personal lives become so intertwined that they are indistinguishable from one another. This is more apt to be true of a couple pastoring in one congregation than with those serving two separate churches. When serving together in one parish the home can frequently become an extension of the office. Then the feeling is that you never leave work, and there is no place to experience renewal.

When serving one congregation the tendency is for mealtimes, playtime, and bedtime to become "churchtime." Couples can find themselves continually at work, having staff meetings over dinner, in the bedroom, or while watching television. And although pastors do not work a 9 to 5 day, they need time away from the job. Even God rested when he finished the job of creating the world. The pitfall of conflation can be overcome by clergy couples through the conscious effort of pursuing something that they enjoy doing together that will take them out of the arena of the church.

In order to continually renew the relationship with one another, time needs to be spent together that is not devoted to discussing the business of the church and its needs. There are different ways of accomplishing this. One way is to make an agreement that mealtimes will be reserved for conversation other than church business. Or a hobby can be taken up together, something that both enjoy doing. For us, bedtime is definitely not a time for shop talk.

The "day off" can become a pitfall instead of a renewal. In order that it may truly be an experience of renewal, try to keep it sacred. There are always the exceptions, of course—funerals or other emergency situations—but if at all possible, the day off should be a day of relaxation and revitalization. Sometimes the only way to do this is to leave the house! Go to visit that new mall, explore a park, or take in an afternoon matinee. Otherwise the phone will ring and it will be business as usual.

My husband was shocked when I said I wanted my own horse. He knew I was a horse lover but had never expected it to come to this. However, we now own two horses and they are our time away. The time and energy that is spent caring for, feeding, and riding them takes our minds off the business of the church and we can concentrate solely on enjoying our time together.

When we are grooming and caring for a horse, our concentration must be on him, totally. We look for signs of good health or illness. Is he off his feed? Is his coat shining? And when we are on the trail our concentration is on the ride or the scenery, the woodland creatures, or the beautiful day. It is time we enjoy spending together and it helps us to relax. Our meals may be interrupted by the telephone and even bedtime can be interrupted by an emergency, but the time spent with the horses is our time, a time of renewal.

Moving on can be a problem for a clergy couple serving two

separate congregations. Two calls in close proximity to each other are not always easy to locate. Some couples choose to move on when one has received a call to a good position in the hope that the spouse will also be able to receive a call nearby.

In serving two congregations that both have parsonages, the problem is: "In which will we live?" One solution might be to request that the congregations provide a housing allowance so that the couple can purchase or rent their own home. The congregations can then sell, rent or utilize their parsonages as they see fit.

A problem that we experienced personally, as did another clergy couple we know of, was that of living in the spouse's parsonage. We had been living in the parsonage owned by my husband's congregation for four years prior to my ordination. The congregation that called me did not own a parsonage. After my call and ordination, some members of my husband's congregation wanted to know if my congregation was going to pay rent. I had been living in this house with my family for four years and now they wanted me to pay rent!

We felt the whole idea of paying rent was ludicrous, of course. We stated that it was their parsonage and my congregation would expect no benefits from their house or property should they decide to sell. We also made them aware of the fact that if I were gainfully employed in some other line of work they would not expect my employer to pay rent for me to live in the parsonage. Thankfully, the situation resolved itself without too much conflict.

When called to a team ministry, salary can become an issue. Unfortunately for women pastors, sexism still exists. And this sexism frequently shows up in the form of salary. In fact, some congregations reportedly have called a woman simply because they feel they can offer her a smaller salary than her male counterpart. When meeting with the call committee, a clergy couple can stress that their ministry is a true partnership by asking for two equal salaries. Clergy couples we know who have settled for sharing one salary instead of two have later said that it was a mistake.

Matt was ordained nine years ago, and I was ordained two years ago. So to many of Matt's parishioners I was still thought of as just the pastor's wife. We have had a difficult time educating them to the fact that I am now an ordained pastor also.

When someone calls our house and I answer, the usual question is, "May I speak to the pastor please?" When I respond that I am one of the two pastors there and ask which one they wish to speak with, frequently there is confused silence on the other end. People, especially those who have had little contact with the church, still have the expectation that the pastor will be a male and are taken back when a female voice responds, "This is the pastor."

Maternity and paternity leave for couples entering the ministry with young children or the prospect of children is a pitfall to navigate around. Most couples today do not consider that raising children is solely the role of the mother. Both parents may desire to participate as fully as possible in raising their offspring. When being interviewed by a congregation, clergy couples may wish to discuss maternity and paternity leave with the call committee. Even though that may be down the road a few years, during the call process is the best time to deal with it.

A detail to be worked out by clergy couples is the scheduling of office hours so that someone is home and able to care for the children, especially pre-school age youngsters. One spouse might even want to work part-time for a while. Or to keep things on an even keel, both may choose part-time or three-quarters time.

Housework needs to be divided up evenly, unless you are lucky enough to afford outside help to come in and clean. Although Matt and I never sat down and worked out a deliberate schedule, as we worked together a pattern fell into place that was satisfactory to both of us. We didn't assign chores but felt as though we were both doing our fair share and that the bulk of the work was not falling more on one than on the other. There was never the expectation that the housework was the wife's job! Also, regarding housework, children, and ministry, it is important that we not attempt to stick the tasks we don't like on our partner. Teamwork doesn't mean only doing the jobs we want and like, and leaving the others for your partner.

Finally, a source of blessing unique to clergy couples is support. Although others frequently offer us support, when working with my spouse, that support can come in the form of a much needed hug in the office, a loving shoulder to cry on, or just in hearing the words, "I love you." Those intimate gestures coming from someone who loves me and whom I love can help drain off fatigue, or bring a moment of cheer to an otherwise bad day.

The Alban Institute conducted research on couples in ministry in the three predecessor bodies of the recently formed Evangelical Lutheran Church in America. Two hundred and nine written surveys were received. This data was the raw material for a conference led by Roy M. Oswald of the Alban Institute.[3] Ninety-seven persons attended the Conference on Couples in Professional Ministry held in Elizabethtown, Pennsylvania, July 16–18, 1985. Matt and I were participants in the conference. The two hundred and nine written surveys broke down as follows:

102 female (72 ordained, 30 lay professionals)
 98 males (96 ordained, 2 lay professionals)
168 total ordained
 32 total lay professionals

The data collected reflects some of the insights already expressed in this chapter. The blessings of serving as a couple in professional ministry extracted from the research are: understanding, support, common interest, flexible work hours, meshing of strengths and weaknesses, androgynous lifestyle and ministry.

Understanding was seen as the most popular advantage for couples in ministry by the respondents. They were not lone rangers in the ministry. There was always someone to share the joys, workload, and disappointments. Many felt that this type of intimacy actually strengthened their marriage.

Flexible hours was viewed as a positive advantage for couples in ministry. These ministers could get together at unconventional hours. Flexible hours enabled them the opportunity to have a greater share in child-rearing. And because these couples shared each other's company during the day, evening appointments and meetings were less burdensome than they might otherwise have been.

The advantage of meshing strengths and weaknesses was found primarily among couples who worked together in the same parish. Few ministers are good at every aspect of ministry. The team approach complements one another's gifts and allows for individual shortcomings. One person's talents and skills may be in the area of worship and Christian education. The other's may be in administration and evangelism. Also, the ability to deal with different, as well as difficult, people varies among ministers. Whereas one pastor may not be able to reach a particular parishioner, the partner in ministry may have that ability.

Another gift that couples serving in the same parish have is the ability of modeling a male and female perspective of the faith to the church. St. Paul's goal of being "all things to all people" is out of reach for most, if not all. Yet a couple in ministry is able to demonstrate that "service" is better realized when it is performed together. However, some respondents stated that for this team approach to ministry to be effective, more attention must be given to nurturing the couple's marriage. A dysfunctioning marriage relationship will certainly disable a couple's ministry.

Although the list of disadvantages of doing ministry as a couple is longer than the list of advantages, most couples in the survey and the conference felt that the advantages far outweighed the liabilities of couples in ministry. The list of disadvantages included: conflation, little time for "us," church conflict spilling over into marriage, lack of support for this style of ministry, difficulty of staying healthy spiritually, jealousy and competition, serving in different settings, sexism in the church.

Time for "Us"

Just because couples are always working together does not mean that these care-givers are taking enough time to care for each other. Couples can borrow from the equity that they have accumulated in their marriage, but there is a limit. Couples in ministry, like the couples in their congregations, must make time for each other. Participants in the conference were asked, "Which vow takes precedence when conflict arises—marriage or service?" Couples are realizing that when their marriage relationship is nurtured and continually renewed, their ministry also thrives. The opposite is not always true. Couples in ministry, in the survey, and at the clergy conference more often gave preference to marriage vows.

Conflicts at work can easily spill over into the marriage. Arguments at church do come home with pastors. Couples need first to be aware of this problem and then to strive not to let the work of the church overwhelm one's marriage.

Couples in ministry experience a general lack of support for their style of ministry. Just as members of congregations have little understanding of the pressures and problems a pastor faces, so too they are rarely cognizant of the problems couples in ministry face. But that is not a condition exclusive to laity; it is also shared by clergy colleagues, bishops, and bishops' staff. Couples in ministry are more often viewed as a placement problem than as a blessing.

Couples also claim difficulty in staying spiritually healthy. They confide that they are often "churched out." This condition can make praying together on a regular basis difficult. Daily devotions more often than not consist of grace before meals. Days of recollection or regularly planned spiritual retreats may benefit the spiritual renewal of couples.

Jealousy and/or competition was seen as a possible stumbling block for couples serving the same parish. "Am I as good a preacher, teacher, counselor, visitor, administrator as my clergy spouse? Am I getting a fair share of weddings and funerals?" Women said that they felt their husbands were taken more seriously as pastors, while men noted that there were more opportunities for their wives to serve on synodical and national boards. Complementary gifts and talents which are sometimes viewed as assets for couples, may appear as liabilities at other times.

Serving in different ministerial settings has its liabilities, too. There are two schedules to juggle. Finding time for each other and the family becomes more challenging. As mentioned earlier, mobility becomes a greater problem. One conclusion from the Clergy Couple Conference was that couples need to be prepared for the fact that during their partnership in ministry, half of the team may be unemployed for a period of time. Of course, couples serving in the same congregation have a mobility problem, too, as there are few congregations that can afford two full-time pastors.

A financial disadvantage that is experienced by one partner of the clergy couples is sexism in the church. In a church that is two thousand years old and has until recently been male-dominated in leadership, the woman pastor receives a less than equal share of acceptance. Too often parishioners, and even male clergy themselves, have deference to the male pastor. Whether it is an unconscious response or learned behavior, it is painfully real to the female pastor.

Although some of the same blessings and challenges that exist for clergy couples also exist in staff ministry. There is one very big difference. TRUST! In a staff ministry a senior pastor is frequently looking over his/her shoulder because there are assistants or associates who could be willing to take his/her job. Competition and jealousy can arise in all working relationships, but it is freeing to know that your partner in ministry loves and trusts you. Therein lies the great strength in couples serving together. This model of ministry, although still new, has the potential of being a great blessing to a congregation and the church at large.

Notes

1. Richard Lund, *One in Marriage, Two in Ministry: Collected Clergy Couple Resources* (Doctoral dissertation, 1987).

2. Personal communication from a denominational executive in the Evangelical Lutheran Church in America, 1988.

3. Roy M. Oswald, research by The Alban Institute, Inc., 4125 Nebraska Avenue, N.W., Washington, D.C. 20016, 1985.

Suggestions for Further Reading

Allen, Arthur and Nancy, *Clergy Couples Connect:* Quarterly publication originating in United Methodist circles. Re-Creation Ministries at RR 1 Box 44; Stuart IA 50250. Subscription cost: $10.00.
American Lutheran Church, Office of Support to Ministries, *Research on Clergy Marriages and Spouses* (Minneapolis, 1978): Unpublished documents from several denominations bound together by the Library at Luther Northwestern Seminary, 2481 Como Avenue, Saint Paul, MN 55108-1496. Available via interlibrary loan.
Anderson, Herbert and Phyllis, *Two Ministries and One Marriage* (Resource: A Continuing Education Cassette Series for Pastors by the Seminary Faculties of The American Lutheran Church, Series 6—May 1979, Side 1. Minneapolis: Augsburg Publishing House).
Bowman, Joan, and Roy Oswald, *Women and Men Together: A Transforming Power for Self, Church and World* (Washington D.C.: The Alban Institute, 1983).
Carroll, Jackson W., Barbara Hargrove, and Adair Lummis, *Women of the Cloth: A New Opportunity for the Churches* (San Francisco: Harper & Row, 1983).
Clergy Couples: Dynamic Duals in Ministry: Occasional newsletter circulated by United Methodist Rex Van Beck from 1976 through 1982. Several issues included in *Research on Clergy Marriages* (cited above). Other *may* be in the United Methodist Archives at Drew University, Madison NJ 07940.
Clergy Couples of the Presbyterian Family. *CCPF Newsletter:* Quarterly publication issues occasionally from 1981 through 1986. Several issues bound in Lund's *One in Marriage, Two in Ministry: Collected Clergy Couple Resources.*
Clergy Couples of the Presbyterian Family, "Two by Two—Partners in Marriage and Ministry," 1983: Twenty minute color filmstrip highlighting ministries of six clergy couples serving in diverse settings across the country. Available from Presbyterian Church (USA) Office of Professional Development, 341 Ponce De Leon Ave NE, Atlanta GA 30365-5401.
Couples in Marriage and Ministry, *CMM Newsletter:* Published summer and fall of 1986, winter of 1987 for clergy couples in the Association of Evangelical Lutheran Churches, The American Lu-

theran Church, and the Lutheran Church in America. Bound in Lund's *One in Marriage, Two in Ministry: Collected Clergy Couple Resources.*

Detrick, Ralph and Mary, "Marriages of Two Clergy-Persons," *Pastoral Psychology,* Vol. 30, No. 3 (Spring 1982), pp 170–178: Succinct description of the relationship, listing advantages and disadvantages for congregations and individuals. Includes mid-1981 summary of numbers in eleven denominations.

Egolf-Fox, Kim, "A Family Affair: Sharing a Pastorate," *Christian Ministry* (January 1986), pp. 14–15: Two half-time Baptist co-pastors divide the load, classing responsibilities as shared, alternated, and divided.

Faus, Nancy Rosenberger, *Clergy Couples: An Analysis of a New Style of Ministry in the Church of the Brethren* (Doctor of Ministry thesis, Chicago Theological Seminary, 1981): Detailed descriptions of the work of seventeen Brethren couples. Little analysis.

Jensen, Charles Henry, *A Study of Career Goal Frustration Among Clergy Couples in the American Baptist Churches* (Doctor of Ministry thesis, Eastern Baptist Theological Seminary, 1979): Studied nine couples, observing frustrations centering about: (1) placement, (2) mobility, (3) spouse competition, (4) time management, (5) sexism, (6) demands of children. One copy at Bethel Theological Seminary Library in St. Paul, Minnesota.

Lund, Richard, *One in Marriage, Two in Ministry: Collected Clergy Couple Resources,* 1987: Original and collected resources of broad interest, narrow distribution. One copy in library of Luther Northwestern Seminary, 2481 Como Ave., St Paul, MN 55108-1496.

Lundahl, Glenn W., *Ministry: Married Couples in Ordained Ministry* (specialization project for Doctor of Ministry degree at Denver cluster of Lutheran School of Theology at Chicago, May 1982): Author sent questionnaires to bishops of The American Lutheran Church and Lutheran Church in America plus nineteen LCA clergy couples. Quotes from most of the responses in detail, albeit with little analysis.

Mitchell, Kenneth, *Marriage and Ministry of Clergy Couples,* 1978: One of four major addresses from the 1978 clergy couples consultation sponsored by National Council of Churches. Transcribed by Richard Lund. Included in his work (above). Summary of the consultation itself written by John and Nancy Jo von Lackum (see below).

Mowrey, James and Thelma, *A Team Ministry Model for a Clergy*

Couple Serving in One Context (Doctor of Ministry project, United Theological Seminary, September 1982): Notes on historical and contemporary clergy couple ministries based on research and questionnaires. Copy available through Library, United Theological Seminary, 1810 Harvard Boulevard, Dayton, OH 45406-4598.

Nordstrom, Carol Shimmin, *Clergy Couples in Shared-Call Ministry* (Doctor of Ministry project, Luther Northwestern Seminary, 1987): Looks with special interest at issues of power as experienced by couples in the Evangelical Covenant Church. Available through the Library, Luther Northwestern Seminary (2481 Como Ave., Saint Paul, MN 55108-1496).

Oswald, Roy M., *Episcopal Couples in Professional Ministry*, 1986: A report, with frequent extemporaneous additions, on survey of Episcopal couples presented to a conference of Episcopalians. Transcribed by Richard Lund and bound in his work (see above).

Tamorria, Dona and Michael, "Couples in Professional Ministry: A Report on Data Collected from 209 Individuals, Each of Whom Is Part of a Couple in Professional Ministry." Washington D.C.: The Alban Institute, 1986: Preliminary report. The Alban Institute hoped by late 1987 to weave material from both the Episcopal and Lutheran studies together in one piece.

Rallings, E.M., and David Pratto, *Two-Clergy Marriages: A Special Case of Dual Careers* (Lanham MD: University Press of America, 1984): Excellent and concise, based on interviews with fifty-four couples in the southeastern United States, primarily United Methodist. The *only* commercially published book on clergy couples to date.

Stenman, Joanne and Eric, "Partners in Marriage: Partners in Ministry," *Lutheran Partners*, Charter Issue (May/June 1985), published at Minneapolis by Augsburg Publishing House, pp. 21–24: Humorous and straightforward reflections by first Lutheran Church in America clergy couple.

von Lackum, John P and Nancy Jo, *A Report on Clergy Couples and The Ecumenical Couple Consultation* (New York: Professional Church Leadership, Division of Education and Ministry, National Council of the Churches of Christ in the USA, 1979): Copies still available from Alban Institute, possibly from Professional Church Leadership (475 Riverside Drive, Rm. 770, New York, NY 10115-0050) as well.

Wayman, Phyllis Tyler, "Building on Noah's Ark: Clergy Couples in Ministry," *The Christian Ministry* 14 (May 1983), pp 31–32.

August G. Lageman, Ph.D.

The Congregation: A Family System

A Unique Marriage

From a systematic point of view, one cannot look at a congregation without looking at the pastor and the pastor's relationship to and participation in the congregation system. Traditionally the image of a "marriage" between pastor and congregation has been used. Theologically the relationship has often been viewed as a covenant. Within this covenant there is, I believe, a multi-level series of contracts. The different levels of contracts in marriages have been delineated by Clifford Sager. Sager maintains that there are three levels to a marriage contract: the first is conscious and verbalized; the second is conscious and not verbalized; the third is the unconscious—the level beyond awareness—dimension of the marriage.[1] In my experience I have found these three levels existing in the relationships I have had with congregations. Some of the difficulties pastors may encounter result from ignoring or refusing to acknowledge that the second and third levels exist.

Using this marriage framework, the relationship between pastor and congregation is unique. From the pastor's perspective it is a polygamous relationship—there are many spouses. From the congregation's perspective it is monogamous—there is often only one pastor. This provides the relationship with unique stresses and opportunities. A prime example is that it creates a relational context in which the pastor is the first candidate for the overfunctioning (the identified patient) position. One person with many bosses creates a context in which burnout is a distinct possibility.

Systems thinking has revolutionized how therapists view individuals, couples, and families. One term frequently used to describe the position of the therapist is that of observer and participant. The therapist becomes a part of the couple's family system. At the same time, the therapist has the responsibility to observe what is happening in the marriage. This duality of observer and participant is the position from which the therapist functions. The key is to balance both in a way that is effective in the therapeutic process. The key is the same, albeit in a different context, for the pastor. It is possible to err by overemphasizing either one dimension or the other. In my experience we clergy tend to get lost in the participant role (the subjective one) and disconnect from the observer position (the objective dimension). Another conceptual distinction from systems therapy may help to clarify the dichotomy of the situation. In working with couples and families, the therapist usually focuses more on process, and the quality and nature of the interactions in the relationship, rather than on the content, the actuality of what the family is discussing. We tend to get caught up in the myriad of content issues in the congregational life and neglect the process issues. Again, as with observer and participant, a healthy balance between process and content is vital.

Boundaries

Boundaries are important both in the relationship between pastor and congregation and in the larger context, i.e. the denomination which institutes policies that may either facilitate or interfere with their establishment of boundaries. In my own denomination—United Methodist—the parsonage system makes the establishment of healthy boundaries difficult in that it creates a dual set of relationships. The congregation, which sets the pastor's salary, functions as the "boss." At the same time the congregation functions as the pastor's landlord. This situation is ripe for the phenomenon of displacement of difficulties and feelings from one dimension of the relationship to the other.

One pastor I currently supervise was describing the hierarchy in his denomination. The congregation forms the base of the pyramid, the pastor is the middle level, and the denominational executive is at the top. As this pastor described his own anger and frustration, it became clear to me that of these three hierarchical levels the congregation was the most powerful and the executive was reactive to the congregation. The pastor was at the bottom of the power pyramid. No wonder he was overstressed!

In understanding boundaries and related issues, it is important to have an understanding of the family lives of the people within the congregation as well as the congregation as a whole. Families are sometimes enmeshed—the boundaries have broken down. Being an individual in such a family is difficult. Such families are fused, i.e.

stuck together. Is this a typical or atypical family pattern in the congregation? At the other end of the spectrum are those families that are cut off from their families of origin and from others as well (often the one-third of the congregation who don't participate). Murray Bowen has pointed out that those who are cut off are just as stuck as those who are enmeshed. Both are responses to family emotional issues that have become toxic. In one congregation I pastored this showed up in an interesting way. The "old guard" was aging and dying off. The surviving spouses generally remarried someone within the same group within one year. This pattern occurred seven times in a five year period, a clear sign of some of the emotional fusion within the congregation. People were remarrying in order to resolve and replace their losses.

The key issue, in my judgment, with regard to boundaries is respect for the privacy of the pastor's personal and family life. Or does the congregation expect the pastor's family life to occur within the congregation's life? Friends and support systems outside the congregation become critical when the pastor is experiencing conflict within the congregation. Establishing clear boundaries is the responsibility of both the congregation and the pastor. Congregations do not automatically form clear boundaries unless the pastor is clear as to where his or her boundaries are.

Power and Intimacy

In family systems theory there are two families with which we have all been involved. The first is our family of origin; in ecclesiastical terms this would be the congregation in which we were raised. Our present family is our family of choice. The congregation as a voluntary organization has many of the dynamics of our present family—our family of choice. All families deal with issues of power and intimacy. Is the life of the congregation such that the events in a family's life cycle are shared and celebrated? The health of a congregation is not a simple matter to assess. Health is characterized by the respect, love and freedom people give and receive. Is the life of the congregation characterized by emotional and spiritual intimacy? Are these dimensions of closeness forced or avoided? Some churches replicate a typical pattern in American families—an over-involved mother and a distant father. I have seen this become typical in congregations where the men work on finance, trustee and administrative boards (paralleling what they do in the work world), while the women do the program dimension of church life. By splitting in this way, growth is avoided and problematic family patterns are reproduced in the congregation's life. Healthy families balance power and intimacy. Likewise, healthy congregations maintain clear lines of structure and authority while at the same time providing a safe place (sanctuary) for people to share the joys and struggles in their own lives.

The word "diagnosis," even in the mental health field, has some negative connotations. It sometimes implies judgment or labeling. Diagnosis means to known through or to understand. The pastor needs to diagnose his or her congregation. What are the idiosyncrasies? What are its strengths and resources? What are the toxic and hidden issues in the congregation? I suggest as a guiding principle the assumption: What you don't know will hurt you. I learned this from a colleague who innocently appointed as co-chairs of a stewardship campaign a man and a woman both from families active in the congregation. After six months of a series of difficulties, my colleague found out that they had had an affair with each other several years before. As clergy, we often shy away from toxic and hidden issues. I once supervised a young pastor working with his first congregation. Prior to his arrival the treasurer of the congregation had embezzled $40,000 from the church funds. The congregation had since divided into three factions: one group wanted to deny that it had ever happened, another group wanted to forgive the treasurer, and the third group wanted justice. After being initiated into the parish life with this issue, that pastor received his second appointment two years later. This time he succeeded a pastor who had been defrocked for pedophilia with a twelve year old boy from the parish. The congregation came to the pastor with a long list of petty issues, all of which had intense emotions attached to them. The congregation kept personalizing the issues. I tried to coach the pastor to avoid the personal nature of the issues and to help the congregation work with the underlying problems. At present both pastor and congregation had been able to move on with the life and work of the church. It is not the toxicity of the issue that determines the outcome; rather it is the manner in which the emotionally charged issue is handled that makes the difference.

Pastors often have more power than they think they do. The church is a volunteer organization and as such brings out the best and the worst in people. I have seen business executives behave at church board meetings in ways they would consider improper in the management of their corporations. This is the phenomenon of displacement which we will consider shortly.

Congregations often give inordinate power to the most vocal members. People act out—attention getting behaviors, sibling rivalries, seduction, scapegoating are all performed on the congregational stage. While dealing with these issues requires skill and patience, it does not necessarily follow that being a pastor includes accepting abuse. I once received from my district superintendent, after the congregation's annual meeting, an anonymous letter enumerating my faults. I was hurt and angry. As I struggled during the week with the topic for Sunday's sermon, I finally decided to preach on the letter. I was able to vent my anger and explain why I did not think an anonymous letter was the appropriate way to deal with the issues. A year later the congregation's annual evaluation listed the "ability to deal with criticism constructively" as my major strength. The message I conveyed was clear: I would deal with criticism, but I would not accept abuse. Pastors educate congregations as to how they expect to be treated.

Your Inheritance

Each congregation has its unique history, and each congregation lives within a denominational context. For churches that function with a "call" system, the process of calling a pastor resembles that of the adoption process. For churches that function with a hierarchical model, the congregation and the pastor inherit the unresolved issues that exist between the congregation and the denomination. The Bowen approach to family therapy was the first to describe the intergenerational transmission process which lives, in different forms, in each congregation. The new pastor inherits the unresolved issues of the congregation and the previous pastor. These unresolved issues are close to the surface when a pastor leaves and a new pastor arrives. Some members of the congregation feel a strong loyalty to the departing pastor, who was the one, perhaps, who buried a spouse, celebrated a baptism, or counseled a marriage. This pastor cannot, in a sense, be emotionally replaced. The issue for these parishioners is whether or not they will be able to move through the grief process. Others, because of hurts and disappointments with the previous pastor, are glad to see a new face. There is both an individual and a congregational grief process taking place. People are sad, mad, and glad. The departure of a pastor provides a window into the life of the congregation. Grief is the residue of the unresolved aspects of a relationship.

The other primary issue in congregational life is a theological, as well as political and systematic, issue. Who owns the ministry? Is the ministry something that the congregation and the pastor share? All too often the congregation sees ministry as residing in the minister. This leads to a common phenomenon—the ecclesiastical version of pilot error. When things go wrong in the parish, it is often easiest to blame the difficulties on the pastor. It is important for the new pastor to look at the congregation's history of blame to explain the source of parish conflict and problems.

Displacements and Triangles

Bowen theorizes that when difficulties arise in a two person relationship the process of triangulation occurs. The emotional process which has become too intense is rerouted through a third person. The pastor is often the first person invited to become the third side of the triangle (remember, a three-legged stool is more stable). This is instigated when a parishioner asks the pastor to act as his or her agent in some respect. Friedman cites a good example:

A woman with a terminal condition gave her minister a letter with specific instructions for her funeral, emphasizing that she desired absolutely no eulogy, nor personal remarks, nor family involvement. She had told her minister that her husband knew about the note, so the minister did not bother to show it to him (which would have been the right detriangling move that might have affected the eventual mourning).

When the woman died, her husband asked to see the note. It turned out that she had not shown it to him, only informed him of its existence. As is characteristic of the state of grief, the family said, "We must follow her wishes." The clergy woman was, therefore, totally unable to convince the family that they should do what was best for the survivors. But the effects of the triangling did not end there. As the minister drove over to conduct the funeral, she found she was also triangled with the rest of the congregational family. The note was preventing her from fulfilling her duty to aid their mourning. She found herself carrying on a monologue with the deceased woman, cursing her for the bind she had put her in.

As she mounted the pulpit for the service, she suddenly realized what to do. She read the note to the congregational family. At that moment, she said, her hostility evaporated like a mist, and she was able to perform the funeral according to the woman's wishes. After the service, the triangle had predictably shifted; the congregation was absolutely furious at the deceased.

Assume that the process of triangulation is occurring. To accept a request at face value is to risk getting lost in the content and being triangulated. Emotionally powerful events in either the pastor's family or in a family in the congregation can cause a displacement. When a colleague's seventeen-year-old son was hospitalized for chemical dependency, the congregation was very supportive, at least on the surface. At the same time, however, a series of parish crises began. A withdrawal of emotional energy is frequently noted on an unconscious level. When a displacement occurs, look for the partner to act in such a way as to reestablish the balance in the relationship. Displacements occur in the extended family as well as the work context and can happen in either direction.

Leadership and Change

In seminary I was taught a model of the minister as a change agent. I have come to realize that this model contains an element of paternalism. It also tends to invite a push/resist dynamic that is familiar to anyone who has done marriage counseling. One person pushes, the other resists. Sometimes the struggle evolves to deciding who is going to change whom. It also tends to evoke rigid inflexible attitudes from the congregation.

Friedman has described a different model that he calls leadership through self-differentiation. The responsibility of the leader is to be clear about his or her role in the system and to be in touch with many dimensions of the congregational system. The job of the leader is to be a non-anxious, non-reactive presence.

Building on Friedman, I suggest the image of the pastor as a catalyst in the congregational growth process. In this model I partici-

pate in the process and expect to grow and change myself. In my
development as a therapist, I have been involved in group therapy. I
learned a model wherein the therapist is responsible for the process.
The therapist monitors the process and teaches the members of the
group to do the actual therapy.

We as pastors need to be clear about the models upon which we
operate and the images that guide our ministry. One of the ministers I
supervise is now doing an interim ministry. Dick has a fascinating
image for his work—that of a bay pilot who comes on board for a
limited period of time to guide the ship through the bay. This interim
pastor knows the dynamics and processes of interim ministry.

Resources and Directions

In terms of understanding the congregation as a family system,
the best place to start is Edwin Friedman's book *Generation to Generation.*[2] It is hoped that Friedman's book will mark the beginning of the
application of family systems concepts to congregational life.

The Alban Institute[3] does not focus on a systematic perspective
but publishes books and articles on the developmental, emotional and
spiritual dynamics of ministry and congregational life.

The Myers-Briggs Type Inventory[4] is based on Jung's psychology
and is a useful instrument to use to understand personality differences. It can be used to with church boards and committees. Training
is necessary in order to purchase and administer the program.

The search for directions and solutions for the issues raised in this
chapter is ongoing, complex, and personal. Two guidelines are appropriate. A consultant trained in organizational and congregational dynamics can be helpful in assessing and helping congregations clarify
their goals. It is crucial that the consultant be knowledgeable in systems concepts and have an understanding of congregational life.

An ongoing process with a supervisor is essential for pastoral
direction. Again, as with the consultant, the supervisor must think in
systemic terms.

Certification by the American Association of Marriage and Family Therapists is a good indication of both experience and expertise.
The supervisor should have experience as a pastor. The contract between pastor and supervisor must be independent of academic or
other programs. This is to ensure that triangles and other complica-
tions will not arise and interfere with the process. Ongoing supervision is essential in helping the pastor refrain from taking congrega-

tional concerns too personally. It will also provide an understanding of what is happening from a systemic perspective. The process of supervision can help the pastor maintain the observer dimension and balance the observer/participant dynamic. Finding a solution to understanding and pastoring congregations is an ongoing process. A good supervisory relationship can serve as the catalyst.

Notes

1. Clifford J. Sager, *Marriage Contracts and Couple Therapy* (New York: Brunner/Mazel, 1976), pp. 19–22.

2. Edwin H. Friedman, *Generation to Generation* (New York: Guilford Press, 1985).

3. The Alban Institute, Inc., 4125 Nebraska Avenue, N.W., Washington, D.C. 20016.

4. Consulting Psychologists Press, 577 College Avenue, Palo Alto, California 94306.

Notes on the Contributors

SARAH CAROL ADAMS, age sixteen, is a junior in high school in Baltimore, Maryland, and is involved in field hockey, tennis, jazz band, student government and creative writing. Future plans include attending college and becoming a psychologist.

VIRGINIA CARSON, M.S., C.T.R.S., is a professionally certified Therapeutic Recreation Specialist currently employed as a Coordinator of Continuing Education and Community Services at Catonsville Community College. She is a registered consultant with the Maryland Recreation and Parks Association in the area of leisure and therapeutic recreation. Ms. Carson received her B.S. degree in Recreation with a Therapeutics Option from the University of Maryland and her M.S. degree in Human Resource Development from Towson State University.

EVELYN RAUCH CHESNUTT, of Wheaton, Maryland, has been the wife of a United Methodist clergyman, the Reverend Lon B. Chesnutt, for twenty-eight years. She is the mother of a son, David, who is a senior at the University of Maryland. She received her B.A. in Sociology from Douglass College at Rutgers University, N.J., and her M.A. in Education from Syracuse University, N.Y. For the last four years she has been a High School Guidance Counselor.

JOSEPH W. CIARROCCHI, Ph.D., is the Director of Addictions Services and Psychological Consultant for the Isaac Taylor Institute of Psychiatry and Religion at Taylor Manor Hospital, Ellicott City, Maryland. He is also Assistant Professor in the Pastoral Counseling Department, Loyola College.

NOREEN SURINER CRALEY, M.Div., is married to Paul E. Craley and the stepmother to two children, Bronwen, 16, and Timothy,

13. She was ordained a priest in March 1977 and has served three congregations since that time. She is currently serving Christ the King Episcopal Church as Rector. Ms. Craley grew up in a small town in western Massachusetts. She represents the first woman ordained priest in that Diocese and was also the first woman called as Rector in the Diocese of Maryland. She currently lives in Baltimore with her husband, stepson, and their beloved animals.

B. JOHN HAGEDORN, JR., Ph.D., an ordained minister in the Evangelical Lutheran Church in America, is the director of the Institute for Pastoral Psychotherapy of the Pastoral Counseling and Consultation Center of Greater Washington, D.C., Inc., where he serves as teacher, supervisor and pastoral psychotherapist. He is an adjunct assistant professor in the Department of Pastoral Counseling of Loyola College, Columbia, Maryland.

DANIEL C. HENDERSON, D.P.C., is a United Methodist Minister and Agency Director, Pastoral Counseling and Consultation Centers of Greater Baltimore. He is a Fellow in the American Association of Pastoral Counselors.

AUGUST G. LAGEMAN, Ph.D., is a United Methodist Minister who serves as the Director of the Harford Pastoral Counseling Service. Dr. Lageman is a Fellow in the American Association of Pastoral Counselors and a Clinical Member of the American Association of Marriage and Family Therapists.

GLENN E. LUDWIG is a Senior Pastor, First Lutheran Church, Ellicott City, Maryland. He received the Master of Divinity Degree, magna cum laude, and was ordained to ministry in the Lutheran Church in America in 1973. Pastor Ludwig served as Chaplain to Susquehanna University, Selingsgrove, Pennsylvania, 1980–1985, and is currently on the Board of Directors of Lutheran Youth Encounter. He is listed in *Who's Who In Religion, Third Edition*, and the *International Book of Honor, 1986*. Glenn Ludwig is the author of *Building an Effective Youth Ministry*, Abingdon, 1979, and *Keys to Building Youth Ministry*, Abingdon, 1988.

R. ALEX LUTZ an eleventh-grade student in Columbia, Maryland, active in football and baseball, and involved in his church. At this time, he plans to attend a culinary arts school upon graduation and pursue a career as a chef.

ROBERT R. LUTZ is a pastoral counselor on the treatment staff of the Isaac Taylor Institute of Psychiatry and Religion at Taylor Manor Hospital, Ellicott City, Maryland. An ordained Lutheran minister, he received the Master of Divinity degree in 1972 from Philadelphia Lutheran Seminary and the doctorate in pastoral counseling (D.P.C.) from Loyola College in 1989.

ROBERT J. McALLISTER, Ph.D., M.D., is Director of the Isaac Taylor Institute of Psychiatry and Religion and Adjunct Professor, Pastoral Counseling, Loyola College, Baltimore. Dr. McAllister is on the Board of Directors of the National Guild of Catholic Psychiatrists. He received his Ph.D. in Psychology from Catholic University, Washington, D.C. and his M.D. from Georgetown University.

REA McDONNELL, S.S.N.D., serves as a spiritual director at the Consultation Center, Adelphi, Maryland. She is the author of five books and numerous articles on biblical spirituality, prayer, ministry, healing for adult children of alcoholics and spiritual issues in pastoral care. She received a Ph.D. in biblical studies from Boston University. She continues to travel to Boston to teach as associate professor in Emanuel College's graduate program for pastoral counselors. Her most recent book, *Hope for Healing: Good News for Adult Children of Alcoholics,* co-authored with psychologist Rachel Callahan, C.S.C., is on the Paulist Press all-time best seller list.

MARY ELLEN MERRICK, M.S., N.C.C., is a member of the Sisters, Servants of the Immaculate Heart of Mary (Scranton, PA). In addition to her clinical responsibilities with the Isaac Taylor Institute of Psychiatry and Religion at Taylor Manor Hospital, she is pursuing a doctorate in Pastoral Counseling at Loyola College in Maryland.

THE REVEREND ROY M. OSWALD, an Evangelical Lutheran Church in America pastor, is the Senior Consultant of the Alban Institute Inc., Washington, D.C. He has served in many capacities in the Church: Director of Clergy and Congregational Development, Metropolitan Ecumenical Training Center, Washington, D.C.; Assistant to the Bishop and Director of Youth Ministry, Central Pennsylvania Synod, E.L.C.A.; and Pastor, St. Mark's Lutheran Church, Ontario, Canada. Roy Oswald earned the B.Ed. degree at the University of Edmonton, Alberta, Canada in 1958 and the M.Div. degree at the Lutheran School of Theology at Chicago in 1962. The author of many publications, he has written extensively in the field of ministry and clergy stress and burnout.

DONNA PAYNE, Ph.D., is the granddaughter of missionaries, daughter of a pastor, daughter-in-law of missionaries, niece of four ministerial and two missionary couples, and an acquaintance of many pastoral families. She has had numerous opportunities to observe children of religion professionals in their natural habitat. Her present activities revolve around husband, two children, church, and work in bio-medical research.

W. BENJAMIN PRATT, D.Min., has been a pastoral counselor since 1974 with the Pastoral Counseling and Consultation Centers of Greater Washington. He is a Fellow with the American Association of Pastoral Counselors and a Member of the American Association of Marriage and Family Therapists. He was the founding pastor of the Good Shepherd United Methodist Church in Dale City, Virginia. He is the spouse of Judith for twenty-five years and the maturing father of Megan and Alexa.

JAMES S. ROSEN is the Associate Rabbi at Chizuk Amuno Congregation, Baltimore, Maryland. He received his Rabbinic ordination and M.A. from the Jewish Theological Seminary of America and his M.S.W. degree from Columbia University. He has served as a visiting faculty member at the Baltimore Hebrew University and worked extensively in the fields of interfaith dialogue and educational outreach to intermarried families.

MATTHEW S. SCHENNING, M.Div., is a 1979 graduate of the Lutheran Theological Seminary at Gettysburg and is currently serving as pastor of St. Paul's Lutheran Church in Upperco. NORMA L. SCHENNING, M.Div., is a 1986 graduate of the Lutheran Theological Seminary and is currently serving as pastor of Christ Lutheran Church in Upperco. They have been married for twelve years and have four sons. Both are active in Synodical work. Norma is a member of the Candidacy Committee of the

Maryland Synod. Matthew is past chairman of the Worship and Music Task Force of the Maryland Synod.

KAY C. SMITH, B.S., is a member of the Isaac Taylor Institute of Psychiatry and Religion at Taylor Manor Hospital. She received a B.S. in Biology and Physical Education from Western Maryland College and has completed additional studies in addiction treatment, Biofeedback and Guided Imagery and Music. Since 1983 she has worked with adult, adolescent, and young adult in-patients with psychiatric and/or addicting disorders in the areas of Stress Management, Relaxation Training, Biofeedback and Leisure Education.

KAY STANFORD, L.C.S.W., A.C.S.W., is a member of the treatment staff of the Isaac Taylor Institute of Psychiatry and Religion and Assistant Director of Social Work at Taylor Manor Hospital, Ellicott City, Maryland. She received the M.S.W. degree from Bryn Mawr College. Ms. Stanford is active in a unique congregation which is a union of both Methodist and Presbyterian denominations. She has had a long-standing interest in working with mental health issues of clergy.

BRUCE T. TAYLOR, M.D. (Introduction) is the Associate Medical Director and Director of Admissions, Taylor Manor Hospital, and President of the Board of Directors, Changing Point, Inc. He also serves as Clinical Assistant Professor, University of Maryland, and Instructor in Psychiatry, Johns Hopkins Hospital. Receiving his M.D. in 1975 from Johns Hopkins Medical School, Dr. Taylor completed his residency in Neurology at Johns Hopkins Hospital and residency in Psychiatry at Phipps Clinic, both in 1979. He has been involved in research, publications, and presentations on Psychophysiology, Psychopharmacology, Biofeedback, Electroconvulsive Therapy, and the Psychiatric Hospital as Treatment Environment.